The C Tutorial/Turbo C

Nigel G. Backhurst

Sigma Press- Wilmslow

First published in 1988 by
Sigma Press 1 South Oak Lane, Wilmslow, SK9 6AR, England.

British Library Cataloguing in Publication Data

Backhurst, N. G.
    The C tutorial-Turbo C
    1. C (Computer program language) 2. Turbo
    C (Computer program)
    I. Title
    005.13'3 QA76.73.C15

ISBN: 1-85058-102-9

Distributed by
John Wiley & Sons Ltd., Baffins Lane, Chichester, West Sussex, England.

Printed by Interprint Ltd, Malta

Cover design by Professional Graphics, Warrington, UK

Acknowledgments: Turbo BASIC is a trade mark of Borland International; various other software and hardware products are mentioned within this text and may be protected by trade marks, in which case full acknowledgment is hereby given.

PREFACE

This book is intended to give you an introduction to the C language. It is not meant to be, and is not designed to be, an expert text or master handbook.

What it is designed to do is to get you quickly and easily programming in the C language. It is then up to you to go on and learn the language in full.

The book has been designed to be used mostly by people working at home or in an office by themselves on a micro system. Probably, they will be working with Turbo C, although they may be using one of the other C compilers. They will, though, find it easier to follow the examples if they are using Turbo C.

As this book is an introductory tutorial I have strictly limited the functions included and the scope of the book. It is hoped that cover has been given to all the main functions which you are liable to need for most user programming. Coverage is not given to those aspects of the language more of use to the systems programmer. These can be looked up once you have a basic understanding of the language.

To use this book you should have access to an IBM PC or compatible computer and the Turbo C compiler. The programs in this book were developed and tested on a Handwell Baby AT and Handwell XT provided by AM Components of Coventry, England, and an Amstrad PC1640HD20 provided by Interspike Intersoft, Apeldoorn, The Netherlands.

Finally, this is a Turbo C tutorial. It is not a replacement for the Turbo C manual. If you do not have a manual, you do not have a legitimate copy of Turbo C. That is a shame. You need the manuals to get the most out of one of the best implementations of C under MSDOS.

Nigel G. Backhurst

Dedication.

To Simon who got this book started, and to Joan who said keep on writing. Above all to Mark for whom it is written.

CONTENTS

BACKGROUND TO C

The C language is a mid-level general purpose programming language which was developed by Dennis Ritchie in the early 1970s at Bell Labs. This statement raises the question, What is a mid-level language?

At the most basic level the way you give instructions to a computer is by way of machine code. Machine code is a series of binary numbers which are understood by the microprocessor as instructions. Such instructions form the lowest level of computer programming languages.

Such low level programming presents problems for the programmers. Binary machine code is not the easiest thing to write or read. It is, in fact, not a very practical method of programming due to the difficulty of dealing with binary numbers:

```
00010110
00101100
10110011
10001101
01000011
10111110
10000111
```

If you have to try and debug binary code, as shown above, you have problems; trying to work out what it is doing is virtually impossible.

Fortunately, we have been saved from the problem of trying to talk to computers in binary code by the development of hexadecimal code, although this makes the problem only a little easier. It was made much easier by the introduction of assemblers. With assemblers, instead of having to give each instruction to the computer in a numeric form it is possible to give it in a symbolic form. A special piece of software, the assembler, then assembles this symbolic set of instructions into actual machine code.

There are still problems with assemblers and these are due to two facts. First, the system must be told every step that has to be undertaken. This results in the programmer having to write quite a lot of code. A second problem is that the code written is specific to one processor and one hardware configuration.

The high level languages like Fortran, Cobol, Basic, Pascal and Comal provide a programmer with a set of instructions which are easier to learn. These languages are far more like the English language with one instruction covering a number of steps. There is, of course, a price to pay for all these benefits.

In general, the high level languages are less powerful than the low level languages. This is because they do not provide you with the ability to undertake the direct manipulation of the computer's memory and processor registers as do the low level languages.

There is a small group of languages which provide you with a programming environment which is fairly portable between systems, yet gives you a great deal of power. As these languages lie in a hierarchy between the low level languages and the high level languages they are referred to as mid-level languages.

Of these languages, C is probably the leader today. There are some computer people who claim that C is the only true mid-level language. That is a view which I do not support. Others claim that BCPL and Forth, together with a handful of specialist languages developed for real time programming and communications software like PLM, are also mid-level languages. This I support.

So, let us consider the advantages and disadvantages of having a mid-level language.

The main advantage is that they combine many aspects of the high level programming languages, such as data types, control statements and structured forms, with the flexibility and efficiency which are normally associated with assembly languages. This provision of facilities associated with assembly languages is clearly found in the wide range of operators which C supports for working on the bit structure of data, an operation far more at home in the world of assembly language programming than in the world of high level language programming.

However, C does not supply many of the features which would be expected from many high level languages. It has no I/O or file handling functions defined within the language. There are no direct facilities for dealing with string variables, array sets or lists. These facilities have to be added to the language by means of function libraries.

This does mean, though, that the language can be very compact. It has only a few basic operators and commands. Recently, these have been under review as part of the formalization of a new standard for C, the proposed ANSI standard. Under this review some additions have been made to the basic set. Turbo C supports these additions plus a few special extensions.

A compact language means you have one which is easy to use and also one which is flexible, for you can build your own functions to do what you want instead of having to use facilities built into the language. A final point about a compact language is that it is more portable as there is less chance of incompatibility.

In Tables 1.1, 1.2 and 1.3 are lists of the Turbo C reserved words. These are divided into three sections. First, the classic C reserved words. That is, those reserved words which are found in versions of C which provide a full implementation of the old Kernighan and Ritchie standard. Second, the ANSI additions which will only be found in versions of C which follow the proposed ANSI standard are shown. Finally, the set of reserved words which are special to Turbo C are given.

Table 1.1 Classic C reserved words

auto	break	case	char	continue	default
do	double	else	extern	float	
for	goto	if	int	long	register
return	short	sizeof	static	struct	switch
typedef	union	unsigned	while		

Table 1.2 ANSI additional C reserved words

const	enum	signed	void	volatile

Table 1.3 Turbo C extension reserved words

asm	cdecl	far	huge	interrupt	near
pascal	_CS	_DS	_ES	_SS	_AH
_AL	_AX	_BH	_BL	_CH	_CL
_CX	_DH	_DX	_BP	_DI	_SI
_SP					

Having a very compact language does have some disadvantages. C can be very cryptic at times. It is possible to write C in what is almost a short-hand way using multistatement lines and maximum abbreviations. When this is done it can be almost impossible for anybody other than the programmer to read the code. It can also, at times, produce some very bad code.

Many programmers have the idea that the shorter they make the code for a program, and the more cryptic it is, the more efficient it must be. Whilst this is sometimes the case, it is not always so, and often highly cryptic code is highly inefficient. This is because the programmer has written code which has the shortest form on paper and not that which is the most efficient.

With modern compilers like Turbo C, the need to write very short code is vastly reduced. Turbo C has an efficient optimizing function in its compile process and will optimize code to an extent beyond that of the average, or even good, programmer. This means that Turbo C can be (and is) very efficient. Well thought out code correctly structured and implemented can often approach assembler in performance. In some cases, a piece of well written Turbo C can actually beat a poorly written piece of assembler code, and it is far easier to write good code in Turbo C than in assembler.

The fact that it is easier to write code in C than in Assembler gives us another major benefit from using Turbo C. With its integrated development environment and built in debugging facilities, program development time is drastically reduced. The man/hour effort to produce source code in C is much less than that required to produce similar source code in assembler. The man/hour effort required to produce finished code in Turbo C is far less than that required with many other compilers which are on the market.

The one advantage of using C which is widely praised is that C is highly portable. Well, in theory it is. In practice, it is not very portable, but for most modern programming, portability that is not very important. First, let us look at the theory. If you stick to the ANSI proposed standard and Classical C reserved words, and use only the basic standard function library then your code should be portable. But even then you could have some surprises. Even very basic library functions like getchar() can work differently and unexpectedly under different compilers. For instance, the standard usage of this function is that it returns the value of the key depressed and echoes it to the screen. This is how Turbo C implements the function and how it is found under Unix. On many MSDOS and CPM compilers you are required to press the RETURN key after the key depression before getchar() operates. Differences like this can pose problems of portability.

Even more problems can be expected once you start to make use of any of the special extensions within a language. Turbo C is specifically designed for the MSDOS environment and has extensions and functions within it to support that environment. These are not found in other compilers. Any functions using them would have to be rewritten if you were moving the code to another compiler on another system. There is little point in moving to another compiler under MSDOS. In practice, as many of these extensions are so specialized it might be impossible to re-write the functions affected.

In general, such lack of portability is not a problem. Most software being written by people using Turbo C is designed to run on the IBM PC and compatibles. There is neither expectation nor desire for it to be run on other systems. It is possible to ensure that your Turbo C code is portable. There is a compile time option which will only compile ANSI standard reserved words and produce an error on any Turbo C extensions. By using this you can make certain that you have portable code.

The ANSI Standard

The ANSI standard is referred to above. At the time of writing a committee of the American National Standard Institute is drawing up a new standard for C. Draft proposed standards have already been issued.

Until recently, most compilers have been based on the description of the C language given in *The C Programming Language* by Kernighan and Ritchie. This is a very good book and one which any serious C programmer should possess. It does have a major fault from the point of view of being a standard for a language: it was not written as such. It contains of description of C, but not a definition of it, so, many of the aspects of how C should work have to be taken by implication from the description. Unfortunately, there is enough scope for interpretation of that description to result in some conflict concerning how C should be implemented.

Since the publication of the draft ANSI proposed standards the trend has been for compilers to follow the new draft proposed standards. These are fully supported by Turbo C.

A Short History of C

It is worthwhile for users to have some background on what C is and where it comes from.

The history of C starts in 1972 at the Bell Laboratories in the USA, where Ritchie was working on a development of the B language. B itself was a language derived from BCPL which started life at Cambridge University in England.

This was the time when Thompson and Kernighan were busy developing the Unix operating system and had already implemented it on a PDP 7; they now had the task of moving it over to a PDP 11. Having once written the Unix operating system in assembler on the PDP 7 they were not too keen on the idea of having to do the whole thing again to get it across to the 11 and any future computer to which they might want to port it. Therefore, it made sense to write as much of it as possible in a higher level language. Fortunately, Ritchie was working on a language intended to undertake such work.

After some reworking of C to make it more suitable for systems work it was used to write the first port of Unix. Since that time most of Unix has been written in C. Only that part of the Unix system which handles the software/hardware interface is written in assembler. This means, of course, that Unix can quickly and easily be transported between different machines. It has also meant that there is a very close relationship between C and Unix.

There are some aspects of C which programmers who have never worked on a Unix system tend to find quirky. These generally reflect something about the operation of a Unix system. One aspect of this is the way that the C standard library I/O routines tend to be biased very much to output on a TTY. This is because it is the most basic type of output and the only one you can presume to have on any Unix system.

With the expansion of Unix into the academic world and the impact this has had on computer training, C has become a widely taught language in Computer Science Departments.

Nowadays, it is the main language used for software engineering. In fact, it is often the only language known to many of the younger software engineers in the industry.

For the foreseeable future C will no doubt remain the leading software engineering language and the main programming language on modern computer systems. However it may not become the 'be all' language which many people like to think it will be. It is interesting to note that even now as C is starting to become popular many of the more specialist programmers who embraced C in the late 70s and early 80s are moving to other languages, and that Forth, a much neglected language (albeit in an altered form) is starting to make a reappearance for application program development.

The introduction of Turbo C with its integrated development environment is an indication of a new role for C. It is now clearly emerging as a primary software development language for application software. It is no longer an esoteric tool used by high level programming experts.

The reason for this is that the Turbo C development environment provides far more extensive support for the programmer. It is important for making the writing of good C code easy for the software writer, fully supporting the writer with extensive libraries, fast compile times, efficient and extensive error checking, and most important of all, a clear message system.

2

PROGRAMMING

Many readers will find that this chapter covers familiar areas. You may feel that you can safely skip it. Don't.

In this chapter two aspects are covered. First, the basic concept of what a program is and how these are developed. Second, the terms used in this book are introduced. It is important that when the terms statement and expression are used, readers understand what they mean.

One of the problems in the computer world is that the use of language tends to be very flexible. A term can mean one thing in one context and another in a different context. Terms such as jumps, calls, blocks and structures can have very different meanings according to when and how they are used. This chapter aims to define the basics of how such terms are used in this book.

First, let us consider what a computer program is. It is a set of instructions which the computer can understand and follow, which result in the computer undertaking a specified series of actions in relation to inputted data.

Computer programs are made up of statements which consist of a combination of commands and expressions. So, first we must define a command and an expression. Essentially, a command is an instruction to the computer to carry out an action using data. An expression is an instruction to the computer to carry out an action on data.

If I give the instruction:

> add A to B and place result in C.

that is an expression. In the C language it would be written as:

```
c = a + b;
```

If I give the instruction:

> take the value of C and display it on the screen.

that is a command. In the C language it could be written as:

```
printf("%d",c);
```

Both of the above are statements, that is, they are instructions given to the system. In this case, the statements contain either a command or an expression. However, statements can contain a combination of the two. I could give the instruction:

add A to B and display the result on the screen.

That is a statement which contains an expression and a command; in C it could be written as:

```
printf("%d", a + b );
```

Any computer program is made up of a series of statements.

It is all very well having a series of statements for the computer to follow, but what you need is to get the computer to follow them in the correct order. One way in which you can do this is to put the statements into a preset order so they are always carried out in the same order every time the program is run. Such a series of statements would be as follows:

Get two numbers.
Subtract the second number from the first.
Display the result.

This approach is fine provided you want the same set of operations carried out each time: but often you do not. Look at the above example again. If we wanted the difference between two numbers and we wanted this as a positive figure, the above set of instructions would let us down if the second number was larger than the first. In such circumstances we would need to have a different set of instructions carried out.

This can be done by using what is known as flow control statements. These are statements which cause the order in which statements are executed to be amended according to the condition of data held in the system. In fact, they may prevent certain statements from being executed at all. So, let us look at an amended version of the above example.

Get two numbers.
If the second number is less than the first.
    Subtract the second number from the first.
    Then display the result.
Otherwise.
    Subtract the first number from the second.
    Then display the result.

Here is a situation where if one condition is true, that is that the second number is less than the first, then a set of statements is carried out. If it is not true another set of statements is undertaken. According to the state of the data in the system, the action of the program will be modified.

There are two types of modifier you can use in controlling the flow of a program. The first is the branch. In this, if a condition is met one set of actions is carried out, otherwise another set of actions is carried out.

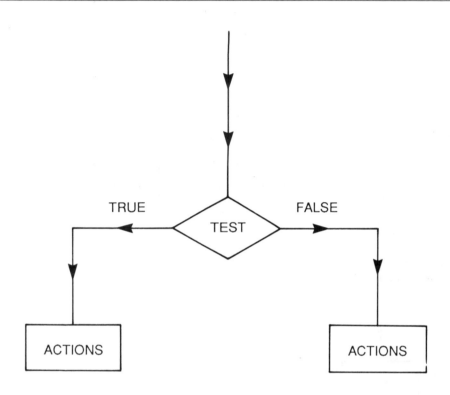

Figure 2.1 The branch .

The second type of modifier is the loop. Actually, a loop is a special type of branch which causes the flow of the program to go round and round in circles until a specific condition is met. There are two types of loop: those where the condition is tested at the start of the loop, start tested loops, and those where the test is made at the end of the loop, end tested loops.

Programming languages can be divided into two classes: lineal languages and block languages. C belongs to the latter type, although it is possible, and occasionally desirable, to program in C using a lineal approach.

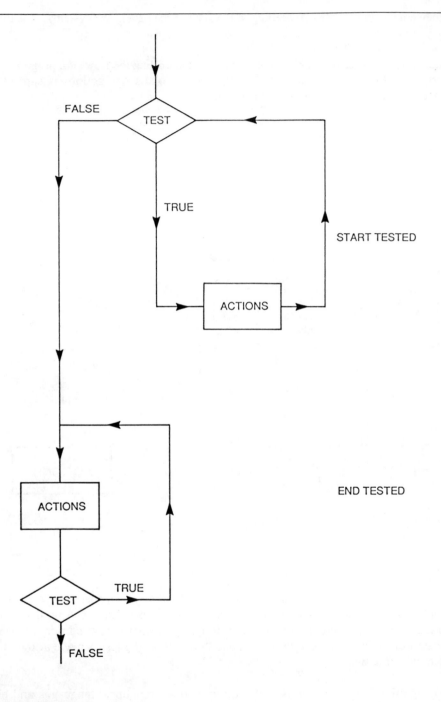

Figure 2.2 The loop.

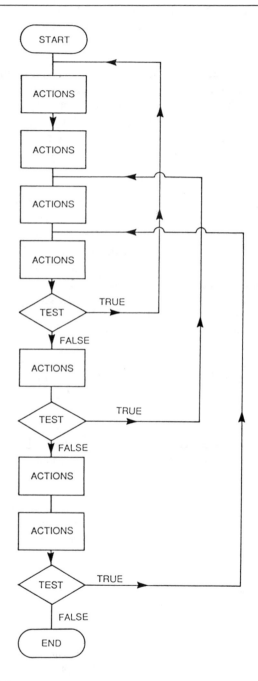

Figure 2.3 Lineal Structure

A lineal program is one in which the statements to be executed follow each other in the order in which they are to be executed. Any modification to the order is undertaken by jumps forward or back in the program.

There are two problems with lineal programming. The first involves all those jumps backwards and forwards. It can become quite difficult to keep track of where you are in a program structure with a number of jumps. In a complex program any attempt to draw a diagram of the program flow can end up looking like spaghetti, which is why many programmers call such programming spaghetti programming. This can result in code which is very difficult to debug.

Another problem is that any commonly used routine must be rewritten every time it is used. This amounts to a tremendous amount of recoding and increases the chance of errors.

The alternative approach is to use block structures. Here, all the actions undertaken in a program are broken down into a set of basic actions. These make up individual blocks which can then be called up by blocks at a higher level. So, in a block structure program you have a top level block which contains a series of calls to lower level blocks and which passes data to them. The lower level blocks then process that data and return the results which can be used in the next call.

One advantage of this approach is that when a commonly used routine exists it only needs to be written once and can be called from a number of blocks. So a single block may be called by more than one block from a higher level.

There is one point which must be made clear. Programming books, magazines, and courses generally place a great deal of emphasis on structured programming and using blocks. This is quite right. However, it is a common mistake to say that lineal code is always wrong. There are times when it is better than even the best block structure.

One example of this is where speed is important. It takes time to do a call to a routine, pass the data to that routine and get the data back. Quite often the time taken to undertake the call can be greater than the time taken to do the processing. In such circumstances there is good reason for using a lineal program structure.

While you should use a block structure approach as much as possible, do not ignore the lineal approach where factors like speed are important or where the program is very simple.

In the above section the terms jump and call have been used. A jump is an instruction which makes the control of the program go to another place in the program from which it will not return. A call is an instruction which makes the control of the program go to another place in the program from where it will return once the set of instructions at the location have been carried out.

Jumps are one of the easiest ways of getting lost in a program and should therefore be avoided as much as possible. Some programmers even go so far as to say you should never use them. That is possibly an extreme, but their use should be kept to a minimum.

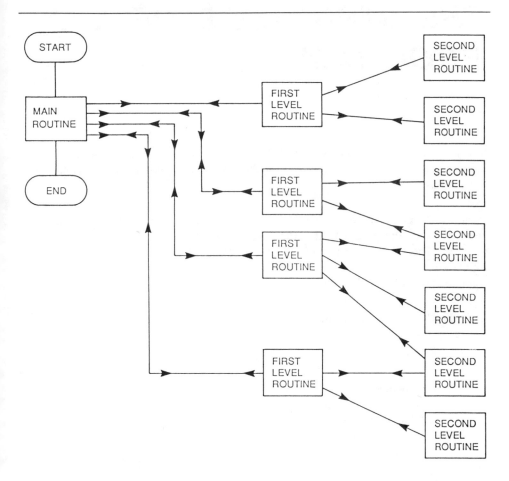

Figure 2.4   Block Structure

3

THE STRUCTURE OF A C PROGRAM

Every C program consists of one or more functions. Each of these functions performs its own tasks. The results generated by these tasks are passed between functions in several ways.

In any C program you must have one function which is called main(). This is the entry point to your program. It is the point from which the program starts when it is invoked. There is no rule in C which states that the function main() has to be the first function in a program, although generally it is. You can put it anywhere you like and some programmers prefer to put it as the last function in a listing.

In Turbo C each function consists of:

-       A heading

        This includes:
          The function name.
          A list of arguments passed to that function.
          Type declaration.

-       A block

        This includes:
          Local variable definitions.
          Statements which may include calls to other functions.

You must terminate each statement within the block with a semi-colon. This semi-colon is known as the statement terminator. If a group of statements have a specific connection to each other you may enclose them within braces. Such groups of statements are known as compound statements.

Given the above, a C program will have the following type of structure:

```
Global  Definitions
main()
{
    function1();
    function2();
}

function1()
{
    statements;
}

function2()
{
    statements;
}
```

This, of course, reflects the type of structure known as a block structure and discussed in Chapter 2. Have a look at Figure 3.1.

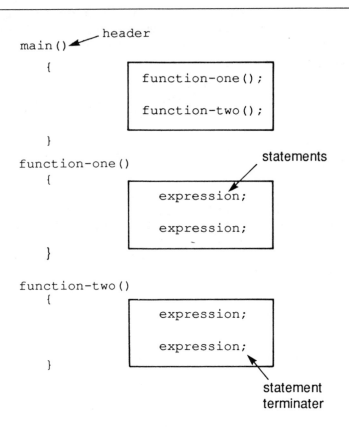

Figure 3.1.

If you consider the example program you will see how such a structure is applied.

```
/*  Example  program  to  show  basic  structure.  */

main()
{
    message1();
    message2();
}

message1()
{
    printf("Hello this is a simple C program \n");
}

message2()
{
    printf("We hope that you will find this tutorial useful.\n");
}
```

Enter this and run it. If you are working from within the Turbo C development environment you can do this direct. It is done either by using Alt-R, or from the main menu. To invoke the main menu use F10. For more details on this you should consult the User's Guide.

In this program you have three functions. The prime entry function main() and two secondary functions, message1() and message2(). The two functions are called up by the statement lines in the block of the function main().

The functions message1() and message2() make a call to a standard function called printf() passing a line of text to that function as an argument to be printed. You should note that printf is a standard function which is supplied with C, it is not part of the C language itself.

If you look at the lines of text passed you will see that each line ends in a special character combination `\n'. In C the backslash character `\' escapes the following character giving it a special meaning, in this case the status of a newline character. So `\n' means print a new line. Some of the other special character combinations in Turbo C are:

> \t   tab
> \b   backspace
> \\   backslash

A complete list can be found in Chapter 8 of the Turbo C User's Guide.

At the start of the program there is a comment telling us what the program is. This is enclosed within a pair of special signs, these are /* and */.

The sign /* tells the compiler that everything which follows, until it is otherwise informed, is a comment and should be ignored. The */ informs the compiler that the end of the comment has been reached and it can start to compile again.

You can place comments across more than one line if you need to. The only thing which you have to be sure of is that they start with /* and end with */. The following is a valid comment:

```
/*

This is a demonstration of the setting up of comments.

This tutorial was written by Nigel Backhurst. Nigel worked mostly
on a Handwell Baby AT and a Handwell PC 8088 which were supplied
by AM Components of Coventry and an Amstrad PC.

*/
```

Perhaps not a very helpful comment, but still a good illustration of placing comments over a number of lines.

When you are using comments you must place the */ at the end. If you do not, the compiler will ignore all the code which follows the comment until it finds the next */. This, as you will no doubt find out, is one of the most common mistakes made by C programmers.

There are a number of ways in which you can avoid such mistakes. They all come down to one basic rule: *establish a standard form for your comments and stick to it.* In this book a well tried style of commenting is used. This is not the only correct way to comment your source code; there are other equally valid methods. However, this system does work and you might like to follow it, or to work out your own variation.

Where a comment is given outside a function I like to include it in a comment block. The opposite corners of the block are formed by the comment start and comment end markers. An example of this would be:

```
/**********************************************************
*   This routine is used to check that the command      *
*   entered is a valid command.  The check is done by*
*   seeking a match for the command letter against a    *
*   letter in the valid command string.                 *
**********************************************************/
```

If there are comments inside functions these can be dealt with in two ways. The first is to put a single comment line after the statement to which it refers:

```
lpi = malloc( strlen( buf ) );
/* Get space to copy buffer into. */
```

There is a problem here that interspersing comment within code can make the code difficult to read. Another method which I prefer is to offset the comments to the right of the code. In this case a line of * is placed down one side of the comment as in the following example:

```
while ( TRUE )
{
    key = getch();
    if ( key == 32 ) break;    /* Endless loop.  Keep
                                * testing until the
                                * space bar is pressed
                                * then break out.
                                */

}
```

An advantage with this type of commenting is that it is fairly easy to write tools to check the comments. Basically, the rule that such a tool should look for is that if there is not a comment cancellation on the same line as the invocation then an * must exist on each line until the cancellation is found. When you have finished this tutorial you might like to have a go at writing such a tool.

Commenting style is a very personal matter. It is important to find a style which suits you and to stick to it. This will mean that any break from the normal can easily be seen. If this practice is adopted, mistakes with comments are less likely.

A further point about comments is that normally you cannot nest comments. The result of this is that if you wrote the following code:

```
/* This function is to be excluded

    delay( int time )
    {
        int i,j;
        for ( i = 0; i < time; i++ )
        /* Empty loops */
            for ( j = 0; j < 1000; j++ );
}

unless the delay is required. */
```

it would not work. The */ in the empty loop comment would be taken as the end of the comment, and the second part of the delay loop and the second part of the comment would both produce errors.

There are times when it might be useful to be able to comment out sections of code. With Turbo C this can be done. There is a compile time option which allows use of nested comments. Generally, such practice is best avoided. If it is necessary to cut out sections of code, it is best to do this by making use of conditional compilation. This is covered later in Chapter 23.

A point to note about declaring functions is that a function cannot be declared from within a function. The following would be illegal:

```
main()
{
    int  fnumber,  snumber;

    fnumber  =  3;
    snumber  =  5;
    print_mes();

    print_mes()
    {
    printf("\nThe  value  of  the  two  numbers  added  is  ");
    }

    printf("%d\n",  fnumber  +  snumber  );

}
```

because we have tried to define the function print_mes() from within the function main(). The legal way to write the above program would be:

```
main()
{
    int  fnumber,  snumber;

    fnumber  =  3;
    snumber  =  5;

    print_mes();

    printf("%d\n",  fnumber  +  snumber  );
}

print_mes()
{
    printf("\nThe  value  of  the  two  numbers  added  is  ");
}
```

Here the function print_mes() is the same, but this time it is declared outside the function main().

4

NAMES, VARIABLES AND CONSTANTS

Variables and Constants - Definition

Computer programs deal with data held in the computer. This data can be of two types: variable values and constant values.

A variable value is:

> A value which may change during the run of a computer program.

A constant value is:

> A value which does not change during the run of a computer program.

Memory Storage

Data values are stored by the computer in its memory. An easy way to visualize this is to imagine the memory being made up of many little boxes. It can be thought of as being somewhat like the old-fashioned 'pigeon hole' system which was used for holding mail. If you look at Figure 4.1 you will see such a representation.

All data is held in the computer as numeric values. Each box can hold a numeric value from 0 to 255. This is shown in Figure 4.2.

This is fine provided you only want to store values up to 255 in memory. If you want to store a value more that 255 you cannot do this in one box. In such cases two or more boxes must be used, each box holding a value up to 255. This is shown in Figure 4.3.

You have to tell the compiler how many boxes (or to be more technically correct, bytes) are going to be required to store the values which you will be placing into

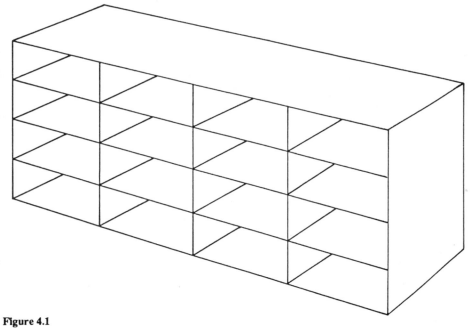

Figure 4.1

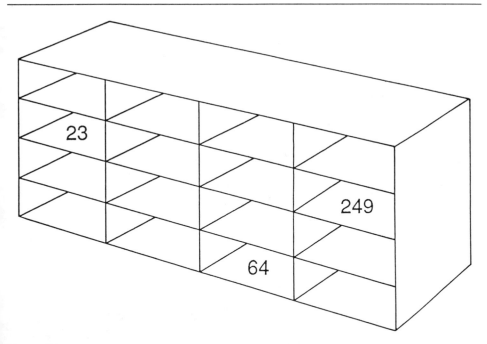

Figure 4.2

memory. This is done by defining constants and declaring variable values within the program. Each variable must be declared to belong to a specific type.

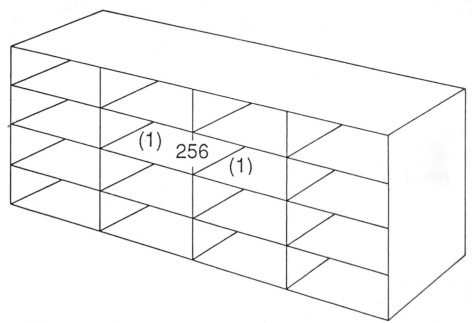

Values over 255 are split across two or more bytes each holding up to 255

Both bytes contain the value 1, the number 256 being made up of 1 from the low order byte + 1 * 255 from the high order byte

Figure 4.3

The C programming language supports a number of different types of variable. To start with, we consider just three: the int, char and float.

The variable type int stands for integer. Integers are whole numbers, not decimal numbers. In Turbo C a variable of type int will take two bytes, that is sixteen bits, to be stored in. With other compilers, on other systems, the amount of space used for storing ints, or other variable types may be different.

The variable type char stands for character. These include the letters of the alphabet, the digits used to write numbers, punctuation marks, space and any special graphic characters which exist on your system. All characters are stored in memory as numeric values. To confuse things, the value stored may have no direct connection with the character. For instance, the character `1' is stored as the value 49, whilst `9' is 57. In fact, all characters are stored in accordance with their ASCII values.

Characters have a numeric value in the range 0 to 255. This means that they can be stored in a single byte.

The variable type float stands for floating point. These are numbers which have a decimal point, the position of which changes according to the value represented. Not all C compilers support this type of variable, but it is fully supported in Turbo C.

Variable Declaration

The declaration of a variable can take place at a number of different points in a program. The point at which a variable is declared will affect the scope of that variable. We look at this later. The form of a variable declaration is always the same:

```
type    identifier ;
```

Identifiers

Each variable, or for that matter constant, has to be given a name. This name is associated with a specific set of bytes and is used by the compiler to identify that set of bytes. It is therefore known as an identifier.

There are some specific rules covering identifiers. These are:

Identifiers must begin with a letter or an underscore character (_).

They can only be made up of alphanumeric characters and the underscore character.

The Turbo C compiler, in common with most C compilers, treats upper and lower case letters as different. This is the C standard. There are a few older C compilers which do not follow this standard so care must be taken when moving source code from old systems.

No identifier can be the same as a keyword.

Each identifier must be unique.

With regard to the last point, although many compilers only recognize the first eight characters and some recognize fewer, Turbo C will recognize the first thirty-two characters of an identifier as being unique. This is in keeping with the newer standards for C.

There can be a source of problems here if you are trying to move code from one compiler to another. This is particularly true if you are moving code written for one of the older C compilers to Turbo C. In one case where I was moving code across, it would not compile. It took many hours of debugging before I found that the problem was that the original compiler for which the code had been written only recognized the first eight characters as being significant. This meant it regarded next_line_current and next_line_held as being the same. Turbo C of course, recognized them as being different. This is in keeping with modern C practice. There is an easy way to avoid this problem if you come across it. You can set the number of characters to be significant as a compile option. See page 198 of the Turbo C User's Guide.

If you are not using Turbo C it is a good idea to run a check to see what your compiler will allow. The compiler check program will undertake this.

```
/* Compiler Check */

main()
{
    float number;
    /* Check compiler supports floating point variables */

    int firstnum;    /* Carry out check to      see if the
                      * compiler differentiates between
                      * upper and lower case      characters.
                      */
    int FirstNum;


    int _newnum;
    /* Check for allowability of lead underscore */

    /* The following check is for number of unique characters */

    int ab3;
    int ab34;
    int ab345;
    int ab3456;
    int ab34567;
    int ab345678;
    int ab3456789;
    int ab34567890;
    int ab345678901;
    int ab3456789012;

    /* End of test */
}
```

If you compile this program using one of the older C compilers you will probably get some errors reported. From these you should be able to tell the specific aspects of your compiler's implementation. It will let you know the limitations of your compiler.

Assigning values

Values are assigned to variables using the assign operator =. The nature of the value assigned will depend on the type of the variable.

```
/* Demonstration of assignment */

main()
{
        int number;
        char letter;

        number = 1;
        letter = 'A';

        printf("\nThe number is %d ", number );
        printf("the letter is %c \n", letter );
}
```

In this example we have the declaration of two variables. The first is an integer variable called number. The second is a character variable called letter. This is followed by the assignment of values to the variables, the value on the right of the assignment operator being assigned to the variable on the left (see Figure 4.4). In this case we have the value one being assigned to the integer number and the value 'A' being assigned to the character letter.

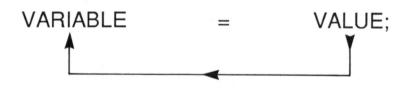

VARIABLE   =   VALUE;

THE VALUE ON THE RIGHT OF THE OPERATOR IS ASSIGNED TO THE VARIABLE ON THE LEFT

Figure 4.4

In the final part of the program the printf() functions are used to output the results of the assignments.

You do not have to assign a specific value to a variable. You can assign the value of another variable. Have a look at the following program and see if you can find out what the final values of fnumber and fletter are. When you have worked it out, enter and compile the program to see if you were right.

We have introduced something slightly different in this program. Here, instead of declaring each variable on a separate line, we have done all declarations of one type on one line, the identifiers being separated by commas. This is a multiple declaration.

```
/* Assignment of variable values */

main()
{
    int  fnumber,  snumber,  tnumber;
    char fletter,  sletter,  tletter;

    fnumber  =  1;
    snumber  =  fnumber;
    tnumber  =  snumber + fnumber;
    fnumber  =  tnumber;

    fletter  =  "a";
    sletter  =  "b";
    tletter  =  sletter + 1;
    fletter  =  tletter;

    printf("\nfnumber = %d ",fnumber);
    printf("\nfletter = %c ",fletter);
}
```

As you have no doubt found out, this is a little trap in the above program. If you look at the first part it is fairly easy to follow. The value of 1 is assigned to fnumber. This means that fnumber is now 1. The value of fnumber is next assigned to snumber. This gives you a value of one for snumber. Now the value of fnumber and snumber are added and the result assigned to tnumber. This results in a value of 2 for tnumber. Finally, we have the assignment of the value of tnumber back to fnumber. So fnumber ends up having the value two.

All this you should have found fairly easy to follow. Now for the more difficult part, the letters.

The value 'a' is assigned to fletter. A has the ASCII value 97, so fletter therefore is given the value 97. Next, the value of 'b' is assigned to sletter. The character 'b' has an ASCII value of 98. The assignment to tletter is the trick, though. Here we have the assignment of the value of sletter, which is 98 plus 1. The result of this is that the value 99 is assigned to tletter, which is the ASCII value for 'c'. The final stage of assigning the value of tletter to fletter gives fletter the value of 'c'.

Coming back to the multiple declaration of variables at the start of the program this can save you quite a bit of typing when entering code. It is often far easier to read code if the variables are declared separately. With good compilers like Turbo C this should make no difference to the size or performance of the final code.

Turbo C and most good compilers support the ability to 'initialize' variables in one statement. That is, to declare the type of the variable and its value at one and the same time. In such cases you get a statement such as:

```
int anumber = 7;
```

However, it should be noted that many compilers do not support this. In such cases, two statements have to be made to achieve the same result:

```
int anumber;
```

```
anumber = 7;
```

Constant values

Often within a program you will have certain values which are used over and over again. These can be stored as a variable. Another approach to handling such values is the preprocessor directive #define.

#define

Let us settle one point before talking about the #define directive. Many programmers tend to think that this works something like defining constants in other high level languages. This, in fact, is not the case.

With the #define directive, a definition' is given to a token. During the compiling process, whenever the compiler meets that token it will replace it with the text held in the definition. It will then continue compiling, reading the new text. In many ways this is similar to a search and replace operation in text editing. All references to one thing are changed into a reference to something else.

One of the main uses for this is in the case of constant values which are used in a program. If we say:

```
#define GIANT 7
```

then every occurrence of GIANT in the source code at compile time will be replaced with 7.

There are three parts to using #define. First, the preprocessing directive #define. There should be no gap between the # symbol and the word define. Some compilers will accept such a gap but most will not. For the sake of safety it is best to get into the habit of not putting a gap.

Second, comes the alias. This is the text which will be put into your source code. Finally, comes the replacement text. You will notice in the above example that we do not put a semi-colon at the end. Anything following the alias is taken as part of the replacement text, that includes semi-colons, quotation marks, etc.

As the #define directive undertakes a replacement of the text before the compilation of that piece of text, it is possible to use it as a means of inserting any standard text, not just for constant values. Thus, it can be used to provide an easy way of entering much used but complex statements, so reducing the risk of typing errors during compilation. For instance:

```
#define TAGLINE "The current situation in %10s is \
currently running at %d %% over the figures for %d.\n"
```

means that for everywhere else in the source code that we want this text all we have to do is enter the alias TAGLINE, eg:

```
printf(TAGLINE,country,gross,year);
```

We have used the \ to escape the carriage return at the end of the first line of the #define. This will result in the compiler viewing the two lines as one. Such procedures allow us to define fairly long pieces of text for replacement.

In theory, you can use the #define directive anywhere outside a function. In practice, you are advised only to use it at the start of a program, immediately after any #include directives. We look at those later.

There are two reasons for placing #define directives at the start. First, the main reason for using #defines is so that if a value has to be changed you only have to do it once in your source code. It is far easier if they are all together at the start when you come to changing values. A second reason is that, although Turbo C will support #defines anywhere outside functions, many compilers will not. If you need to produce portable code it is best not to presume you can use #defines elsewhere in your source code.

It is said that C is a standard and highly portable language; somebody should have told the compiler writers. Fortunately, with Turbo C, Borland provided the information so that you can make your code portable, but you will need to read both the User's Guide and the Reference Guide to make sure you write portable code.

Pointers

Pointers are one of those aspects of C which tend to cause major problems for people trying to learn the language. This is especially the case for those coming from languages like BASIC which do not make use of pointers.

What pointers are is explained here, although not in any depth. As the different topics concerning pointers come up during the course of the book we will look at them.

When you first make use of a variable, an area of the computer's memory is allocated to hold the values which you allocate to that variable. Note that this is different from many other languages. The memory is not taken up until use is made of the variable. With many languages the memory is allocated as soon as the variable is defined.

On a standard MSDOS system an integer variable is stored as two bytes in the memory of the computer. So, if you have, at the start of your program, the line:

```
int num_one = 10;
```

somewhere in the memory of the computer two bytes are reserved to hold the value allocated to num_one. The location at which this memory is reserved is an address which has an integer value. If you want to refer to this address you can do so by putting the address operator, an ampersand (&) in front of the variable name, eg:

```
&num_one;
```

which means the address of num_one. This can be seen in Program 001 which you should enter and try.

On the system used to test the software this returned a value of -10 as the memory location at which the variable num_one was stored. Different values will result depending on the system used is set up.

```
/ * * * * * * * * * * * * * * * * * * * * * * * * * * * * * * * * * * * * * * * * * * * * *
*    Program 001                                            *
*    Demonstration of memory address operator               *
* * * * * * * * * * * * * * * * * * * * * * * * * * * * * * * * * * * * * * * * * * * * * * /

main()
{
        int num_one = 10;

        printf("\nThe value of num_one is %d \n",num_one);
        printf("The address of num_one is %d \n",&num_one);
}
```

The memory location will always be an integer number.

As you can refer to the location in memory where a variable is stored you therefore have two ways of addressing any variable in memory. First, you can use its name. The second method is to use the location of the variable in memory. This is done by assigning the memory address to a class of variable known as a pointer. Pointers are indicated by having an asterisk (*) in front of their name at declaration.

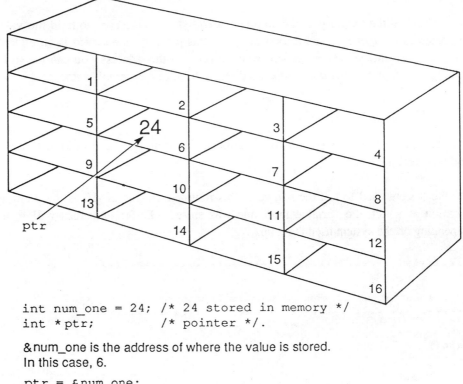

```
int num_one = 24;  /* 24 stored in memory */
int *ptr;          /* pointer */.
```

&num_one is the address of where the value is stored.
In this case, 6.

```
ptr = &num_one;
```

```
ptr is therefore equal to 6.
```

*ptr is the value held at location 6, which is 24.

Figure 4.5

So, if we want a pointer to num_one we can have Program #002.

```
/****************************************************
*    Program 002                                    *
*    Demonstration of memory address operator  and  *
*    pointers.                                       *
****************************************************/

main()
{
    int  *p_one;
    int  num_one = 10;
    p_one = &num_one;
    printf("\nThe value of num_one is %d \n",num_one);
    printf("The address of num_one is %d \n",&num_one);
    printf("The value of p_one is %d \n",p_one);
    printf("It points to the value of num_one %d \n",*p_one);
}
```

In this program the address of num_one is assigned to the pointer p_one. The first printf() line prints out the value of num_one. The second prints out the address of num_one. Next, we get the value held in the pointer (note you do not use the * here). This is followed by the value pointed to by the pointer. In this case, as you want to point to something, you use the * to indicate the nature of the pointer.

The question of why pointers are useful is considered later in the book. For the time being just try and understand what they are.

There is one other factor which you need to keep in mind about pointers. They behave differently from normal variables when you carry out incremental or decremental operations on them. Have a look at Program 003.

```
/****************************************************
* Program 003                                       *
* Incremental effect on pointers                    *
****************************************************/

main()
{
    int  f_num, *p_one;

    f_num = 0;
    p_one = &f_num;

    while ( f_num < 5 )
    {
        printf("Current value of f_num is %d \n",f_num);
        printf("Current value of p_one is %d \n",p_one);

        f_num = f_num + 1;
        p_one = p_one + 1;
    }
}
```

In this program we start with the declaration of two variables. One f_num is of type integer. The second p_one is a pointer to type integer. The value 0 is assigned to f_num and the address of f_num is assigned to p_one.

Next, a loop is set up in which the current values of both f_num and p_one are printed out and then the values are increased by adding one. All you have to do is enter Program 003 and run it.

You will find (as could be predicted) that the series of values printed for f_num will be 0, 1, 2, 3, 4. You may be surprised when you look at the values for p_one. This will be different on different systems, but on my system I got -10, - 8, -6, -4, -2. What you should find is that the value of the pointer is increased by two, not by one.

The reason for this is that when you increase or decrease a pointer, the pointer carries out that increase or decrease in the number of units appropriate to the class of the pointer. In our case we were pointing to an integer on an MSDOS system. Under Turbo C these occupy two bytes. Therefore, if you wish to increase the pointer to point to the next variable of this type in a sequence stored in memory you have to increase it by two bytes. The compiler automatically does this for us so that when I add one to the value of p_one it takes this to be one unit which for an integer pointer is two.

This should be remembered at all times when you are working with pointers. If it is not, you can find yourself faced with problems because the increase occurring is not what you expected.

The const Modifier

The const modifier is one of the three modifiers defined in the proposed ANSI standard. The other two are signed and volatile. The signed modifier is dealt with next, but the volatile modifier is really outside the scope of this book. Information on it can be found in the Turbo C User's Guide.

The const modifier is used to define an object as being unalterable. In fact, it makes it have a constant value. In classic C this was not possible. If you had a constant value in a program you could deal with it in three ways.

First, you could enter it in full at each point it was used. This did produce extensive typing and an increase in the chance of typographical errors, especially if the value was fairly long like that of pi. Consider the following example:

```
area = 3.1415926 * radius ^ 2;
```

All right, you might not think it is all that much. But if you had to type the value pi into a program 80 or 90 times, can you be certain you would never get it wrong? The compiler will not check it.

The second method was to use the #define directive as discussed earlier in this chapter. So you could use:

```
#define PI 3.1415926
```

at the start of the program and would use:

```
area = PI * radius ^ 2;
```

in the code. This does have the advantage that it saves all the typing and significantly reduces the chances of a typographical mistake. However, it does have a disadvantage in that when the program is compiled the macro is expanded to the full value of pi and it is stored as a constant at each use. Now pi is a float, so it takes up four bytes. If you have it occurring 300 times in a program, that is over a kilobyte of code just used to store one set of values. Not very good if you are working with a restricted memory. (By the way, if you think 300 occurrences of one constant is a bit heavy, I have come across one piece of code where the value of pi had to be used over 2,000 times.)

A third way was to declare pi as a variable. This saved memory. However, it had the disadvantage that there was always the chance that it might be amended by mistake. That is something which you do not want to happen to a constant.

The const modifier gives you a way around this. You can declare an object as you would a variable but modify the declaration so that it is declared const. So your declaration of pi will read:

```
const float pi = 3.1415926;
```

This means that although we can now use pi in an expression as if it were a variable, we can do nothing to it which would change its value.

The const modifier can be applied to all types of values, ints, floats, doubles, characters and pointers.

The signed and unsigned modifiers

Another addition from the proposed ANSI standard is the signed modifier. This is a counterpart to the unsigned modifier which is found in classic C. First, we will look at the operation of the unsigned modifier.

A normal int variable can contain values from -32768 to 32767. Often, though, you will have situations where you will never need to store a negative value in a variable. In such cases you can declare a variable as being unsigned. Then it can only be used to store positive numbers; in the case of integer variables, numbers from 0 to 65535.

There are certain types of variable under classic C which were always unsigned. These were the character variables. The reason for this is that they were needed to hold the ASCII character set plus the extensions which occupy the values from 0 to 255, that is, the values which can be held in a single unsigned byte.

In practice, character variables are often used to store low value numbers, especially the single numbers from 0 to 9. This is fairly common, especially in applications which are handling many small numbers and where there is a need to save memory. To be able to declare a character variable as a signed variable and store negative numbers in it is therefore most useful.

With the Turbo C compiler you can decide whether you want to have your character variables default to signed or unsigned type. The standard default is to signed. Whichever type you use you must be certain of specifically modifying your declaration to either signed or unsigned when you are making use of variables specifically in a signed or unsigned role.

From the point of view of documentation and as it makes life easier (in that you do not have to bother to make sure you have the correct compiler option set to the mode you require for the compilation) it is probably best always to declare variables to be either signed or unsigned. This is the practice which we will follow from now on in the tutorial.

5

WORKING WITH
FUNCTIONS

In the last chapter we looked at functions briefly. Now we consider them in more depth.

A function is a self-contained set of instructions which carries out a specific task within a program. A C program is made up of a series of these functions. There is a theory in C programming that no function should carry out more than one task. In practice, this is not always desirable or possible.

Each C program must have a function called main(). This is the entry point to your program. It is the function within which you normally set up the top level of program flow control.

There is no rule which says that you have to put the function main() at any specific place in the source code. Nonetheless, it is good practice to put it somewhere where it can be found without difficulty. This will make life much easier for you when you need to debug it or amend it. The tradition is to put main() as the first function in your source code. However, there are some programmers who like to put it at the end of the source code. The choice is yours, you can put it wherever you like: just make sure you always put it in the same place.

Variables and functions

Variables which are declared outside of functions are known to all functions following their declaration. In theory, you could declare variables outside functions anywhere you like in the code. In practice, it is best to put all such declarations at the start of the source code.

As the variables are known to all functions, such variables are said to be global to the program. They are therefore known as global variables.

Variables which are declared within a function are known only to that function. Such variables are said to be local to the function. They are therefore called local variables. An important point here is that if you have two variables of the same name in two different functions, they are different variables. This is illustrated in Program 004.

```
/****************************************************
 * Program 004                                      *
 * A demonstration of local and global variables    *
 ****************************************************/

unsigned int mas_num;   /* Variable declared global */

main()
{
    unsigned int a_num;   /* Variable declared local */

    a_num = 5;
    mas_num = 10;

    first_fun();
    second_fun();

    printf("End of main mas_num = %d, ",mas_num);
    printf("a_num = %d\n ",a_num);

}

first_fun()
{
    int a_num;              /* Variable declared local */

    a_num = 4;

    printf("\nmas_num = %d\n", mas_num);

    mas_num = mas_num + a_num;

    printf("mas_num = %d\n", mas_num);
    printf("a_num = %d\n", a_num);
    printf("This is the end of first_fun \n");
}

second_fun()
{
    int a_num;              /* Variable declared local */

    a_num = 3;

    printf("\nmas_num = %d, a_num = %d\n", mas_num, a_num);

    mas_num = mas_num + a_num;

    printf("mas_num = %d, a_num = %d\n",mas_num, a_num);
    printf("This is the end of second_fun \n");
}
```

If you enter this program, compile and run it, you will find that at the end of the run the last value printed for the variable a_num which is first declared in main() is the value allocated to it in main(). All the other assignments to a_num in the other functions were to a variable local to that function. Although they had the same name they were different variables. The value of mas_num has been altered from the value assigned to it in main() because it is defined outside the functions. It is a global variable.

Coming back to a point which was made earlier, you can declare a global variable under Turbo C at any point in the source code. You should remember though, that it will only be known as a global variable to those functions which follow the declaration in the source code. The fact that global variables are not known to functions which precede them can occasionally be useful. Not often, but do not dismiss it. The rule is that global variables should be declared at the start of the program.

Remember that the art of good programming is to follow the rules; the art of brilliant programming is to know when to break them.

The ability to make use of both global and local variables gives a great deal of flexibility to the handling of values within C. It can also present a difficulty. Often you want one function to know the value associated with a variable in another function but you need to keep the variables local.

Function Arguments

One way in which this can be done is by the passing of arguments to functions. An argument is a value which is passed from one function to another in the call to the second function. Have a look at Program 005.

```
/*********************************************************
 * Program 005                                          *
 * Demonstration of function arguments                  *
 *********************************************************/
main()
{
    int  f_number, s_number;

    f_number = 5;
    s_number = 6;

    calc( f_number, s_number);

    printf("\nf_number = %d, s_number = %d\n", f_number, s_number);
}

calc( int num_1, int num_2 )
{
    int  r_num, s_num;

    printf("num_1 = %d, num_2 = %d   \n", num_1, num_2);

    r_num = num_1 + 5;
    s_num = num_2 + 7;
```

```
    printf("r_num  =  %d,  s_num  =  %d \n",  r_num,  s_num);

    num_1  =  0;
    num_2  =  0;

    printf("num_1  =  %d,  num_2  =  %d \n",  num_1,  num_2);
}
```

Here we have a nice illustration of argument passing. In the first function main() we declare two local variables f_number and s_number, assigning values to them. A call is then made to the function calc(). In this call the values f_number and s_number are passed as arguments.

In the second function calc(), we receive these arguments as num_1 and num_2. Note that we declare the type of these variables in the function argument list. This is in keeping with the new ANSI standard which is supported by Turbo C. In the older Cs the variables would have to be declared immediately after the function name line. So the start of our function would read:

```
calc( num_1, num_2 )
          int num_1, num_2;
{
```

Turbo C will support this method of function declaration if required. It can be confusing at times to come across both types of declarations for passing arguments. It is my view that where possible it is best to use the ANSI form and declare the passed variable in the function declaration. This removes the chances of making a mistake in the declaration list, which was a common form of error under the older compilers. Also, it allows the compiler to undertake more checking at compile time.

As num_1 and num_2 are declared inside the function they are local variables. Anything done on them will not affect f_number and s_number in main, although the values assigned have come from those variables.

We now go into the block of the function calc(). Here we declare two more variables, then carry out a series of operations displaying the results with the function printf(). This shows the passing of the values and their resetting.

Finally, we return to main() and using the function printf(), confirm that the values of f_number and s_number are still in the form in which we left them.

There is, of course, more argument passing in here: the passing of the argument to the function printf(). Here we are passing, as an argument, the material which we want to have printed out.

Returning Values

Sometimes you want to return a value to the calling function. You can do this by making use of the keyword return.

The return command also has another function. It can be used to cause a function to terminate and return control to the calling function, whether or not the function has finished.

First, we will look at the case where it is being used to terminate the operation of a function.

```c
/******************************************************
* Program 006                                        *
* Demonstration of return from a function            *
******************************************************/

#include <stdio.h>

main()
{
    printf("\nThis is now calling the function \n");

    first_fun();

    printf("\nNow we have returned to the main function. \n");
}

first_fun()
{
    char a_char;
    int a_num;

    a_num = 0;

    while ( a_num < 10 )
    {
        printf("\n%d Enter a letter : - ", a_num);
        a_char = getche();
        if( a_char == 'q' ) return;
        a_num = a_num + 1;
    }
}
```

Here is a program which will keep looping until either a lower case 'q' is pressed, or it has looped ten times. A test is included for the detection of the lower case 'q'. When it is detected the return takes us back to the function main().

The rule with return is that when it is encountered, the program will return to the calling function.

Now have a look at Program 007.

```
/ * * * * * * * * * * * * * * * * * * * * * * * * * * * * * * * * * * * * * * * * * * * * *
 *  Program 007                                              *
 *  Demonstration of return of a value                       *
 * * * * * * * * * * * * * * * * * * * * * * * * * * * * * * * * * * * * * * * * * * * * * /

#include  <stdio.h>

main()
{
    int  f_num;

    printf("\nThis  is  now  calling  the  function  \n");

    f_num  =  first_fun();

    printf("\nNow  we  have  returned  to  the  main  function.  \n");
    printf("You  took  %d  trys  before  returning.\n",f_num);
}

first_fun()
{
    char  a_char;
    int   a_num;

    a_num  =  0;

    while  (  a_num  <  10  )
    {
        printf("\n%d  Enter  a  letter  :  -  ",  a_num);
        a_char  =  getche();
        if(  a_char  ==  'q'  )  return  (  a_num  );
        a_num  =  a_num  +  1;
    }
}
```

In this second example, the value a_num is returned to the function main() where it is
assigned to f_num. Here you can see the use of a function call as one side of an
assignment. This is something which we had already used with the getche() function.
The value to be returned is placed in brackets immediately following the return
keyword. Note that we leave a space between return and the opening bracket. This is
done to clearly indicate that return is a keyword and not a function.

A couple of small points about return which brings up again the subject of
incompatibility between compilers. First, in the theory of classic C, return () should
be the same as return. At least, that is what the text books say. In my experience this
is very rarely the case. A number of compilers will flag return () as an error. This is
the action taken by Turbo C. As a result of this if you are using return without a value
to be returned you should use just return.

There is a very good reason for this approach. It allows Turbo C to carry out a higher
level of error checking. If there are brackets then a value must be returned. The
compiler can check if a value is expected and that one is being returned.

The other question is that of brackets around the returned value. In fact, these are optional under Turbo C which will accept both:

```
return a_num;
```

and:

```
return (a_num);
```

as being valid. There are some compilers that insist on brackets. It is, therefore, safer to use brackets, and this makes the code easier to read.

A final point about the above programs. You will notice that we have used the command:

```
#include <stdio.h>
```

The file stdio.h is a special file which contains certain standard definitions and define directives. The command #include tells the compiler to read this file and include it as part of the program.

Pointers

Another method of transferring values between functions is by pointers. They are very much more versatile than arguments and return values. They are also more complex.

Class and Variables

In addition to type, that is the nature of a variable, C variables also have a quality which is called class. The nature of a variable's class defines how long it will exist and maintain its value.

There are two classes of C variable: static and auto. Basically, the easiest way to understand this is to say that an auto variable is automatically disposed of as soon as it has been finished with whilst a static variable will remain holding its value. In practice, all variables other than global variables are automatically declared as auto unless otherwise specified. Therefore, if you wish to declare a variable inside a function as static that must be done specifically.

Program 008 displays the difference between auto and static variables within a function.

This program is fairly straightforward. The interesting point is in the function increment. Here, the variable integer f_num is declared and initialized to zero. It is of type auto. The variable s_num is not initialized; it will automatically be given the value zero on the first call to the function. After that it will hold whatever value it had when you left the function last.

```
/ * * * * * * * * * * * * * * * * * * * * * * * * * * * * * * * * * * * * * * * * * *
*  Program 008                                                *
*  Demonstration of automatic and static       *
*  variables in functions                                 *
* * * * * * * * * * * * * * * * * * * * * * * * * * * * * * * * * * * * * * * * * /

main ()
{
    int count = 0; /* Declare and initialize local variable */

    while ( count < 10 )              /* Start loop */
    {
        printf("\n count = %d ",count);
        count = count + 1;
        increment();
    }
}


increment ()
{
    int f_num = 0;
    static int s_num;

    f_num = f_num + 1;
    s_num = s_num + 1;

    printf("f_num = %d, s_num = %d \n", f_num, s_num);
}
```

Register Variables

There is a third form of variable: the register variable. Technically, register variables are a third class of variables, but it is easier to think of them as a modified form of automatic variable.

The actual workings of a register variable are really for the advanced C programmer and therefore beyond the scope of this tutorial. Briefly, you can declare a variable in a function to be a register variable and the compiler will then attempt to hold that value in the processor registers rather than in memory. This, of course, means that it can be accessed quicker. However, unless you know exactly what you are doing, forcing the compiler to treat a variable as a register variable can lead to a reduction in performance. Turbo C has an effective optimization system in it which is usually far better than most programmers at selecting which variables in a routine to treat as register variables.

If you do feel that you need to make use of register variables, read the Turbo C User and Reference Guides and some of the standard text books on advanced C.

Type and Functions

All functions have a type. This is dependent on the type of the return value of the function. By default, the type of any function is int. If a function has a type other than int, then this must be specifically known to the function calling it. This can be done either by declaring the function globally so that it is known to all functions in the program, or by declaring it specifically in the calling function. There are two ways in which such a function declaration can take place. The first is the method used in classic C. This is fully supported by Turbo C. In this form the declaration of a function takes the form:

```
type  function_name();
```

So if we have a function called words, which is returning a pointer to a character, our declaration of that function would be:

```
char  *words();
```

One fact about this is that no information is given about what arguments, if any, are required to be passed to the function. This means that there is no way in which the compiler can check for you that the right number of arguments have been passed to the function. To overcome this the ANSI extension supported by Turbo C contains the option to prototype functions. The form to do a function prototype declaration is:

```
type  function_name( argument list );
```

so in our example we could have:

```
char  *words( char vowels[], char noun[] );
```

Also, as we have seen , Turbo C supports full function definitions. This means that rather than having the classic C declaration for the function word in the form:

```
char  *words( vowels, noun)
     char vowels[];
     char noun[];
{
```

we can make use of the fuller function definition which allows far more error checking on the part of the compiler of the function call:

```
char  *words( char vowels[], char noun[] )
{
```

Even where prototyping has not been used, the fuller form of the function declaration allows the compiler to undertake a higher level of error checking than with the more traditional C style of function definition.

There is, however, a problem with this. If you are writing code which has to be portable to other systems there is a chance that you may find that the older compiler on that system will not support the new form. Fortunately, Turbo C supports both forms. This means that if you need to write portable code, then you can still use the older and less efficient form of declaration for functions.

The Void Type

As described above, the presumption in C is that every function returns a value. The function has the type of the returned value. If this is not declared then the value is presumed to be of type int. Many functions do not have any return value. It was the custom with the older versions of C to define a type VOID using the #define expression in the form:

```
#define VOID int
```

This meant that if you had a function declaration you could make it clear that it was not returning any value by including the VOID word. This, on compilation, would be expanded to int so making no change:

```
VOID delay()
{
      int i;
      for ( i = 0 ; i < 10000 ; i++ )
      ;
}
```

In Turbo C, in keeping with ANSI, there is now a new standard type. This is the type void. The easiest way to think of this is as a null type. If you have any function which does not return a value then it should be declared as being of type void. You can also use void to show that no arguments can be passed to a function, so with the above example we would have:

```
void delay( void )
{
```

Another useful aspect of the type void is that it can be used to handle untyped pointers. These are pointers which are returned by functions, but do not point to a specific type. The most common form is that which is returned by the function malloc() and which actually points to a block in memory. This block may be of any size. In classic C these pointers have been declared as type char *. (They had to point to something, so saying they pointed to a single byte worked.) With the introduction of the void type you can now declare them as being of type void *. This has been done in Turbo C with many of the routines such as malloc() which handle memory blocks.

One advantage of using the void pointer is that you can assign its value to pointers of other types without having to cast them. This was something which you often had to do with the older compilers.

6

SOME INPUT AND OUTPUT

One task which you will need to perform in any language is to handle the input of data to your program and the output of data from it. In this chapter we introduce some of the basic functions used.

printf()

You have already come across the printf() function in the demonstration programs. Until now, we have not given any explanation of what it is or what it is doing.

The function printf() is a member of the standard function library of the C language. Being a print formatting function, printf() provides us with a very powerful way of outputting data. Incidentally, print formatting means that it will format your output according to the specifications you give the function in the call to it.

To use printf(), you have to send it two arguments. The first of these arguments is mandatory. This means that it must always be included. It is known as the 'control string' although for some reason people have now started to use the term format string' to describe it. This latter is the term used in the Turbo C documentation. The control string can be either a string contained within double quotation marks, or a pointer to a string.

The second argument is optional. Its use will depend on the contents of the format string. It is a list of variables, which are to be formatted and included in the printout.

First, let us consider the use of printf() with just a control string:

```
printf("Hello.");
```

In this case everything within the double quotation marks will be printed. As a general rule with printf() everything inside the double quotation is printed. However, there are two exceptions to this. These are the cases where either escaped character codes or format control directives are used.

Escaped character codes are a set of characters which are given a special meaning by being 'escaped'. That is, removed from their normal meaning. In C this is done by preceding the character with a backslash. They are, therefore, often known as backslash directives.

The escaped character codes are:

\n	Linefeed or Newline
\r	Carriage return
\t	Tab
\b	Backspace
\f	Formfeed
\0	The NULL value
\<character>	Ignore any special meaning given to the character.
\nnn	Where nnn is a three or less digit octal number that value is passed as a control character.
\xHHH	Where HHH is a three or less digit hex number that value is passed as a control character.
\a	The ASCII code 7, the audible bell or buzzer.

Most of these are fairly clear in their usage. Indeed, you will be very familiar with the \n directive which has been used in the example programs. The one aspect of the backslash directive which does cause problems is the escape mode when it is used to escape a special meaning which C gives to a character.

For instance, if we want to print a backslash in a piece of text we experience problems. The way around this is to escape it. If you wanted to print on the screen:

```
The \n is used to generate a new line.
```

It would be no use you giving the call:

```
printf("The \n is used to generate a new line.");
```

as C would treat your \n as a backslash directive and what will be printed is:

```
The
    is used to generate a new line.
```

What you have to do is escape the \ so that it is ignored by the compiler. To do this you precede it with a backslash. So what you will have is:

```
printf("The \\n is used to generate a new line.");
```

The same applies to the other symbols which have special meanings. A list of these is given on page 201 of the Turbo C User's Guide. One point here is that this list includes the single quote (apostrophe) and the question mark. Although these characters can take on special meanings which in some circumstances have to be escaped, this is not the case within printf() statements.

If you have any characters which have special meanings being used inside the control string which you intend to be printed, then you will have to escape them. For instance, if you wanted text displayed inside double quote marks you would have to use the backslash so that:

```
printf("The answer was given \"That's right.\"");
```

would produce:

```
The answer was given "That's right."
```

This can be confusing to start with but you will soon get the hang of it, and if you want to program in C you will have to!

A final point with regard to the escaped characters: the \a and the \xHHH form part of the new ANSI standards. They are not found on many older compilers. If you want to use these make sure you are using Turbo C.

Format control directives are preceded by a % sign. They are therefore often known as percent directives.

The % sign is used to tell the printf() function that it has to print a value at that point in the text. This value is obtained from the list of values given as the second argument in the function call.

The type of value which will be printed is indicated by a letter which follows the % sign. Before looking at those there is one point to consider. The % sign has a special meaning in printf() function calls. If you want to actually print the % sign in your text you have to handle it in a special way. Unlike the other special characters you do not escape it with the backslash. To print the % sign you must put in two of them. That is %%. In this case, the % directive is used to escape the % sign. Therefore:

```
printf("The dividend is expressed as a %% of gross.");
```

will print:

```
The dividend is expressed as a % of gross.
```

Now on to value types.

%d	will print an integer value.
%c	will print a character value.
%f	will print a floating point value.
%s	will print a string.
%o	will print an octal value.
%x	will print a hexadecimal value.

For each of the percent directives which appears in the control string there must be a corresponding value in the value list. The values in the value list must appear in the same order as the associated percent directives in the control string.

This means that if the first percent directive in the control string is a character percent directive and the second is an integer percent directive, then the first value in the value list must be a character value and the second an integer value. Have a look at Program 009.

```
/***********************************************
* Program 009                                  *
* Demonstration of printf()                    *
***********************************************/

main()
{
    char  a_let;
    int   a_num;

    a_let = 'a';
    a_num = 1234;

    printf("The letter = %c, the number %d \n",a_let,a_num);
}
```

The printf() function allows you to include many formatting commands. One useful aspect of the percent directives is that you can include flags to tell the function how to print the values. These can specify the field size, left or right justification and form. The field size and justification can be very useful if you are working in columns.

You specify field size by placing a numeric value between the % sign and the designation letter. If the numeric value is unsigned then the value will be printed right justified. If the minus sign is included to indicate a negative value then it will be printed left justified. If the field size designation is preceded by a 0 then the field will be zero filled.

Note that if you give a field size which is smaller than the amount of space required for the value, then the field will be expanded to make space. Consider Program 010.

If you enter and run this you will get the following results:

```
Justify to the right    The number is :1234
Justify to the left     The number is :1234
Cut it to 3 places      The number is :1234
Zero fill to 7 places   The number is :0001234
```

```
/************************************************
* Program 010                                  *
* Demonstration of field setting in            *
* printf() functions                           *
************************************************/

main()
{
        int a_num = 1234;

        printf("Justify to the right   ");
        printf("The number is  :%7d\n",a_num);
        printf("Justify to the left    ");
        printf("The number is  :%-7d\n",a_num);
        printf("Cut it to 3 places     ");
        printf("The number is  :%3d\n",a_num);
        printf("Zero fill to 7 places ");
        printf("The number is  :%07d\n",a_num);
}
```

As you can see, where we have tried to cut the number back to three places, it has not worked. The space has been expanded to allow the total value to be printed.

In the case of floating point values you may want to specify the degree of precision with which you want them printed. For instance %5.2f will print the number to two places of decimals.

If you want to print to two decimal places without setting the field size, you can do this by putting just the number of decimal places to be printed to the right of the decimal point. So %.3f will print the value to three decimal places with no setting for the field size. Have a look at Program 011.

```
/************************************************
* Program 011                                  *
* Demonstration of decimal place               *
* formatting with the printf() function        *
************************************************/

main()
{
        float num = 49.123456;

        printf("The number is %f \n",num);
        printf("The number is %5.3f \n",num);
        printf("The number is %.3f \n",num);
        printf("The number is %04.4f \n",num);
}
```

This will produce the following output:

```
The number is 49.123455
The number is 49.123
The number is 49.123
The number is 49.1235
```

You will notice that the printout is not accurate beyond the third decimal place. This is something which you should keep in mind when working with floating point numbers in C. Accuracy is not one of their greatest attributes.

There are a number of other aspects to the printf() function for formatting output. They are not used so often as those given above. As such, they are left out of this section to try and keep it fairly simple. The whole of printf() under Turbo C is explained fully in the Reference Guide. Once you are confident in your basic usage of printf() sit down and read the relevant section in the Guide.

The same advice will apply to all the standard functions discussed later. The aim of this book is to give you a basic introduction to programming in Turbo C. If you want to know all the ins and outs of the language, read the Reference Guide.

scanf()

The complementary function to printf() is the input function scanf(). This again is part of the standard library. It takes input from the standard input, this is usually the keyboard, and places that input in a designated address.

Like printf() scanf() requires two arguments passed to it. The first is the control string which will consist of percent directives, informing it what type of input to accept. The second is a list of addresses telling it where to place the input.

The form of the percent directives is the same as for printf().

To input an integer number the function would be used in the form:

```
scanf("%d", &a_num);
```

where a_num is a declared integer variable. The & before a_num refers to address. A simple way to think of this is to read the & as being short for at. So what you are saying is 'store at a_num'. What has been expressed in the above statement is take the input of an integer value and place that value in the address associated with the variable a_num.

```
/******************************************************
 * Program 012                                        *
 * Demonstration of input using scanf()               *
 ******************************************************/

main()
{
      int a_num = 0;

      printf("The value of a_num is %d.\n", a_num);
      printf("Please enter new value ... ");

      scanf("%d", &a_num);

      printf("\n\nThe new value is %d\n", a_num);
}
```

This is, of course, a very simple demo program. Study it and understand how scanf() is working. Try a few experiments of your own and see how you can develop the use of the function.

Although versatile, there is a problem with scanf() which throws many programmers. If you ask printf() to print a string:

```
printf("%s", a_string);
```

the whole string will be printed right up to the terminating 0. Many programmers, especially when they are starting, tend to think that scanf() will work the same with inputted strings: it does not.

First, scanf() ignores leading white space, that is spaces, tabs and newlines. It does not start to read the string in until it comes across a character which is not white space. Second, it terminates its read at the first white space character it comes across.

This means that if the name Mike Richards is entered as a response to a scanf() input call, only Mike would be entered. Enter and run Program 013 and see how scanf() reacts to different string inputs.

```
/ * * * * * * * * * * * * * * * * * * * * * * * * * * * * * * * * * * * * * * * * * * * * * *
* Program 013                                          *
* Demonstration of scanf()                             *
* * * * * * * * * * * * * * * * * * * * * * * * * * * * * * * * * * * * * * * * * * * * * * /

main()
{
        int i;
        char string[30];

        for ( i = 0; i < 10; i++ )
        {
        printf("\n%02d : Enter a word or phrase .... ");
        scanf("%s", &string);

        printf("\n\nThe accepted input was %s \n",string);
        }

        printf("\n\nRun Finished.\n");

}
```

This program uses a for loop to take an input of strings. Do not worry about how it is working as we will be looking at that in depth later. All you need to note is how it reacts to different input. When I entered the phrase "Turbo C is the greatest", all that was printed out was "Turbo".

getchar()

Another input function is getchar(). This function is defined in the file stdio.h. To use it, therefore, you must include the contents of that file in your program. This is done by making use of the preprocessor directive #include:

```
#include <stdio.h>
```

This will tell the compiler to include the system header file stdio.h. This file, in fact, includes a number of standard routines and definitions for input and output functions. You will come across its use quite often.

The getchar() function when called waits for a key to be depressed and returns the value of the key pressed. There is a problem here in that it appears to operate slightly differently on different systems. This appears to be a reflection of the version of MSDOS you are using. On some systems it will return a value the moment the key is depressed. With other systems you will have to press the RETURN key. In these latter cases this is taken as a second input. Enter and run Program 014 and see how your system reacts.

```
/***********************************************
* Program 014                                  *
* Demonstration of getchar()                    *
***********************************************/

#include <stdio.h>

main()
{
      int keypress = 0;
      char letter;

      while ( keypress != 32 )
      {
            keypress = getchar();
            letter = keypress;
            printf("The letter was %c.\n", letter );
      }

}
```

getche()

If you do want to have a single character get call, which does not wait for the RETURN key to be depressed you are probably better off using getche(). This gets the value of the key depressed and echoes it to the screen. Again, you have to include stdio.h to use this call. Have a look at the previous example program but written this time with getche() in Program 015.

```
/************************************************
* Program 015                                   *
* Demonstration of getche()                     *
************************************************/

#include <stdio.h>

main()
{
      int keypress = 0;
      char letter;

      while ( keypress != 32 )
      {
          keypress = getche();
          letter = keypress;
          printf("The letter was %c.\n", letter );
      }

}
```

getch()

The function getch() works very much like getche() which we looked at above. The difference is that it does not echo a character to the screen. This can be very useful, especially if you are using the key depression as a single rather than a character input. Consider the following code fragment:

```
disk_err_message()
{
    printf("\nAn error has occurred on the disk\n");
    printf("read/write operation.The program will\n");
    printf("now abort.  Please check your system\n");
    printf("before rerunning the program.\n");
    printf("\n\nPress any key to finish. \n");

    getch();

    return;
}
```

In this case a message will be printed and the system will then wait until a key is pressed.

A word of warning about the portability of getch() and getche(). The Turbo C Reference Guide states that they are found on Unix Systems. That tends to be the only place you do find them. A number of MSDOS compilers do not support them.

The above three functions all belong to a family of related functions based on the function getc(). This is one of the basic functions defined in Kernighan and Ritchie. When you are using them remember that they will wait for a key to be depressed. This is not always what you want. Often you want to do one thing if a key has been depressed and something different if a key has not been depressed.

kbhit()

To meet the above requirement, Turbo C provides the function kbhit(). The prototype for this function is held in a header file called conio.h and this must be included in your code if you want to use the function.

When invoked, if a key has been depressed kbhit() will return a non zero value. If there is no key read available it will return zero. In Program 016 I have used kbhit() and getch() to test for an abort situation.

```
/************************************************
 * Prog 016                                     *
 * Demonstration of kbhit() and getch()         *
 ************************************************/

#include <stdio.h>
#include <conio.h>        /* contains prototype for kbhit() */

main()
{
    int i = 0;
    printf("Press \"q\" to stop display\n");

    while ( 1 )            /* This is setting up anendless
                            * loop because the while will always
                            * be one therefore true.
                            */
    {
        printf("%d ", i);
        i = i + 1;

        if ( kbhit() )     /* Test for key depression. */
        {
            char let;
            let = getch();  /* Get value ofkey but
                             * do not echo it to the
                             * screen.
                             */

            if ( let == 'q' ) exit (0);
            /* If q was pressed finish. */

            printf("The key hit was %c \n",let);
        }
        else printf("No key was hit \n");
    }
}
```

This program uses what is known as an endless loop in which to test for the input of a key depression. So far, we have not looked at loops but we will do so in Chapter 9. For the time being note that in the form given the while command will result in the program looping forever. To escape from the loop I have set up a test condition. This tests if the value of the key pressed is equal to a lower case q. If it is, the exit command is used to leave the program, and thereby escape from the loop. The function kbhit() is used to detect if a key has, in fact, been depressed. A check is only made on the value of the key if one has been pressed. Otherwise, the program carries on and prints the information that no key was pressed.

putchar()

Just as getchar() is a special library function to allow you to have an input of a single character, there is also a special library function to allow the output of a single character. This is putchar(). Note once again that with Turbo C this will require you to have #include <stdio.h> at the start of your program. In fact, the inclusion of this file is so common in C programs, it is very unlikely that you will find a C program more than a few lines long without it.

A couple of points with putchar(). It can only be used to print single characters at a time. Control characters like \n have to be passed to it in single inverted commas. Have a look at sample Program 017 below.

```
/ * * * * * * * * * * * * * * * * * * * * * * * * * * * * * * * * * * * * * * * * * *
* Program 017                                              *
* Demonstration of putchar                                 *
* * * * * * * * * * * * * * * * * * * * * * * * * * * * * * * * * * * * * * * * * * /

#include <stdio.h>

main()
{
        int  num,scount;
        char buf[] = "Turbo C";
        char ch;

        for ( num = 0; num <= strlen(buf); num++)
        {
                ch = buf[num];

                for( scount = 0; scount <= num; scount++)
                {
                putchar(32);
                }
                putchar(ch);
                putchar('\n');
        }

}
```

In this program we are using another form of loop which we demonstrate later in Chapter 9, the for loop. Do not bother now with how the loop is working, just look at the use of putchar(). In the inner loop we are using putchar() to put down spaces. It is passed the value 32 which is the ASCII value for a space. Once the number of spaces which are required for the offset have been produced by the loop, putchar() is again invoked. In this invocation, the variable ch is passed to it. This has been given a value equal to one of the letters of the string 'Turbo C'. Finally, after this has been printed, putchar() is passed the control character for a newline, this being passed inside single inverted commas.

The printing of single characters is a fairly common activity in C programming and putchar() is somewhat more efficient at doing this than using the single character print facility in printf().

7

THE C OPERATORS

Operators are instructions, usually represented by single symbols, which when combined with values instruct the program to carry out some form of operation of the values.

This concept may seem complicated, but it is quite simple. If I say "ADD TWO TO THREE", the values would be two and three. The operator in that statement is the instruction add. It may be represented in arithmetic form as:

```
2 + 3
```

In this case the operator is "+".

Table 7.1 Operator Descriptions

Type of operator	Description
Additive	The addition and subtraction operators. + - .
Multiplicative	The operators which handle multiplication, division and modulo. They are *, /, and %.
Relational	The operators which test the relationship between two values. They are greater than, less than, greater than or equal to, less than orequal to. >, <, >=, <=.
Equality	A special pair of relational operators which test for values being either equal or not equal. They are equals == and not equal !=.
Logical	The operators which carry out 'logical' comparisons, 'and' and 'or', && and ||.
Unary	These are operators which carry out an operation on a single value. They are the unary minus, - and the logical negation !.
Incremental	The operators which increase or decrease a value by one unit, ++ and --.
Bitwise	These are a special set of operators which carry out functions on bytes at the bit level. They are covered in detail in Chapter 15.

In the C language there are a number of types of operator. Do not expect to memorize them all now. The only way you will learn them is to use them. Read through and become familiar with them.

The Additive Operators

Addition and subtraction are as one would expect. There are no nasty surprises here. Have a look at Program 018.

```
/***********************************************
* Program 018                                  *
* Demonstration of additive operators          *
***********************************************/

#include <stdio.h>

/* Declaration of global integer variables. */

int f_num, s_num, t_num, r_num;

main()
{
        get_num();
        add_num();
        results();
        sub_num();
        results();
}

/******************************************************
* The function get_num takes the input of three       *
* integers and assigns it to the global variables.    *
* In this function a dummy getchar() is used to        *
* dispose of the unwanted return left behind by        *
* getchar.                                             *
******************************************************/

get_num()
{
        printf("\nEnter three single digit numbers. \n");
        printf("\nFirst Number : ");
        f_num = getchar() - '0';
        getchar();
        printf("\nSecond Number : ");
        s_num = getchar() - '0';
        getchar();
        printf("\nThird Number : ");
        t_num = getchar() - '0';
        getchar();
        printf("\nThank you.\n\n");
}
```

```
/ * * * * * * * * * * * * * * * * * * * * * * * * * * * * * * * * * * * * * * * * * * * * * * * *
* The function add_num adds three numbers         *
* together and assigns the result to r_num        *
* * * * * * * * * * * * * * * * * * * * * * * * * * * * * * * * * * * * * * * * * * * * * * * * /

add_num()
{
        printf("\nAdding Numbers.\n");
        r_num = f_num + s_num + t_num;
}

/ * * * * * * * * * * * * * * * * * * * * * * * * * * * * * * * * * * * * * * * * * * * * * * * *
* The function sub_num subtracts three numbers    *
* assigning the result to r_num.                  *
* * * * * * * * * * * * * * * * * * * * * * * * * * * * * * * * * * * * * * * * * * * * * * * * /

sub_num()
{
        printf("\nSubtracting Numbers. \n");
        r_num = f_num - s_num - t_num;
}

/ * * * * * * * * * * * * * * * * * * * * * * * * * * * * * * * * * * * * * * * * * * * * * * * *
* The function results() prints out the state of*
* the variables and the result of the operation *
* * * * * * * * * * * * * * * * * * * * * * * * * * * * * * * * * * * * * * * * * * * * * * * * /

results()
{
        printf("\nFirst number    = %d ", f_num);
        printf("\nSecond number   = %d ", s_num);
        printf("\nThird number    = %d ", t_num);
        printf("\nThe result of the calculation was ");
        printf("%d \n", r_num);
}
```

There is nothing particularly complicated about this program. However, there are a few touches which are worth noting.

First, we have proceduralised the program quite a bit. This means that we only have to write the printout sequence for the results once, even though we make use of it twice.

As far as possible you should try to break your programs up into small, self-contained procedures.

Note how each of the functions is commented, telling you what it is going to be doing. At the moment, these comments are fairly informal. As you work further into this tutorial you will find that the comments become more formal and more informative. The commenting of a program is important. If you ever have to go back to maintain a program months after you have written it, you will be grateful for good comments.

One practice which you will notice here is that use has been made of a dummy getchar() to remove the unwanted return left behind by getchar(). This is a very useful technique. Many of the input functions give problems with unwanted returns at the end of the input. The function scanf() is a particularly difficult one at times. Placing a getchar(), the return value of which is not assigned to anything, after the reading function can clean up the unwanted returns.

In this program I have used the getchar() function to get the input of a number. The reason for this is that in this example only single digit numbers are required. The function getchar() will return a single character value. That value, though, is an ASCII character value. To use it as a number from 0 to 9, I have to strip off the difference between its ASCII value and the number it represents. This I have done by subtracting the value of the character '0' from the returned value.

You will find techniques of this kind very useful when you want to limit the scope of input which may be given.

The Multiplicative Operators

In C there are three multiplicative operators. They are the multiplication operator, *, the division operator, /, and the modulo operator %.

Multiplication works in the way familiar from normal arithmetic. From 4 * 5, that is four times five, you obtain the result 20. However, division can present a few surprises.

If you are working in integers, and divide an integer by an integer, you will get an integer result. Any remainder that there might be is discarded. This is something which can be confusing if you are not expecting it.

Should you need to know what the remainder of a division is this can be obtained by using the third of the multiplicative operators, the modulo operator. This also carries out a division. In this case, though, it only gives you the remainder as a result. Incidentally, the modulo operator can only be applied to integer variables.

Program 019 gives a demonstration of the basic usage of the multiplicative operators.

```
/******************************************************
* Program 019                                        *
* Demonstration of multiplicative operator           *
******************************************************/

#include <stdio.h>

/* Declare Global Variables. */

int f_num, s_num, r_num;
```

```
main()
{
        getnum();
        multiply();
        divide();
        modulo();
}


/*****************************************************
* The function getnum() takes the input of two     *
* single digit numbers and assigns them to the     *
* global variables.                                *
*****************************************************/

getnum()
{
        printf("\nEnter a single digit number - ");
        f_num = getchar() - '0';
        getchar();

        printf("\nEnter a second number        - ");
        s_num = getchar() - '0';
        getchar();

        printf("\nThe numbers selected are ");
        printf("%d and %d \n", f_num, s_num);
}


/*****************************************************
* The function multiply() carries out a multi-     *
* plication operation on the two numbers.          *
*****************************************************/

multiply()
{
        r_num = f_num * s_num;

        printf("\nThe multiply operator gives the ");
        printf("result %d \n", r_num);
}


/*****************************************************
* The function divide() carries out a division     *
* operation on the two numbers.                    *
*****************************************************/

divide()
{
        r_num = f_num / s_num;
        printf("\nThe divide operator gives the ");
        printf("result %d \n", r_num);
}
```

(handwritten annotation: subtract the Ascii value of '0', i.e. 30 decimal.)

```
/ * * * * * * * * * * * * * * * * * * * * * * * * * * * * * * * * * * * * * * * * * * *
*  The  modulo()  function  carries  out  the  modulo     *
*  operation  on  the  two  numbers.                        *
* * * * * * * * * * * * * * * * * * * * * * * * * * * * * * * * * * * * * * * * * * * /

modulo()
{
        r_num = f_num % s_num;
        printf("\nThe modulo operator gives the ");
        printf("result %d \n", r_num);
        }
```

Notice that use has again been made of the dummy getchar() call to cope with the problem caused by unwanted return key values.

You should have a basic understanding of some aspects of C by now, so why not write a program on your own? One task you could try is write a short program to do the following:

> Take the input of two numbers.

> Divide the first number by the second number.

> Print the result with the remainder.

One way of doing this is given in Answer 1 in Appendix 4. Before you look at it, try and work it out for yourself. Remember, the answer is just one way of doing it. There are a number of others. That is one of the enjoyable aspects of C, there are many different ways of using it to solve a problem.

The Incremental Operators

It is common when writing programs to increase or to decrease the value of a variable by one unit. In C you are provided with two operators to do this, they are the ++ and --. These are very useful operators, but should be used with care.

It is important to remember that it increases or decreases by one unit or you might get some very nasty surprises. The incremental operators take into account the type of variable on which they are working. They adjust the amount of the numeric change in accordance with the type of variable.

With the normal numeric variables, they work as expected. If you have a variable f_num and use the expression:

```
f_num++;
```

the value of f_num will be increased by one. For example, if f_num was 1048 it will be increased to 1049. The difference comes when the variable is a pointer. In the case of a pointer the numeric change will be equal to the size of the object in bytes to which the pointer is pointing. If you have a pointer of type integer, it is pointing to a two byte object. To increase the pointer to point to the next object in memory will require an increase of two. If you use the incremental operator on a pointer to type integer, the change will be two. So if our pointer p_fnum is pointing to a location -102 and we use the expression:

```
p_fnum++;
```

the pointer will now point to location -100.

The placement of the operator has an effect on how the operation is carried out. You can place the incremental operators either before the operand, that is the value they are operating on, or after it. If you are using the operation in an expression this will make a difference. Note that:

```
a = ++b;
```

is not the same as:

```
a = b++;
```

The first expression says increase the value of b by one unit then assign that value to a. The second expression says assign the value of b to a then increase b by one unit. You must keep this in mind at all times when working with the incremental operators inside expressions.

Have a look at Program 020 which illustrates this.

```
/ * * * * * * * * * * * * * * * * * * * * * * * * * * * * * * * * * * * * * * * * * *
 *  Program 020                                        *
 *  Demonstration of incremental operators       *
 * * * * * * * * * * * * * * * * * * * * * * * * * * * * * * * * * * * * * * * * * * /
# include    < std io. h >
main()
{
        int i, r_num, f_num;

        f_num = 1;
        r_num = f_num++;

        printf("\nr_num = %d, f_num = %d", r_num, f_num);

        f_num = 1;
        r_num = ++f_num;

        printf("\nr_num = %d, f_num = %d", r_num, f_num);
}
```

This produces the output:

```
r_num = 1, f_num = 2
r_num = 2, f_num = 2
```

In the first stage of this program one is assigned to f_num then the value of f_num is assigned to r_num and f_num is increased by one. The results of this are then printed out. In the second part one is assigned to f_num, f_num is then increased by one. Only then is the value of f_num assigned to r_num and the results printed out.

It is surprising how often even quite experienced C programmers are confused by positioning of either -- or ++ and get a result they did not expect. This is so frequent that it calls into question the use of these operators.

Saying:

```
f_num++;
```

is equivalent to saying:

```
f_num = f_num + 1;
```

although the latter is a great deal easier to read and understand. I am not saying that you should avoid using the ++ and -- operators. What I am saying is that you should use them with care and consider using the full assignment form rather than the incremental operators when you can. It may take more typing in, but it is far easier to read when you come to maintaining code.

This brings us to the question of 'shorthand' forms in C. Very often you will find that C provides you with two ways of writing something: one which takes quite extensive typing in and another which takes less. In most circumstances with compilers like Turbo C the optimization routines will compile these to the same code. The use of the shorthand form can save you considerable typing in, but it can also make code difficult to read. As it does not really fit in anywhere else we will look at one of these shorthand forms now.

The OP operator

A common practice in programming is to do something on a variable and assign the result to the variable upon which the operation has been carried out. The increment of a variable is probably the most common example:

```
num = num + 2;
```

In this case we have a variable num, which we have increased in value by 2. A similar sort of action would be:

```
num = num * 9;
```

Here we assign to num the old value of num times 9.

This type of action is so common in programming that C has a special set of operators to handle this situation. The operator takes the form of the mathematical or bitwise operator immediately followed by the equals sign. It says take the value on the left of the operator, carry out the operation indicated using the value on the right and store its result back in the variable on the left. Consider the following:

```
num += 2;

num *= 9;
```

The OP form of the operators will work with all the mathematical operators and the bitwise operators with the exception of ~, the bitwise ones-complement, which is a unary operator.

Using the OP operators can save you a great deal of typing. They also tend to make the programs rather more cryptic when you come to read them. Again, what I am saying here is use them by all means but take care that they do not impinge on the readability of the code.

There are many C programmers around, usually from an assembler background, who think that short and cryptic code is good code. To an extent, in the early days of C, this was often the case. Operations like:

```
num++;
num *= 3;
```

would produce less code than:

```
num = num + 1;
num = num * 3;
```

This is generally no longer the case. Turbo C, in common with most modern compilers, has quite an efficient optimization routine which will usually make a better job of code optimization than you can by selecting between the different ways of writing an expression.

My advice is: try and write code which is in the form that is easiest to read. This is usually the least likely to have bugs in it, and the easiest to maintain.

The additive, multiplicative and incremental operators explained in this chapter are the arithmetic operators within C. Four of the other operator sets: the relational, equality, logical and unary operators, are involved in truth testing. These are studied in Chapter 8 when we look at the if statement. The final set of operators are the bitwise operators which are dealt with on their own in Chapter 15.

8

TESTING RELATIONSHIPS

The relational, equality and logical operators, together with the unary operators are all concerned with relational values. The testing of the relationship between values is a major element in most programming work. Take, for example, the following piece of specification:

> Take input from keyboard.
> Assign input to variable key_in.
> Test if key_in is the letter y or the letter Y.
> If the test is positive go on to the next stage.
> Otherwise return to main menu.

Here we have to compare the input from the keyboard and test it against two possible values, y and Y. This sort of procedure is fairly common in programs.

True and False

An important concept which you must understand is that of True and False. In the above specification we have a condition. Does the input from the keyboard match either y or Y? If it does, the condition is said to be true, otherwise it is said to be false.

In the C language, as with most but not all computer languages, the value zero is used to represent false. As you can only have one of two results, either something is true or it is false, any other value than zero must be regarded as true. So if a test is constructed to test if the input from the keyboard is either y or Y, it will return a non-zero value when the input is y or Y and a zero value when it is not.

The if Command

The if command carries out a test of a condition. If the condition is true, then it carries out an action specified in the statement. If it is not, the action is ignored. The basic form of the command is:

```
if ( condition ) action ;
```

Often, you will want to carry out more than one action. In such cases, a series of statements can be included in the if command by using the following construction:

```
if ( condition )
{
        action1 ;
        action2 ;
        action3 ;
        :
        :
        actionn ;
}
```

The structure of an if statement is such that if the condition is true an action is carried out. If not, control moves onto the next statement. This is shown in Figure 8.1.

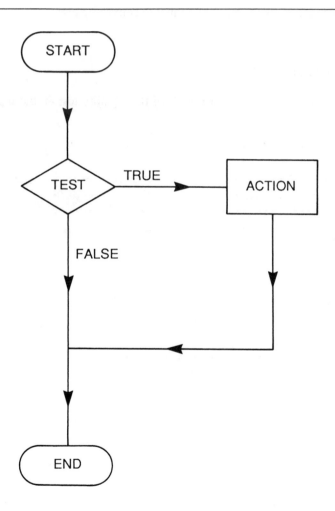

Figure 8.1

The Equality Operators

The simplest type of test is to test if something is equal to, or not equal to, something else. Tests of this kind are done using the equality operators, == and !=.

The == operator tests if something is equal to something else. So :

```
a == b
```

is saying is a equal to b?

The != operator tests if something is not equal to something else. So :

```
a != b
```

is saying is a not equal to b?

Program 021 gives a simple demonstration of the equality test on the input from the keyboard.

```
/*****************************************************
* Program 021                                       *
* Demonstration using equality operators to test*
* input from the keyboard                           *
*****************************************************/

#include <stdio.h>

main()
{
        char letter;

        while ( 1 )
        {
                printf("\nEnter a letter : ");
                letter = getche();
                if ( letter == 'y')
                {
                        printf("\nLetter was y, now exiting. ");
                        exit (0);        return (0); (for C++)
                }

                if ( letter != 'y' )
                        printf("\nLetter was not y.");
        }
}
```

In this program a character is entered from the keyboard and the value of that character is assigned to the character variable letter. This is done inside a while loop. Two tests are now carried out on the variable letter. If it is equal to y a message is printed and the program is exited, thereby escaping the endless loop. The second test checks if the letter was not equal to y and then the loop continues.

The else command

If you think about Program 021, if the first test is false, the second must be true. The second test is immaterial. We could have just had one test. Sometimes though, you need to carry out an action if the test is true, and another if it is false. This is where the else command comes into use.

```
/ * * * * * * * * * * * * * * * * * * * * * * * * * * * * * * * * * * * * * * * * * * * * * * * * *
* Program 022                                        *
* Demonstration of else                              *
* * * * * * * * * * * * * * * * * * * * * * * * * * * * * * * * * * * * * * * * * * * * * * * * */

main()
{
        char letter;

        while ( 1 )
        {
                printf("\nPress a key ");

                letter = getche();

                if ( letter == 'y' )
                {
                        printf("\nThe letter was y. ");
                }
                else
                        printf("\nLetter was not y.");

                if ( letter == 'q' ) exit (0);
        }

}
```

In Program 022 one of two actions is carried out depending on the result of the condition in the if statement. The basic structure of an if..else statement is that if the condition is true, one action is carried out, if it is not, another is carried out (see Figure 8.2).

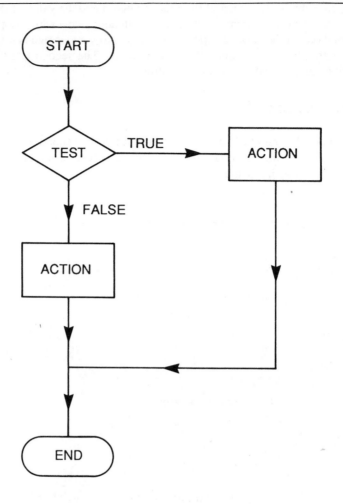

Figure 8.2

The relational operators

These operators test for the relationship between values. The value on the left-hand side of the operator is compared with the value on the right-hand side of the operator and if the relationship is that indicated by the operator, then the test is regarded as true. The relational operators are:

>   is greater than.
<   is less than.
>=   is greater than or equal to.
<=   is less than or equal to.

You can see how these are used in Program 023.

```
/ *************************************************
* Program 023                                   *
* A demonstration of the relational operators.   *
* This routine converts lower case letters        *
* to upper case.                                  *
************************************************* /

#include <stdio.h>

/* function prototype */
char make_upper( char let );

main()
{
        char ch;

        while(1)
        {
                printf("\nEnter any character    : ");
                ch = getchar();
                getchar();

                ch = make_upper(ch);
                printf("\nThe character was %c ",ch);
                if ( ch == 'Q' ) exit (0);
        }                         return
}


char make_upper( char let )
{
                if ( let < 'a' ) return (let);
                if ( let > 'z' ) return (let);
                return ( ( let - 'a' ) + 'A');
}
```

This program takes the input of characters inside an endless loop. We look at the workings of such loops in Chapter 9. The inputted character is passed as an argument to the function make_upper(). As this function is not returning the default type int we have specifically prototyped it at the start of the program. In the function make_upper() two tests are carried out to check that the character is a lower case letter. If it is not, then it is returned unchanged. If it is, the value 'a' is subtracted from it and the value 'A' added. Due to the arrangement of the ASCII code this has the effect of changing the value to that of an upper case letter. This is then returned.

In fact, this is all rather a waste of time as Turbo C has a function in its standard library which will do this for you. That is toupper(). It is good practice, though, to write your own version of functions like this. How about writing one which will convert upper case to lower? An example of such a function is given in Answer 2 in Appendix 4.

The Logical Operators

Quite often you need to have a command carried out if one or another condition is true, or sometimes only if all conditions of a set of conditions are true. You can, of course, cover this by using complicated if structures. Consider the example of Program 024.

```
/ * * * * * * * * * * * * * * * * * * * * * * * * * * * * * * * * * * * * * * * * * * * * * * * * *
* Program   024                                         *
* Complicated if structures                             *
* * * * * * * * * * * * * * * * * * * * * * * * * * * * * * * * * * * * * * * * * * * * * * * * * /

#include  <stdio.h>

main()
{
        char  f_let, s_let;

        printf("\nEnter  a  character  :  ");
        f_let  =  getchar();
        getchar();
        printf("\nEnter another       :  ");
        s_let  =  getchar();
        getchar();

        if  (  f_let  >=  '0'  )
        {
                if  (  f_let  <=  '9'  )
                        printf("First  character  is  a  number.\n");
        }
        if  (  s_let  >=  '0'  )
        {
                if  (  s_let  <=  '9'  )
                        printf("Second  character  is  a  number.\n");
        }
}
```

It works, but any C programmer opening this book at random and seeing this example would be very shocked. The C language supports two logical operators which allow you to combine conditions in truth tests. The operators are:

The AND operator &&

and:

The OR operator ||

If you look at the following:

```
if( (x<5 && y>5) || (x>10 && y<10))    .....
```

what is being said here is:

if x is less than 5 and y is greater than five carry out the action, or alternatively if x is greater than 10 and y is less than 10 carry out the action.

If we replace the multiple if statements in the above program with if statements using && we can have a much shorter program. Study Program 025.

```
/********************************************
* Program 025                              *
* Demo Using if with && so that two conditions *
* are required to be true before action is  *
* taken.                                    *
********************************************/

#include <stdio.h>

main()
{
    int f_let, s_let;

    printf("Enter a character ");
    f_let=getchar();
    getchar();
    printf("Enter a second character ");
    s_let=getchar();
    getchar();

    if(f_let >= '0' && f_let <= '9')
        printf("First character is a number\n\n");

    if(s_let >= '0' && s_let <= '9')
        printf("Second character is a number\n\n");
}
```

Having entered the above and found out how it works, try altering parts of it and see what effect this has. You should now try the following. Write a short program making use of the || operator to accept as a true input either upper or lower case y without having to do a case conversion.

Such a routine can be very useful once you have written it. It is quite common in programs to require a Yes or No input to be given with a single key entry of the Y or N keys. The problem is that you must allow for it being given in either upper or lower case. To convert all input to upper case or *vice versa* then do the test takes much more coding and run time code than a test which allows for both options.

The Unary Operators

These are operators which operate on a single variable or expression. There are two in the C language, they are:

      The NOT operator   !

      The NEGATION operator -

Let us consider the NOT operator first. A common type of test in programming is to see if a variable has a value of zero. Such a test could be written as:

```
if(f_num == 0) ....
```

As we explained above, the value 0 is false in the true/false testing. Therefore, if f_num is equal to 0 in the above value the result returned is a value other than 0. If we had written:

```
if(f_num)...
```

the action will only be carried out when the f_num is a value other than 0 which is not what we want. The NOT operator, however, inverts the truth of a variable or expression. So if we write:

```
if(!f_num)...
```

it is the same as writing:

```
if(f_num == 0)...
```

This is because when f_num is equal to 0 false is returned but this is inverted by the NOT operator into true. Just as when f_num is equal to any value other than 0 f_num would return true but the not operator inverts this into false.

The NOT operator is a way of writing (f_num == 0) more briefly. It is more difficult to read and understand, and many programmers prefer to use (f_num == 0) rather than the shorter (!fnum). With modern optimizing compilers like Turbo C there is little or no advantage in using the NOT operator rather than the test for equal to zero. The compiler will normally compile both to the same code.

The other unary operator is negation. This is a - sign placed in front of any variable or expression and has the effect of reversing the sign of that variable or expression.

For example, if the value of (x-y) is positive, then -(x-y) will be negative.

The ? and : operators

One of the most common types of selection using the if else structured test is to return one of two values depending on the truth of a condition. Consider the following code fragment:

```
if ( ch >= 'a' && ch <= 'z' )
        dduct = 32;
else
        dduct = 0;
```

In this fragment a test is made to find out if the character ch is a lower case letter. If it is, the integer variable dduct is then given the value 32, if not, it is given the value 0.

The important point about this is that the test can only return one of two results depending on whether it is true or false. Such tests are so frequent in programming that C has two special operators to deal with it; they provide a shorthand way of expressing such situations. The two operators are ? and : which are used in the manner:

```
<allocation> = (test) ? <result if true> : <result  if false>;
```

So the above example can be rewritten as:

```
dduct = ( ch >= 'a' && ch <= 'z' ) ? 32 : 0;
```

These structures can be used to combine the test within another expression. For instance, the test for printing the largest of two numbers could be combined with the print command as:

```
printf( "%d",(num1 >= num2) ?num1:num2);
```

This is illustrated in Program 026.

```
/****************************************************
* Program 026                                       *
* Demonstration of ? and : operators                *
****************************************************/

main()
{
        int num1, num2;

        printf("Enter two numbers ");
        scanf("%d%d",&num1,&num2);
        printf("\nThe largest number is : ");
        printf("%d\n",(num1 > num2 ) ? num1 : num2 );
}
```

Although the ? and : operators can be very useful, especially when writing code macros, they should be used with care. Although they take less typing and produce less code than the if else tests they are always less easy to read. This can result in difficulty in debugging and maintaining code.

As a basic rule it is advisable not to use the ?: operators outside the definition of code macros unless a speed or code size advantage can be demonstrated which is important in the situation where they are used.

9

GOING ROUND IN CIRCLES

More often than not, in a program you will want to do something a number of times. In fact, we have already done so in some of the examples , although use of the while statement has not been explained.

The method used to carry something out a number of times is looping. There are three looping statements in C. They are:

> while
>
> do-while
>
> for

The while Loop

With the while loop the syntax is:

> while(condition)
>   action;

While the condition is true, the action will be repeated. Multiply actions can be included by using curly brackets in the form:

> while(condition)
>   {
>   action1;
>   action2;
>   action3;
>   {

The important point to remember about the while statement is that the condition is tested at the start and the actions only carried out if the condition is true (see Figure 9.1).

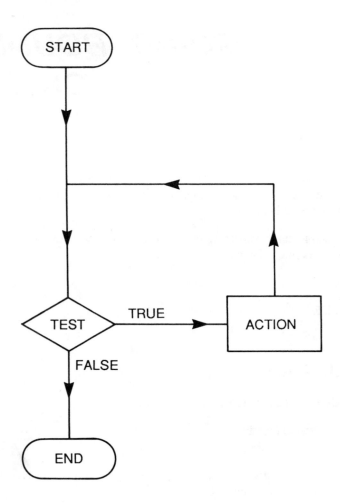

Figure 9.1 The while loop

The do-while Loop

The reverse of this is the do-while statement. This has the form:

```
do action;
  while(condition);
```

Whilst some compilers will accept a do statement in the above form, many insist that curly brackets are used even when there is only one action. As this also makes the do-while statement more readable they should always be used. So the form should be:

```
do
{
action;
}
while(condition);
```

Here the test is made at the end and a do-while loop will always be performed at least once before the test is made (see Figure 9.2). This is not the case with a while loop.

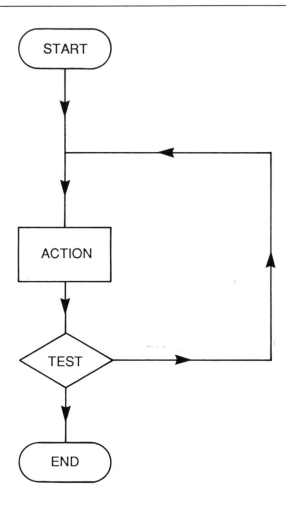

Figure 9.2 The do-while loop

Have a look at Programs 027 and 027a.

```
/ * * * * * * * * * * * * * * * * * * * * * * * * * * * * * * * * * * * * * * * * * *
* Program 027                                                   *
* Demo of while loop                                            *
* * * * * * * * * * * * * * * * * * * * * * * * * * * * * * * * * * * * * * * * * * /

#include  <stdio.h>

main ()
{
        char  ch;
        int  f_num;

        f_num = 0;

        printf ("Enter  a  character  ");
        ch=getchar ();
        getchar ();

        while (ch  !=  'q')
        {
                printf ("%d\nEnter  a  character  ",++f_num);
                ch=getchar ();
                getchar ();
        }

}

/ * * * * * * * * * * * * * * * * * * * * * * * * * * * * * * * * * * * * * * * * * *
* Program 027a                                                  *
* Demo of do-while loop                                         *
* * * * * * * * * * * * * * * * * * * * * * * * * * * * * * * * * * * * * * * * * * /

#include  <stdio.h>

main ()
{
        char  ch;
        int  f_num;

        f_num = 0;

        printf ("Enter  a  character  ");
        ch=getchar ();
        getchar ();

        do
        {
                printf ("%d\nEnter  a  character  ",++f_num);
                ch=getchar ();
                getchar ();
        }
            while (ch  !=  'q');
}
```

Enter and run both these programs and try them out. You will find that so long as the first character entered is not a lower case 'q' then they will work exactly the same. But if the first character entered is a lower case 'q' then the first one will not carry out anything whilst the second one will print up the value 1 and ask you to enter a character.

Another fact you should notice here is the inclusion of the incremental operator upon f_num inside the printf statement. This is a shorthand method of writing:

```
++f_num;
printf("%d\nEnter  a  character  ",f_num);
```

and in this case does produce less object code.

The for Loop

The for loop has the following form:

> for (initialization; condition; change) action ;

multiply actions may be included by containing them inside curly brackets:

> for (initialization; condition; change)
> {
> action1;
> action2;
> action3;
> }

Program 028 is a simple counting program which demonstrates the use of the for loop.

```
/****************************************************
* Program 028                                      *
* Demonstration of a for loop                      *
****************************************************/

main()
{
   int f_num;

   for ( f_num = 0 ; f_num < 10 ; f_num++ )
      {
      printf("The value of f_num is now %d\n",f_num);
      }
}
```

Try this one out and then try playing around with it. What happens if you alter the change section of the for statement from f_num++ to ++f_num, or if you alter the initialization value?

Try a few different things and see what the result is.

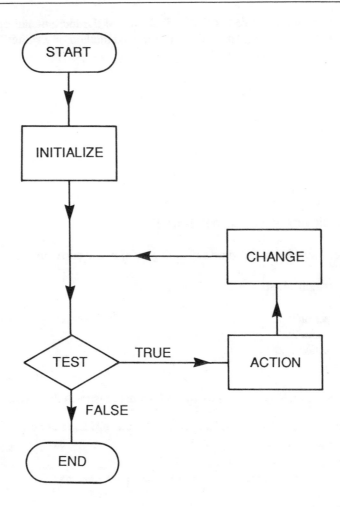

Figure 9.3 The for loop

Getting Out of Loops

Normally, a loop will execute until the exit condition is met. In the case above, it will execute until the value of f_num is greater than or equal to 10. Sometimes you will want to get out of a loop before such a condition is met.

This can be achieved by using the break keyword. The normal way in which this is used within a loop, and we have seen others but will not go into them, is in conjunction with an if statement. Programs 029, 029a and 029b show the use of the break statement with all three types of loop. Each of these loops should operate 20 times. However, if either q or Q is entered you will jump out of the loop. Try them and see.

```
            break

            while()
            {
                    c = getchar ();
                    if (c = = 'q') break;
                    putchar (c);
            }
            printf ("hoop ended \n");
```

Figure 9.4 The break statement

```
/***************************************************
 * Program 029                                     *
 * Break from while loop                           *
 ***************************************************/

#include <stdio.h>

main()
{
   int f_num;
   char ch;

   printf("This is the start of the loop ");
   printf("f_num is set to zero.\n\n");
   f_num = 0;

   while ( f_num < 20 )
   {
        printf("%d Enter a character ",f_num);
        ch=getchar();
        getchar();

        if ( ch == 'q' || ch == 'Q')
            break;
        f_num++;
   }

   printf("The end value for f_num is %d\n\n",f_num);

}
```

83

```
/******************************************************
* Program 029a                                        *
* Break from do_while loop                            *
******************************************************/

#include <stdio.h>

main()
{
    int  f_num;
    char ch;

    printf("This is the start of the loop ");
    printf("f_num is set to zero.\n\n");
    f_num = 0;

    do
    {
        printf("%d Enter a character ",f_num);
        ch=getchar();
        getchar();

        if ( ch == 'q' || ch == 'Q')
             break;
        f_num++;
    }     while ( f_num < 20 );

    printf("The end value for f_num is %d\n\n",f_num);

}
/******************************************************
* Program 029b                                        *
* Break from for loop                                 *
******************************************************/

#include <stdio.h>

main()
{
    int  f_num;
    char ch;

    printf("This is the start of the loop ");
    printf("f_num is set to zero.\n\n");

    for ( f_num = 0 ; f_num < 20 ; f_num++)
    {
        printf("%d Enter a character ",f_num);
        ch=getchar();
        getchar();

        if ( ch == 'q' || ch == 'Q')
            break;
    }

    printf("The end value for f_num is %d\n\n",f_num);

}
```

Jumping to Start of Loop

Sometimes, if a certain condition is met within a loop you will not want to go on with the rest of the operations within the loop, but at the same time will not want to abandon the loop. This can be achieved using the continue keyword. Have a look at Program 030.

```
/ * * * * * * * * * * * * * * * * * * * * * * * * * * * * * * * * * * * * * * * * * * *
* Program 030                                           *
* Use of continue                                       *
* * * * * * * * * * * * * * * * * * * * * * * * * * * * * * * * * * * * * * * * * * * /

#include <stdio.h>

int f_num;
char ch;

main()
{
   printf("Now setting up loop with f_num = 0\n\n");

   f_num = 0;

   while(f_num < 26)
   {
      printf("Enter a letter ");
      ch = getchar();
      getchar();
      if(ch < 'A' || ch > 'z')
          continue;
      printf("The ASCII code for the letter %c is %d\n",ch,ch);
      if( ch == 'q')
          break;
   }
}
```

Here we are taking the input of a single letter and printing the ASCII value of the letter. We do not want the ASCII value printed if it is not a letter, therefore in the if statement we test for a none letter and if the test is true the continue statement jumps the operation back to the start of the loop.

Incidentally, this program is not correct. It works because the letters are in sequence. Unfortunately, there is a small group of none letters with ASCII values 91 to 96 in the middle which break up the sequence. This program does not test for them. Try amending the program to exclude this small group.

```
        for (i = Ø; i < 100; i++)
        {
            c = getchar ();
            if (c < 32)
                continue;
            mem [++q] = c;
        }
```

Figure 9.5 Using continue

Something which must be kept in mind with the continue statement is that the jump will be made to the test in both while and do_while loops, but to the change in a for loop. This is important when making use of the continue statement.

Endless Loops

There are times when you want to continue without end, or at least without the loop test producing an end. If an empty test is given to a loop condition, C will always treat it as true. Consider the following examples:

```
while ()
{
    let = getch;
    if ( ( let >= 'A' && let <='Z' ) || (let >= 'a' && let <='z'))
    putchar(let);
    else
          if ( let == 27 ) break;
}
```

This loop will continue to take input and put any letters to the screen until the Escape key is pressed. In a for loop the empty condition takes the following form:

```
for ( ; ; )
{
statements;
}
```

Although having an empty condition in a loop is interpreted as TRUE it is often not clear what is happening when you try to read the code. A far better method is to declare a value for TRUE and then set your loop with:

while (TRUE)

or

for(;TRUE;)

Although this will take fractionally more code, the benefit to debugging and maintenance of code is well worth it.

Problems with Floats

There is a problem which arises when using floats in relational tests. It usually comes to light when working with loops. If you consider how computers deal with numbers it soon becomes clear that they do not have an accurate method of representing certain floating point numbers. One aspect of this is that there is no way of exactly representing the value 0.1 in binary, which is the way computers deal with numbers.

Study Program 030a.

```
/*****************************************************
* Program 030a                                      *
* Problems with floats in loops                     *
*****************************************************/

#include <stdio.h>

main()
{
        float num;
        char let;

        num = 0;

        while ( num != 1.3 )
        {
                printf("Press a key ");
                let = getch();
                printf("%f,  %c\n",num,let);
                if ( let == 'q' ) break;
                num = num + 0.1;
        }
}
```

If you enter and run this program, it requires you to press a key before it prints out the current value of num and let. What you expect is that it will stop when num gets to 1.3. You will find it will not, and that you will have to press 'q' to escape. Look at the test. It reads, ' while num is not equal to 1.3 do '. This means that when num gets to 1.3 it should stop. Unfortunately, it will not. The reason for this is that the binary system used within the computer cannot exactly represent 1.3, therefore the chances of an exact match being made are very slim. Having said this, due to a certain degree of randomness (which exists in such representations) you may find on some systems, in some circumstances, an exact match will be made.

The way around problems of this type is not to test equality or inequality on floats. If you are using floats you should not use == or !=; that is a basic rule. The rule is so basic that there have been suggestions that the standards should be written to make it impossible to use these operators with floats. Fortunately, this has not been done. There are a few (and that is very few) times when using the equality and inequality operators on a float is useful, especially when you want to test the accuracy of your system's binary representation of floats.

Returning to the main point, if you need to use floats in a comparative test, do so using the less than and greater than tests. In this way you can test within a degree of accuracy which you desire. For instance, if you want to check if something is equal to 2.35 to a degree of 0.001 you could write:

```
if ( ( num > 2.349 ) && ( num < 2.351 ) )
```

Here we are testing that a number is greater than 2.349 and that it is less than 2.351. If this is true it means that the number is equal to the value we seek within the degree of error we are prepared to allow.

In Program 030a our intention was to stop the loop when num got to 1.3. We did not want the loop to be performed when num was 1.3 so our interest was in those values of num below 1.3. It is, therefore, possible to write the program as shown in Program 30b and obtain the required result.

Many of the bugs created in C programs are caused by the unexpected behaviour of floats in relational tests. Treat them with care, and if possible, avoid using them in relational tests.

```
/****************************************************
* Program 30b                                      *
* Problems with floats in loops                    *
****************************************************/

#include <stdio.h>

main()
{
        float num;
char let;

        num = 0;

        while ( num < 1.3 )
        {
printf("Press a key :");
                let = getch();
                printf("%f,  %c\n",num,let);
                if ( let == 'q' ) break;
                num = num + 0.1;
        }
}
```

Enter and run it, noting the difference.

10

GETTING THE MATHS RIGHT

One of the problems with mathematics is knowing how an expression will be interpreted. Thus, if we have an expression:

    2 + 4 * 6

we could first add two to four to give six, then multiply by six to give thirty-six. Alternatively, you could multiply four by six to give twenty-four and then add two to give twenty-six.

Mathematics has very strict rules for the interpretation of expressions. The rule is that you do multiplication first, and then addition, so the correct answer is twenty-six.

With computer programming languages we have the same problem. If we write a statement we must be certain how it will be interpreted. The C language has a set of rules for the interpretation of expressions. These rules cover all the C operators, but we are only concerned with the mathematical operators at this stage.

The rule is that the mathematical operators, that is multiply, divide, modulo, add and subtract, are contained in two groups. The members of each group have the same level of priority. However, one group has higher priority over the other. The first group consists of:

        multiply   *
        divide   /
        modulo   %

The second consists of:

        add   +
        subtract   -

Within any statement, operations of a higher priority are undertaken before those of lower priority, but where there are a number of operations of equal value they are interpreted from left to right. So, in the following case:

```
r_num = 3 * 4 + 8 / 2;
```

three will be multiplied by four to give twelve, then eight will be divided by two to give four. Finally, twelve will be added to four to give sixteen, that answer being assigned to r_num. It might be that what you actually want is three times the sum of four plus eight, the total divided by two. You can, however, force the compiler to carry out certain operations in precedence to others by enclosing them in brackets. Anything in brackets will be evaluated first. So to get the required result we would have to write:

```
r_num = 3 * ( 4 + 8 ) / 2;
```

The correct use of brackets can be important. First, it forces the compiler to undertake the calculation in a specific way. More significantly though, it makes it much clearer what is happening. This is especially true when you have operators of equal precedence. Consider the following:

```
r_num = 15 / 3 % 2;
```

This is far clearer if it is written as:

```
r_num = (15 / 3) % 2;
```

even though this will make no difference to the result. The compiler will evaluate the expression left to right anyway; or at least it should. Using brackets is also a safety precaution in case you have to move a program to another compiler which is not executing the statements quite as it should. It is, therefore, advisable to use brackets in any calculation, to force the order of the calculation even when there is no specific reason for doing so.

Incidentally, when you have brackets inside brackets as in:

```
r_num = 13 * ((f_num - (s_num % 2) + 5) % 6);
```

the innermost set of brackets will be evaluated first. So in this case, if we give f_num the value 4 and s_num the value 6 the calculation will be as follows:

```
13 * ((4 - (6 % 2) + 5) % 6)
```

```
13 * ((4 - 0 + 5) % 6)
```

because the first operation carried out is the innermost set of brackets, in this case 6 % 2 which is 0. We now get:

```
13  *  (9  %  6)
```

because again the innermost brackets is calculated, and in this case it was 4 - 0 + 5 which is 9. Now the last set of brackets is dealt with:

```
13  *  3
```

because 9 % 6 is 3, and we get the final result which is:

```
39
```

Be careful about the use of the operators. Although with arithmetic operators the order of operation is always from left to right, eg 9 / 3 means divide 9 by 3, with some operators the order is from right to left.

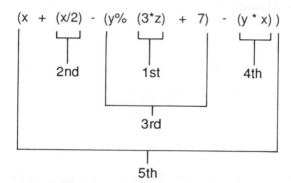

The innermost bracket set is dealt with first. Where two sets are at the same depth the leftmost will be dealt with first.

Figure 10.1 Order of precedence of brackets

11

ARRAYS

So far, we have looked at variables as single entities. A special type of variable is an array.

An array is a collection of variables which are all of the same type and are organized sequentially and accessed under a single name. Let us consider an illustration. We could have a series of ten integer numbers. These could be declared as ten integer variables so we would have:

```
int  first_num,
     secon_num,
     third_num,
     forth_num,
     fifth_num,
     sixth_num,
     seven_num,
     eigth_num,
     ninth_num,
     tenth_num;
```

Provided we are using all these singularly, there would be no problem, but if we are using them in block form, problems would arise. If we need to use the sixth element in the block we first have to go through a long procedure to find the name of that element. We can, however, declare ten integer variables as an array:

```
int  numbers[10];
```

In such a case each element of the array is specified by its offset from the start, the first element having an offset of zero. So if we list the array it would have the following form:

```
numbers[0]
numbers[1]
numbers[2]
numbers[3]
numbers[4]
numbers[5]
numbers[6]
numbers[7]
numbers[8]
numbers[9]
```

Note that although there are 10 elements to the array they are numbered from 0 to 9.

Each element in an array can be addressed by using the offset to that element in the array. So if we wanted to put the value f_num into the sixth element in an array called numbers we could with:

```
numbers[5]  =  f_num;
```

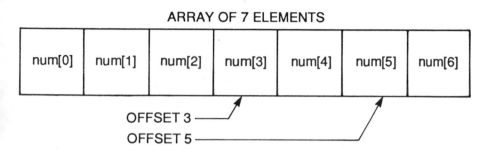

ARRAY OF 7 ELEMENTS

Figure 11.1

More useful is the fact that the offset can be represented by a variable to which the value 5 could be assigned. In such a case you would have:

```
index = 5;
numbers[index]  =  f_num;
```

Have a look at Program 031 which uses two for loops and an array to take the input of ten numbers and print them in reverse order.

```
/****************************************************
* Program 031                                      *
* demonstration of array of integers               *
****************************************************/

#include  <stdio.h>

int  numbers[10];

main()
{
          get_num();
          rev_num();
}
```

```
get_num()
{
        int index;

        for ( index = 0; index < 10; index ++ )
        {
        printf("%-2d Enter number  :",index);
        scanf("%d",&numbers[index]);
        getchar();
        }

        printf("End of input.\n\n");
}

rev_num()
{
        int index;

        for ( index = 9; index >= 0; index -- )
        {
        printf("%2d, ",numbers[index]);
        }

        printf("\n\nEnd of output.\n");
}
```

Let us analyse what we are doing in this program. First, we have declared an array of integers with ten elements under the name numbers. The declaration is global, that is, known to all functions within the program.

Next we have the main() function. This calls two functions up, get_num() and rev_num().

The function get_num() takes the input of the numbers to the array. In this function we declare a local integer variable, that is one known only to this function, called index. This will be used for the offset of the members of the array.

A for loop is set up in which index is initialized to 0; a test is made for index being less than 10 and the change is set to the one unit incremental. Within this loop a message is printed using the printf() function requesting the input of a number. Note that we have formatted the printing to left justify the number printed at the start of the line.

The input of the number is done with scanf() the value inputted being assigned to the array member with the offset indicated by the value of index. Here again we have used the dummy getchar() to deal with the unwanted carriage return.

Finally, in this function we have a message stating that you are at the end of the input.

Next we go on to the function rev_num. Again, index is declared as a local variable. The for loop is used again but this time it is a decreasing loop with the change being the decremental operator −. Two points to note here are that the value to which index is initialized is 9, not ten, even though there are ten elements in the array. Remember the array elements start at 0 not 1. Also, as the last element in the array (if we do a count down) is 0 the test is greater than, or equal, to zero.

In the printf() function again the numbers outputted have been formatted. This time though, they have been right justified. Note also that there is no line feed in the function argument so all the results are printed out on one line. For this reason we have to start the final message with two line feeds to get spacing correct.

Now look at Program 032 using an array of integers. This takes the input of 10 values then sorts them into descending order.

```
/ * * * * * * * * * * * * * * * * * * * * * * * * * * * * * * * * * * * * * * * * * * * * *
* Program 032                                          *
* 2nd demonstration of array of intergers              *
* * * * * * * * * * * * * * * * * * * * * * * * * * * * * * * * * * * * * * * * * * * * * * /

#include  <stdio.h>

int  numbers[10];      /* global declaration */

main()
{
    get_num();
    printf("The  unsorted  array.\n");
    print_array();
    sort_num();
    printf("The  sorted  array.\n");
    print_array();
}

get_num()
{
    int  index;

    for ( index = 0; index < 10; index ++ )
    {
    printf("%-2d Enter  number  :",index);
    scanf("%d",&numbers[index]);
    getchar();
    }
```

```
        printf("End of input.\n\n");
}

print_array()
{
    int index;

    printf("The array is as follows :\n");

    for ( index = 0; index < 10; index ++ )
    {
    printf("Element %-2d : %5d \n",index,numbers[index]);
    }
}

sort_num()
{
    int index, hold, flag;

    flag=0;
    while(flag==0)
    {
      flag=1;
      for(index = 0; index < 9; index ++)
      {
        if( numbers[index] < numbers[index+1])
        {
          hold = numbers[index];
          numbers[index] = numbers[index+1];
          numbers[index+1]=hold;
           flag=0;
        }
      }
    }
}
```

In this program the get_num() function is identical to that used in the previous program. The function print_array is fairly straightforward and should not require any explanation. This leaves the function sort_num(). We are not going into a full explanation of this; you should by now be able to follow it. There is just one point to note. We have used the test in the while statement (flag == 0). We could have used (!flag) that is NOT flag and this might have produced less code. However, flag == 0 is far more readable, and the resultant code is easier to maintain. If you wish, try changing (flag == 0) to (!flag) to prove that they are the same in operation.

Array Class

Arrays, like variables, can be auto or static. When an array is within a function it must be specifically declared static if you want to initialize it.

Array Initialization

Like variables, arrays can be initialized when declared, although this facility is not present in all compilers.

To initialize an array the general form would be:

```
int numbers[4] = { 1, 2, 3, 4 };
```

where the values to be allocated to the array are held in a set of curly brackets. These values will be read into the array in order from left to right, starting from offset 0.

With Turbo C and some other compilers, if the size of the array is not specifed, then the compiler will construct an array of sufficient size to take the values specified. In the following example:

```
int numbers[] = { 1, 2, 3, 4, 5, 6 }
```

will set up an array of 6 elements.

Note that if an array to be initialized is not global, then it must be of class static.

Look at Programs 033 and 034. The first is a very simple demonstration of initializing an array:

```
/**********************************************
* Program 033                                 *
* Demo of an initialized array.               *
**********************************************/

int numbers[5] = { 1, 2, 3, 4, 5 };

main()
{
  int test;

        test=0;
   (    while ( test < 5 )
        {
          printf("%3d,",numbers[test]);
          test++;
        }
}
```

The second shows the initialization of an array within a function. It is basically the same program as 033 but the array has been declared within the function.

```
/*************************************************
* Program 034                                   *
* Demo of an initialised array within a         *
* function                                       *
*************************************************/

main()
{

  static int numbers[5] = { 1, 2, 3, 4, 5 };
  int test;

        test=0;
        while ( test < 5 )
        {
          printf("%3d,",numbers[test]);
          test++;
        }

}
```

Strings

A string is a group of characters. Many computer languages have a special type of variable to handle strings. C does not. In C, a string is an array of type char which is terminated with the value 0.

The value 0 has the character representation \0.

If we wish to have a string to hold the name Nigel we can do this by initializing an array:

```
char  name[]  = {'N','i','g','e','l',0}
```

Note that the last character in the array is not enclosed in single inverted commas. This is because we are giving it the numeric value 0 not the ASCII value of the character 0.

The above method of initialization has been used in the demonstration program 035.

```
/*************************************************
* Program 035                                   *
* Demo of string as array                       *
*************************************************/

char  name[]  = {'N','i','g','e','l',0};

main()
{
   printf(name);
}
```

Such an initialization is, however, somewhat clumsy. C provides us with a far better short-hand way of doing this as is shown in Program 035a.

```
/*******************************************
* Program 035a                            *
* Demo of string as array                 *
*******************************************/

char  name[]  =  "Nigel";

main()
{
   printf(name);
}
```

In this case, everything within the inverted commas is assigned to the array, and the Turbo C compiler automatically supplies the terminating 0 value.

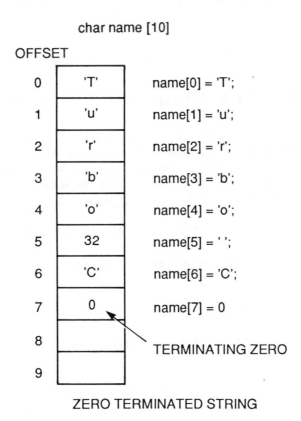

char name [10]

OFFSET

OFFSET		
0	'T'	name[0] = 'T';
1	'u'	name[1] = 'u';
2	'r'	name[2] = 'r';
3	'b'	name[3] = 'b';
4	'o'	name[4] = 'o';
5	32	name[5] = ' ';
6	'C'	name[6] = 'C';
7	0	name[7] = 0
8		TERMINATING ZERO
9		

ZERO TERMINATED STRING

Figure 11.2

Another point which comes up in these two programs is the fact that what we have passed to the printf() function is just the name of the array with no offsets given. This

99

has the address of the start of the array. When printf() gets such an address it starts to print whatever is found at that address and carries on until it meets the 0 value terminating the string.

This is what happens whenever you use printf(). If you have the following in a program:

```
printf("Hello");
```

the compiler will store the string Hello in memory, terminating it with a null character (the 0 value). It will then give the address of the string to the function.

Although the name of the array without any offsets given is the address of the array, this is not a pointer. It is a constant reference to an address; pointers are not, they can have their values changed.

We look at strings in more detail in the next chapter on string handling.

Arrays in More than One Dimension

Quite often you will need to work with an array of arrays. A typical example will be when you need to deal with a list of names. You could define a number of arrays, one for each name you will be working with. In practice, it is far easier to work with a single array, which is an array of arrays. This can be done by declaring a multi-dimensional array. Such arrays are declared in the following way:

class type name [1st dimension] [2nd dimension];

So, to declare an array to hold 10 names of up to 20 characters each, we would use the form:

```
static  char  names[10][20];
```

Have a look at Program 036 which demonstrates the use of a character array of two dimensions to hold a series of names.

In this program we have used a new input function. This is gets(), called get s, not gets. This stands for get string and is dealt with in the next chapter.

Most of this program should be fairly easy to follow. One aspect which would improve it is the addition of a function to sort the names into order. Why not try and add one?

```
/*********************************************
* Program 036                                *
* Demo of two dimensional array              *
*********************************************/

#include <stdio.h>

char  names  [10][20];

main()
{
   get_names();
   print_names();
}

get_names()
{
   int  index;

   for ( index = 0 ; index < 10 ; index ++ )
   {
    printf("%-2d Enter  Name :  ",index);
    gets( &names[index][0] );
   }
}

print_names()
{
   int  count;

   for ( count = 0 ; count < 10 ; count ++ )
   {
     printf("Name  number  %-2d  =  %s\n",count,names[count]);
   }
}
```

Beyond Two Dimensions

There is no reason why you should stick to just using two-dimensional arrays. In fact, for certain work you will find using multi-dimensional arrays useful. In theory, you should be able to have arrays in as many dimensions as you want. Turbo C will allow this, but many compilers will not, stopping you with a maximum of three dimensions.

A THREE DIMENSION ARRAY CAN BE THOUGHT OF AS A BLOCK OF CUBES EACH OF WHICH CAN BE LOCATED BY ITS CO-ORDINATES. WE CAN HAVE 4 DIMENSION ARRAYS BUT CANNOT GIVE THEM GRAPHICAL REPRESENTATION.

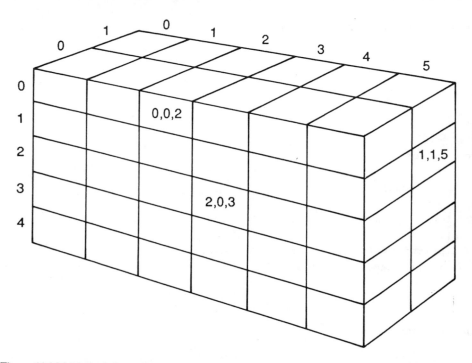

Figure 11.3 Multi dimension arrays

When you are doing some obscure maths, or handling a statistical problem, a limitation of three dimensions can be a handicap, but in general practice it is advisable. Once you start going beyond three dimensions life becomes difficult. First, it can be quite a programming problem to keep track of all the offsets. Second, you quickly start to run out of memory. Just think of the maths. An array of characters takes up one byte per character, so an array of 10 takes up 10 bytes. A two-dimensional array of 10 in each direction will take up 100 bytes, and if you move into a third dimension you are up to 1000 bytes. Four gives you 10,000, add a fifth dimension, ten, and you are up to 100,000 bytes and your memory is quickly vanishing.

The largest dimensioned array which I have worked with under Turbo C was a 7 dimension array. However, it did have very small dimensions and is given below:

```
int  nums[10][2][2][2][2][2][2];
```

I have had Turbo C refuse to accept a five dimension array when the numbers were larger. This means that if you are going to work with multi-dimension arrays you must give careful thought to the demands they will be placing on memory.

Passing Arrays to Functions

You can pass an array to a function in a similar manner in which you pass other variables as arguments. However, you must make sure that you declare the arguments as the appropriate type to go with the array.

Look at the following:

```
main()
{
  char letters[] = "abcdefghijklmnopqrstuvwxyz";
  mix_up(letters);
  order_list(letters);
}

order_list(char list[])
  {
```

Here we have the start of a function order_list(). The name of an array is given as the argument in the calling function and this is named as list in the function argument. The argument is declared as an array of characters.

Note here that the size of the array is not given. The array will be initialized to the correct size according to the array passed.

What is important about passing arrays as arguments to a function is that unlike variables you are not passing a copy of the variable to the function but the actual address of the array. In this case any alteration you make to the array in the function will be effective in the main array. Consider the illustration given in Program 037.

This is quite a simple program. An array is declared called letters, and initialized. This is passed to a function which adds one to the value of each character. When it returns to the main function the value of the array has altered. If it had been a normal variable it would not have altered.

```
/****************************************************
* Program 037                                      *
* Demonstration of passing array to function       *
****************************************************/

char letters[] = "abcdefg";

main()
{
   printf("%s\n",letters);

   inc_let(letters);
```

103

```
   printf("%s\n",letters);

}

inc_let(char  incer[])
{

   int  i;

   for ( i = 0 ; i < 7 ; i++ )
    {
      incer[i] = incer[i] + 1;
    }
}
```

12

HANDLING STRINGS

Having found out that strings are nothing more than a type of array, how do you deal with them? Unlike other languages C does not have any specific built in functions for string handling. If you want a function to handle a string it has to be written.

This has two effects. First, basic string handling in C is much more difficult than it is in other languages. Second, you can do much more with strings in C than you can in many other languages, for the simple reason that if a facility is not there to do what you want, all you have to do is write it.

Fortunately, having established that C does not have any built in functions for handling strings, and as strings are dealt with so much in programming, library functions were quickly developed to deal with the basic operations. These library functions have become fairly standard, to the extent that some compilers are now automatically incorporating them as part of the main compiler and not as an included library.

The basic way of printing a string is to use the printf() functions. To do this (as discussed in Chapter 6) you have to pass the address of the first element of the array to the function. Note that there can be two ways of doing this. Look at programs 038 amd 039.

```
/****************************************************
* Program 038                                      *
* Passing of array to printf() method 1            *
****************************************************/

char name[] = "The C Tutorial";

main()
{
  printf(&name[0]);
}
```

```
/*******************************************************
* Program 039                                         *
* Passing of array to printf() method 2               *
*******************************************************/

char name[] = "The C Tutorial";

main()
{
  printf(name);
}
```

In Program 038 we have passed the address of the array by using the address of the first element of the array in the form &name[0]. In Program 039 we have just given the name of the array. If you enter and compile the two programs you will find that they work just the same.

This again emphasises that the name of the array gives the address of the array. It should not, however, be confused with the pointers.

Pointers are useful when it comes to handling string constants. Study the following code fragment:

```
char *p;

p = "The Turbo C Tutorial";
printf("%s",p);
```

In this case we have defined a pointer of type character. We then assign to this pointer the location occupied by the character constant so the pointer points to the constant in memory. After that the printf() function works as normal.

Assigning pointers to point to constants like this is a perfectly legal and valid move; one which is frequently used. What would not be allowed is:

```
char message[30];

message = "The Turbo C Tutorial";
printf("%s",message);
```

When you declare the array message[] space is allowed for it in memory. The name of the array, message, is the address of that space. It is not a pointer, so its value cannot be re-assigned to point to the address of the constant. If you wanted to get the constant into the array, the way to do it is to copy it into the array.

Putting and Getting Strings

Two very useful and almost universally standard functions are puts() and gets(). As the names suggest these put strings and get strings.

The puts() function will put a string to the standard output device on your system. This is normally the video display, but this could be re-directed. The gets() function will get a string from the standard input device on your system. This is normally the keyboard, but again this may be altered with re-direction.

To put a string to the standard output (we will start to use that term now rather than screen) you need to pass to the function the address of the array containing the string. This can be done in one of two ways. Either you pass the array name or a pointer to the array. Look at Programs 040 and 041.

```
/*****************************************************
 * Program 040                                      *
 * Passing of array to puts()                       *
 *****************************************************/

#include  <stdio.h>

char  name[]  =  "The  Turbo  C  Tutorial";

main()
{
   puts(name);
}


/*****************************************************
 * Program 041                                      *
 * Passing of array by pointer to puts()            *
 *****************************************************/

#include  <stdio.h>

char  name[]  =  "The  Turbo  C  Tutorial";

main()
{
   char  *ptr;
   ptr  =  &name[0];
   puts(ptr);

}
```

One fact you will notice is that, apparently, there is little difference between printf() and puts(). Well, there is one big difference which the above programs do not show. Look at Program 042.

```
/ * * * * * * * * * * * * * * * * * * * * * * * * * * * * * * * * * * * * * * * * * * * *
* Program 042                                            *
* Comparison of puts() and printf()                     *
* * * * * * * * * * * * * * * * * * * * * * * * * * * * * * * * * * * * * * * * * * * /

#include<stdio.h>

char words[] = "This is a test.";

main()
{
  char *ptr;

  printf(words);
  printf(words);

  printf("\n\n That was with printf now with puts \n\n");

  ptr = words;

  puts(ptr);
  puts(ptr);

}
```

Enter this program and run it. You will find that the two printf() functions cause both messages to be printed on the same line. This is because there is no \n for a new line. The puts() functions, however, automatically supply the new line at the end of a string.

Often, this can be an advantage. It can also be a disadvantage. This is the case when you do not want a line feed or if you want a conditional line feed.

The complementary function to puts() is gets(). This reads a string in from the standard input device and places that string in a buffer.

A buffer is an area of memory which is reserved for data. The easiest way, but not the only way, to create a buffer is to use an array. So, consider Program 043.

Here we have a buffer of 20 characters called buffer. We pass the address of this to gets() and the input is placed in the buffer by gets(). The final part prints out what you have put in. All well and good.

What happens, though, if you type in more than 20 characters? Well, in that case you have a problem: it will mess up everything. Some compilers have a clever version of gets() which requires you to state how many characters it can take as a maximum.

This, though, is not standard and can create problems with portability. It should be noted that this approach is taken with fgets(), which is a companion function of gets().

```
/ * * * * * * * * * * * * * * * * * * * * * * * * * * * * * * * * * * * * * * * * * * *
* Program 043                                              *
* gets() function with a array as a buffer                *
* * * * * * * * * * * * * * * * * * * * * * * * * * * * * * * * * * * * * * * * * * * * * /

#include <stdio.h>


char buffer[20];        /* Create buffer */

main()
{
  puts( "Please enter your name ");

  gets( buffer );

  puts( "Hello" );

  puts( buffer );
}
```

The Turbo C library does not support a clever version of gets() which is in many ways an advantage, as such variations are non-standard. You could try writing one yourself. A way of doing this is given in Answer 3 in Appendix 4. You can extend this by putting in facilities which will allow you to backspace, delete, insert, etc.

You might also like to have a go at writing your own puts() function. This should be quite simple so no answer given. A couple of tips though: use putchar() and remember it needs a new line at the end.

Copying Strings

One task which you will almost certainly want to do is to copy the contents of one string to another. Basically, this is simply a matter of copying the elements of one array to another. It can be done in a number of ways. Fortunately, there is one quite simple way and the standard C library contains a function to do it. It is strcpy().

In use strcpy() needs to be passed two arguments. The first is the address of the array into which the string is to be copied, and the second is the address of the array containing the string. Have a look at Program 044.

```
/*************************************************
* Program 044                                   *
* Copying strings                               *
*************************************************/

#include <stdio.h>

char  name[20];

main()
{
  char  buffer[20];

  printf("Please  enter  your  name ");

  gets( buffer );

  strcpy( name,  buffer );

  puts( name );

}
```

The program demonstrates that the strcpy() function works, but there is not really much point to it. You might as well just print out the contents of buffer rather than copy them to name, then print them. If, however, you want to do a series of inputs then the ability to copy over starts to become useful. Look at Program 045.

Here we have declared a multi-dimensioned array of characters called name. We input to a buffer, then using pointers to provide the address, copy from the buffer into the name array. The final part prints out the list of inputted names in reverse order.

```
/*************************************************
* Program 045                                   *
* Copying strings second demo                   *
*************************************************/

#include <stdio.h>

char  name[5][20];

main()
{
  char  buffer[20],*ptr;
  int  count;

  for ( count = 0; count < 5; count ++ )
  {
```

110

```
   printf("Please  enter  a  name  ");

   gets( buffer );

   ptr  =  &name[count][0];

   strcpy( ptr,  buffer );
   }

   for ( count = 4; count >=0; count --)
   {
    ptr  =  &name[count][0];

    puts( ptr );
    }
}
```

Joining Strings

Another task with strings is that of joining them together. This is so common that many languages allow you to do it by using the + sign, but unfortunately, not C.

Joining two strings together is technically known as concatenating them, so the function to do it is called strcat(). Look at Program 046.

```
/ * * * * * *'*'* * * * * * * * * * * * * * * * * * * * * * * * * * * * * * * * * * * * *
* Program 046                                              *
* Demonstration of strcat()                               *
* * * * * * * * * * * * * * * * * * * * * * * * * * * * * * * * * * * * * * * * * * * /

#include  <stdio.h>

char  name[]  =  "Richard  Thomas  ";
char  hname[]  =  "Janet  Rhodes";
char  buffer[80];

main()
{
   strcpy(buffer,name);

   strcat(buffer,"marries  ");

   strcat(buffer,hname);

   puts(buffer);
}
```

First in this program we copy the contents of name into buffer using strcpy(). Then to this we concatenate the string "marries " using the strcat() command. Finally, we join on the contents of hname[] and print it all out with puts(). An easy little exercise.

There is, as always, a slight problem. No check is made by the standard version of strcat to see that the size of the target array, in this case buffer, is not exceeded. It should not be too difficult, though, to have a go at writing a version which does it for you.

Finding the Length of Strings

If you want to join strings, it is wise to check that they are not too long first. For this you need to know the length of a string. Here, there is a fairly simple function which you can use: strlen(). You pass to strlen() the single argument of the address of the string and it will return to you the length of the string.

Have a look at Program 047.

```
/***********************************************
* Program 047                                  *
* Demonstration of strlen()                    *
***********************************************/

#include <stdio.h>

char  name[80];

main()
{
  int  length;
  puts("Enter your name ");
  gets(name);
  length = strlen(name);
  printf("Your name is %d characters long. \n",length);

}
```

This is all fairly simple.

Comparing Strings

The final, standard function for string handling that we are going to look at is the strcmp(). This is the compare function, which is a string equivalant of ==. What it does is take two strings and compares them. If they are the same it returns 0, otherwise it returns another value. Look at Program 048.

```
/******************************************
* Program 048                            *
* Demonstration of strcmp()              *
******************************************/

#include <stdio.h>

char answer[80];

main()
{
  static char capital[]="London";
  puts("What is the capital city of the United Kingdom?");
  gets(answer);

          if ( strcmp( capital, answer) == 0 )
              puts("That is correct. ");
          else puts("That is wrong");
}
```

This is a basic program, but one which demonstrates how to use the function. You pass, as the argument to the function, the addresses of the arrays holding the strings. If the strings match you get a zero back, otherwise some other value. Actually, the value returned is the difference between the ASCII code for the characters, which explains why you can have a negative value returned and gives some indication how the function works.

Concatenation of Constant Strings

One of the major problems with old style C was that if you were setting up string constants, especially for messages, you had to be very careful about how you entered them. The classic C compilers would not accept breaks in your lines, unless you escaped them. Turbo C is much more friendly. Study the following:

```
char *cptr;

cptr =   "This is a message to be displayed on the "
         "screen at different\n points during the run "
         "of the program.\n  It contains line feeds "
         "and formatting information.\n  It will be "
         "handled as one string by Turbo C.";
```

Turbo C will read all this in and handle it as one string. When you give the command:

```
puts(cptr);
```

you will get:

```
This is a message to be displayed on the screen at different
points during the run of the program.
It contains line feeds and formatting information.
It will be handled as one string by Turbo C.
```

This facility in Turbo C for the concatenation of constant strings makes code far easier to enter and read.

13

FILES

A file basically is a sequence of data. As far as C is concerned this is all that is involved in the handling of files. Where they exist is a matter for the programmer, the operating system and the hardware, but not for C.

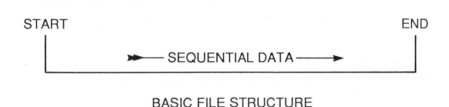

BASIC FILE STRUCTURE

Figure 13.1

This results in you, the programmer, having a great deal of freedom and very little assistance from the language.

The other point which must be remebered, is that all input and output is handled as files. So far as C is concerned, what you type in comes from a special file which is designated as the standard input device, and the display to the screen is also sent to a special file, the standard output device.

There are three things you can do with a file: you can open it, you can access it, and you can close it.

You do have to say exactly how you want to open it, whether to read it or to write to it; but you are still opening it.

C itself does not provide direct support for these functions in the language. Fortunately, the support is provided in the standard function library. The functions used are:

```
fopen()
```

and:

```
fclose()
```

Once a file has been opened it may be accessed with any one of a number of C functions. The main ones which you will find in the standard library are:

```
fprintf()
fscanf()
fputs()
fgets()
fgetc()
fputc()
```

You should be familiar with these. They are the standard input/output routines we have been working with until now but with F added to the front, although their workings are not always quite the same.

With some compilers, file access is even easier. Turbo C can use getc() and putc() as the basic I/O for all file access. You do not need to use fgetc() and fputc().

This is true of most compilers in their structure, but some have built in 'error' checking to force you to use the file form of a command if you are passing it a file pointer. Look at Programs 049 and 050.

```
/*************************************************
* Program 049                                    *
* Writing to a disk file using putc()            *
*************************************************/

#include  <stdio.h>

char message[] = "This is a test of writing to a disk\n";

main()
{
   int count;
   FILE *fp;
   char ch;

   count = 0;

   fp = fopen("holdtest","w");
   while( message[count] != 0 )
```

```
    {
        ch = message[count];
        putc(ch,fp);
        count ++;
    }

    fclose(fp);
}
```

This is fairly simple. We have declared an array message to hold the string "This is a test of writing to a disk". Three variables are declared: one integer, a file pointer and a character. The integer variable count is set to 0. Next, we open the file "holdtest" with fopen(), it is opened in the write mode, "w". The value returned by fopen() is assigned to the pointer fp.

File pointers are the way you tell C which file you are working with. They are a pointer to a special type of structure (we look at structures in Chapter 17) which holds information about the file you are working with. The C calls used make use of this information to find the position in which they are located in the file, which file they are working on, and the mode in which they can access a file.

The while loop is set up which will continue until we come to the end of the string. Remember, the last character in a string has the value 0. The value of each character in the array is assigned one at a time to ch, then this is written to the file with the putc() function, the character ch and the file pointer fp being passed to it as arguments. The value of count is increased and the loop repeated until we get to the end. Finally, we close the file with fclose().

This is fairly simple. Now look at how we read it back in Program 050.

```
/************************************************
* Program 050                                  *
* Reading from a disk using getc               *
************************************************/

#include <stdio.h>
main()
{
char message[80], ch;
int count;
FILE *fp;

count = 0;
fp = fopen( "holdtest","r");

while( (ch = getc(fp)) != EOF )
```

```
{
  message[count] = ch;
  count ++;

}
message[count]=0; /* add a Ø */
printf("%s",message);
fclose(fp);
}
```

There is nothing really surprising here. You should be able to follow it from Program 049. There are just two points to consider. First, this time the file is opened in read mode, that is the "r" argument to fopen(). To getc() we pass the file pointer fp as an argument. The while test looks complicated but is, in fact, fairly simple. Study it a bit and work it out for yourself. Second, notice we add a zero value to the end of the string. The reason for this is that a string must end with the null value and we stripped this off when we were writing it to the disk. Remember the while test in Program 049:

```
while ( message[count] != 0 )
```

which means that when it is equal to zero (that is at the end of the string) the while loop will not be carried out, so the zero value is not written to the disk. This is often an advantage, but occasionally you may want to have the 0 value written to the disk. In such cases use the do-while loop structure, where the test takes place at the end of the loop, not at the beginning. The final value will have been written before the test is made.

The function fprintf() works basically the same as the function printf() with the exception that a file pointer has to be added, so the syntax is:

```
fprintf( filepointer, "control string", arguments );
```

As with printf() arguments need only be supplied when required by the control string. The file pointer must be included. Therefore, to print the string "Hello" to the file pointed to by the pointer *fp our command would be:

```
fprintf( fp, "Hello" );
```

As scanf() is the complementary function to printf() so fscanf() is the complementary function to fprintf(). In this case again we have the addition of a file pointer. So, to take input of a character from a file pointed to by the pointer *fp and assign it to the variable ch our command would be:

```
fscanf( fp, "%c", &ch );
```

There can be a problem with fscanf() on some operating systems. The C language expects the end of a file to be marked with a designated marker, normally -1. This is the case in Unix where all files are a sequence of characters, and the last position in the file is marked with the End Of File marker (EOF) -1. Unfortunately, with other operating systems this is not so simple.

The result of this is that on some operating systems if you are using fscanf() you will not find the EOF. We therefore prefer not to use fscanf() for disk access.

Accessing a file, character by character is quite practical, but also quite long-winded, especially when you are dealing with a number of strings. Here we can use the functions fputs() and fgets().

The function fputs() is fairly straightforward to work with. You have to pass it the address of the string and the file pointer, so the syntax for it is:

```
fputs(string,filepointer);
```

There is no real problem using this. The only major difference between this and puts() is that unlike puts() it does not write a '\n' newline character to the end of the string.

The counterpart function fgets() is more complicated than gets() and also has a surprise up its sleeve for the unwary programmer who does not read the technical documentation. fgets() needs three parameters: buffer address, maximum number of characters to read, and then the file pointer.

With fgets() the string will be read from the file and placed into the buffer until either a newline character is encountered or the number of characters defined in the maximum number of characters to be read -1 have been read into the buffer. This, of course, reflects the clever versions of gets() which we looked at earlier.

The surprise which fgets() holds in store is the return value for End of File. It does not return the EOF value, normally -1, but the End of String value, NULL. Look at Program 051.

Here we are reading a text file called testtext.doc. You will have to create this file in order to try this program out. You should be able to use any file produced by a standard word processor in ASCII file mode, or a text file produced by the Turbo C editor. There is no reason why you cannot use it for text processing.

The program is fairly simple. We start by defining MAX as being 80 and then define a character array called buffer to be 80 characters.

- Program 051 is on the next page -

119

```
/*********************************************
* Program 051                                *
* File read using fgets()                     *
*********************************************/

#include <stdio.h>

#define MAX 80

char  buffer[MAX];

main()
{
  FILE *fp;

  fp = fopen("testtext.doc","r");

  while( fgets(buffer,MAX,fp) != NULL )
  {
    puts(buffer);
  }
fclose(fp);
}
```

When using this program to read data an extra LF is added. Look into this later!

In main the file pointer fp is declared, then the file to be read is opened using the "r" parameter for reading. The value returned by fopen() is assigned to the file pointer. Then the while loop is started and a test set up for the return of NULL which would indicate that we have reached the end of the file. Whilst we have not, the string held in buffer is outputted to the screen using puts(). Finally, we close the file using fclose().

One point about the use of fclose(). The format for this with Turbo C and most modern C compilers, is:

```
fclose( filepointer );
```

The file pointer must be included and each file closed specifically. With many older compilers you can use fclose() without any parameters being given. This will result in all the files being closed.

The function of closing all open files is performed in Turbo C and similar compilers with the call fcloseall().

Now look at Program 052.

This is a simple program for inputting text then saving it to a file. There are a couple of points which should be noted. To understand the program we will go through it from the start.

```
/***************************************************
* Program 052                                      *
* Base for text editor                             *
***************************************************/

#include <stdio.h>
#define CLS printf("%c[2J",27)
#define MAX 80
#define LINES 300

char  text[LINES][MAX],buffer[MAX];

main()
{
  get_text();
  store_text();
}    /* END of main() */

get_text()
{
  char  buffer[MAX],*ptr;
  int x;
  CLS;
  x = 0;
  while( x < LINES )
  {
    gets(buffer);
    ptr = &text[x][0];
    strcpy( ptr, buffer);
    if (buffer[0]==0) break;
    x++;
  }  /* END of while */
}    /* END of get_text() */

store_text()
{
FILE *fp;
int x;
char *ptr,chr,ch1;
chr='\n';
x=0;
fp = fopen("text","w");

while( x < LINES )
  {
  ptr = &text[x][0];
  fputs(ptr,fp);
  putc(chr,fp);
  if (text[x][0] == 0) break;
  x++;
  } /* END of while */
  fclose(fp);
}  /* END of store-text() */
```

The program starts with the preprocessor declarations to include the stdio.h header file.
This contains the prototypes for the file handling functions and the type definition of
FILE.

The next line carries a definition for CLS. Here we come to a point of disagreement amongst many C programmers. We have here a definition of a function call which is made quite often in many programs: a call to clear the screen. The call here is for the Amstrad PC running under MSDOS. If you are using a different operating system and computer you will have to check what the terminal control sequence is on your machine. You will notice in this define definition we have not included the semi-colon at the end. This means that when we put CLS into the main program text we must follow it by a semi-colon. There are some C programmers who state that calls like this should have a semi- colon included in their definition, and so you do not have to put them in the inline call. This is very much a matter of personal preference. It is recommended that you do not include the semi-colon in the definition but put it on the programming line, then you become used to always putting semi-colons in the program. Next we define MAX as 80 and LINES as 300. These two definitions are used in the initialization of the arrays text and buffer.

There are two working functions in this program, get_text() and store_text(). The function get_text() takes an input of text and places it in the array text. This is done until either the array is full, while(x < LINES), or the first character entered in a line has a NULL value. This can be obtained by just pressing return. This produces an empty string, with gets() just inserting NULL at the first position in the string.

The second function store_text() writes the text to a file called "text". This is opened with the "w" write mode set. An important point to note in this function is that we set the character variable chr to be equal to the new line character '\n'. Then, after writing each line to the disk with the fputs() function we write a newline with the putc() function. The reason for this is that fputs() unlike puts() does not add a newline to the string. We do, however, need one to replace the carriage return lost using gets() for the input. We therefore add it with putc(chr,fp).

The rest of the program should be fairly easy to understand. The whole program provides a basic way of entering text and saving it to disk. With Program 051 you had a way of getting text from the disk and putting it on screen. So now try and combine the two and see if you can build yourself a very small text processor.

Getting Hard Output

Up to now we have dealt with reading and writing to disks. What must be remembered is that the C language treats all input and output by way of files (sometimes called streams). This includes output to the printer.

This is one of the points where we start encountering trouble with operating systems. You need to know the file name for a printer in order to be able to use it. It will usually be PRN or LPT1 under MSDOS, but this is not always the case. With Unix you have problems, the printer can be anything the System Manager decides to call it.

Anyway, as an MSDOS system is being used to write this, we will work with the MSDOS file name. Basically, all we have to do is open the printer as a file for output (that is one to write to) and send the output to it. Look at Program 053.

```
/ * * * * * * * * * * * * * * * * * * * * * * * * * * * * * * * * * * * * * * * * * * * * * *
* Program 053                                                *
* Hard output to printer                                     *
* * * * * * * * * * * * * * * * * * * * * * * * * * * * * * * * * * * * * * * * * * * * * * /

#include  <stdio.h>
#define  MAX  80

char  file[]  =  "testtext.doc";
char  printer[]  =  "LPT1";          "PRN";

main()
{
  char  buffer[MAX];
  FILE  *fp,*fpo;
  long  offset;      I don't think this is used in this program!

  fp = fopen(  file, "r");
  fpo= fopen(  printer, "w");
  while(  fgets(buffer,MAX,fp)  != NULL  )
    {
    fputs(buffer,fpo);
    }
fcloseall();
}
```

Here we take the input from a text file called TESTTEXT.DOC which we created before for the file reading program, and we output it to the file LPT1 thus obtaining a print out of TESTTEXT.DOC on the printer. If you have a problem with this not working check what your printer is designated as in your system. LPT1 is the designation of the parallel printer port on the Amstrad PC1640HD20 on which the program was developed. You will probably find the designation will be either LPT1 or PRN, but if you are using a serial printer, or a second printer card, it will be different.

You can use basically the same method to direct output to any device file of which you know the name. So if you had a modem connected to the serial port (which is called COM1) to send the file via the modem you would replace LPT1 in Program 053 with COM1.

Adding Things On

So far, we have opened files, written to them from the start, and read them. Unfortunately, these are not the only tasks you want to do with files. Sometimes you want to add data onto the end. Well, you can. Instead of using the "w" parameter to the fopen() function to write, you use "a" to append. Look at, Program 054a and b, enter them and run them.

```
/****************************************************
* Program 054a                                     *
* Demonstration of append. Part 1                  *
****************************************************/

#include <stdio.h>

char mes1[]="This is the first line.\n";

main()
{
  FILE *fp;
  int i;

  fp = fopen("ftest","w");
  i=0;

  while( mes1[i] != NULL )
  {
    printf("%d",i);
    putc( mes1[i], fp);
    i++;
  }
  fclose(fp);
  printf("That is the end of part one.");
}
```

Program 054b appends the line to the file opened and written to by Program 054a. Incidentally, to check the files use Program 051 that we wrote earlier to read a file, or write another of your own.

```
/****************************************************
* Program 054b                                     *
* Demonstration of append. Part 2                  *
****************************************************/

#include <stdio.h>

char mes2[]="This is the second line.\n";

main()
{
  FILE *fp;
```

```
   int i;

   fp = fopen("ftest","a");
   i=0;

   while( mes2[i] != NULL )
   {
     printf("%d",i);
     putc( mes2[i], fp);
     i++;
   }
   fclose(fp);
   printf("That is the end of part two.");
}
```

Finding Out Where You Are

It is often useful to know where you are in a file. This is especially true when you are doing random accessing of a file. The function ftell() returns the offset of the file pointer from the start of the file. Look at Program 055.

```
/*************************************************
* Program 055                                   *
* Demonstration of ftell()                      *
*************************************************/

#include <stdio.h>
#define MAX 80

char file[]="testtext.doc";

main()
{
  char buffer[MAX];
  long offset;
  FILE *fp;

  fp = fopen(file,"r");

  while(fgets(buffer,MAX,fp) != NULL )
  {
    offset = ftell(fp);
    printf("%d ",offset);
    puts(buffer);
  }

  fclose(fp);
}
```

Random or Direct Access

All the file work we have dealt with so far has been on the basis of sequential access: starting at the beginning and reading or writing to the end. The only variation on this theme has been the use of the append mode to add data onto the end of a file, but here also we have written onto the end. Sometimes it is useful to be able to read or write something from the middle of the file.

This ability to go directly to a specific part of a file is called random or direct access. The function ftell() which allows you to find out where you are in the file is useful in this respect. More useful, though, is the function fseek(). This enables you to place the file pointer to a specific position in the file.

To do this, fseek() requires that you pass it three parameters: the filepointer, an offset, and a value telling it how to use the offset. The standard syntax is:

```
fseek( filepointer, offset, how);
```

The filepointer is fairly simple. You have been using this already in this chapter. The offset and how can cause confusion so to start with we will just cover the basic way of doing it. This is using how with a value of 0 in which case the offset has a value which represents the number of bytes from the start of the file. Look at Programs 056 and 057, enter them and compile them. Note that if you are working with a compiler other than Turbo C you may have a different set of include files and you will need to consult your documentation.

```
/*************************************************
 * Program 056                                  *
 * Random writing of records to a file          *
 *************************************************/

#include <stdio.h>

#define MAX 80
#define CLS printf("%c[2J",27)

char buffer[MAX];
char names[10][10];

main()
{
get_name();
store_name();
}

get_name()
{
```

```
int  x,y,z;
char  *ptr;

CLS;
for ( x = 0; x < 10; x++ )
  {
    printf("\nEnter  Name  ");
    ptr = &names[x][0];
    gets(ptr);
  }
}

store_name()
{
  FILE  *fp;
  int  i,off;
  char  *ptr;
  CLS;
  puts("Storing  Names");

  fp = fopen("workfile","w");

  for ( i = 0; i < 10; i++)
    {
      off = i * 12;
      fseek(fp,off,0);
      ptr = &names[i][0];
      fputs(ptr,fp);
      putc('\n',fp);
    }
  fclose(fp);
}

/********************************************
* Program 057                               *
* Random reading of records from a file     *
********************************************/

#include  <stdio.h>

char  buffer[12];

main()
{
  FILE  *fp;
  int  i,off;
  fp = fopen("workfile","r");

  for ( i = 10; i > 0; i--)
    {
```

127

```
    off = (i-1) * 12;
    printf("\nOffset = %d ",off);
    fseek(fp,off,0);
    fgets(buffer,10,fp);
    puts(buffer);
  }
fclose(fp);
}
```

Let us now consider at what these two programs are doing.

Program 056 takes an input of names and stores them in an array. This is all very simple. However, there is no check to stop you trying to put in a name bigger than the ten characters allocated to it. Try writing a check into the program for yourself.

The next part of the program then stores the array to disk. Here though, instead of storing it in a normal sequential manner, it uses direct access. Each name is stored starting at a byte in the file which is 12 bytes further on than the start of the last name. This is achieved by setting off which will be passed as the offset parameter to fseek() to the value of i multiplied by 12 where i is the number of the entry in the array. The rest of this section is very much the same as in earlier example programs.

One interesting point remains. You will note that after using the fputs() to write the string to the file, we use a putc() to write a newline character to the file. The reason for this is that we are using the fgets() to read back. This will end its read when it finds the newline character. Without such a control you may find yourself getting rubbish characters at the end of the read. Try removing the putc() and see what happens.

Now the names are in and stored. What next? Have a look at the file. The result will depend on what operating system you are using and what tool you use to look at the file. We used the type command under MSDOS, the first name followed by some rubbish, then the second name, each name being separated by a gap. Where there was existing material in this gap it had not been overwritten.

The result was different when we compiled the second program and looked at the file using this. In this program the file pointer is moved to a specific position in the file and the file is then read from that position. This results in us being able to read the records in the file in reverse order. Note that we are reducing the value of i by one before calculating the offset. This is to take into account the fact that there are ten records in the file, but the offset to the first record is 0.

Having looked at the basic way of using fseek() let us look at the other ways of using the offset and how parameters. The first is to move the file pointer to a position relative to its present position. Movements of this kind are quite useful.

If the how parameter to fseek() has the value one then the offset will be interpreted as a number of bytes to be moved from the present position of the file pointer. If the offset is positive the file pointer will be moved forward towards the end of the file, if the offset is negative then it will be moved back towards the start.

The other value that how can be given is two. In this case the file pointer will be set to a number of points from the end of the file, and the file pointer must be negative. Look at Program 058.

```c
/*****************************************************
 * Program 058                                      *
 * Using fseek() to read a file backwards           *
 *****************************************************/

#include <stdio.h>

char ch;

main()
{
  FILE *fp;
  int hold,off;

  fp = fopen("testtext.doc","r");
  off = -1;
  for (hold = 0; hold < 100; hold++)
  {
    fseek(fp,off,2);
    ch = getc(fp);
    printf("%c",ch);
    off--;
  }
  fclose(fp);
}
```

This reads the last 100 characters from a file backwards. You must make sure that there are at least one hundred characters in your file testtext.doc as we are setting the how parameter to fseek() to 2 and offset has a negative value.

- Figure 13.2 is on the next page -

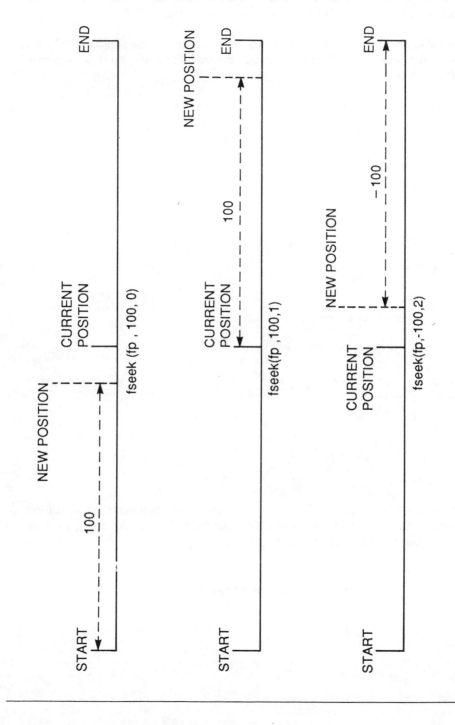

Figure 13.2

14

THE COMMAND LINE ARGUMENTS

It is fairly common to want to pass an argument to a program when the program is invoked from the command line. For instance, if you are using a database program like Lutterworth Software's Microfile you might invoke it with the command:

```
m  agency.
```

In this case you are passing the name of a data file 'agency' to the program 'm' as an argument on the command line.

Such arguments are known as 'command line arguments'. Information about command line arguments is passed by the operating system to the entry function of the invoked program. In the case of C this is the function main().

To make use of the command line arguments which are passed to a program the function main() needs to be told two things. First, how many arguments there are and second, where to find them. This is achieved by two special variables. These are the first and second parameters of the function main(). They can be called anything you like, but by tradition they are usually called argc and argv. In Turbo C these are usually declared as:

```
main(int argc, char *argv[] )
{
```

although if you want to you can still use the older form to keep compatibility with old source code:

```
main(argc,argv)
int argc;
char *argv[];
{
```

In these declarations we meet something new: a declaration of an array of pointers. What we have in the declaration *char[] is a declaration of a pointer, which itself points to an array which is made up of pointers which point to strings. This is complicated and many C programmers become totally lost with them. For the time being, just accept that it works; you can find out more about them later.
Look at Program 059.

```
/ * * * * * * * * * * * * * * * * * * * * * * * * * * * * * * * * * * * * * * * * * * * * * * * * *
*  Program 059                                           *
*  The passing of command line arguments                 *
* * * * * * * * * * * * * * * * * * * * * * * * * * * * * * * * * * * * * * * * * * * * * * * * * /

#include <stdio.h>

main(int argc, char *argv[])
{
     int i;
     printf("The number of arguments is %d\n",argc");

     for ( i = 0; i < argc; i++ )
     {
printf("Argument number %d is : %s\n",i,argv[i]);
     }
}
```

What happens here is that you pass a series of arguments on the command line and they are printed out together with a statement telling you how many there are.

There are some interesting points here. The C standard is that argv[0] points to the program name. This is the case under UNIX. Unfortunately, neither CP/m nor MSDOS below version 3 stored the program name. This resulted in argv[0] pointing to rubbish. Most compilers avoided this by the simple expedient of setting argv[0] to point to an empty string. MSDOS 3.00 and above does support the passing of the program name as argument argv[0]. This aspect of MSDOS is fully supported by Turbo C. However, if you are running Turbo C under a version of MSDOS prior to version 3, then Turbo C will return an empty string as the first argument, that is argv[0]. If you are using another compiler then you will probably get rubbish or an empty string.

Have a look at Program 060.

This is a very primitive word count program. It regards words as being any collection of characters which are contained between two spaces or a space and a newline. The #include statement is used to include the code macro for getc() in Turbo C. If this is not included Turbo C will link in from the library rather than make use of inline code.

```
/*******************************************************
* Program 060                                        *
* Demonstration of command line arguments            *
********************************************************/

#include <stdio.h>

FILE  *fp;
int    count;

main(int argc,char *argv[])
{
        if ( argc <= 1 )            /* Test if arguments passed */
        {
             char name[30];         /* Set up buffer for file name */
             printf("Enter file name ");
             gets(name);
             process(name);
        }

        else                        /* Arguments have been passed */
        {
             int i;
             for ( i = 1; i < argc; i++ )  /* Set up loop to process
                                            * arguments.
                                            */
             {
                    process(argv[i]);
             }
        }
}

process(char *fname)
{
        count = 0;
        fp = fopen(fname,"r");

        while(getword())
        {
        count++;
        }

        fclose(fp);

        printf("\nThe number of words in %s is %d\n",fname,count);
}
```

133

```
getword()
{
        int flag = 0;
        char let;

        while ( ( let = getc(fp) ) != EOF )
        {
            switch (let)
            {
                case 32:                        /* Space */
                        if (flag) return (-1);
                        break;
                case '\n':                      /* Newline */
                        if (flag) return (-1);
                        break;
                default:
                        if ( !flag ) flag = 1;
            }
        }
        return(0);
}
```

The function main() is declared with argc and argv to indicate that command line arguments are expected, the declarations of argc being of type int and argv as an array of pointers to type char. Now for the interesting part.

When we enter the main function a test is made to see if the value of argc is greater than one. Remember that there is always one argument, the program name. If argc is not greater than one then there is not a command line argument to be processed. In this case, the program will ask for the input of the name of the file to be processed. This name is then passed to the function process.

If argc is greater than one, then command line arguments have been passed. In this case a for loop is set up which passes the arguments to the function process. Notice that the loop is initialized to one and not to zero as is common practice with for loops in C. The reason for this is that we are not interested in argv[0] which will point to the program name, only in those names which have been passed to the program as file names on the command line. These will start at argv[1].

The rest of the program is fairly simple, most of the work being done in the switch case statement. A small amount of work here could bring about a major improvement in the program and allow it not to be fooled into counting tabs, etc., as words. Why not have a try and see what you can do?

Passing Numbers

One point about command line arguments is that often you will not want to pass a string, but a number, to the program. Unfortunately, the command line argument only works with strings. What is needed is a way to change strings to numbers. This is provided by the function atoi(). Example Program 061 is written for Turbo C but should work with most standard compilers.

```
/**************************************************
* Program 061                                    *
* Passing numbers                                *
**************************************************/

#include <stdio.h>

main(int argc, char *argv[])
{
        int  i,total,num;

        total = 0;

        for ( i = 1; i < argc; i++ )
        {
          num = atoi( argv[i] );
          total = total + num;
          printf("Argument %d has the value %d\n",i,num);
        }
printf("The total of %d arguments is %d\n",argc,total);
}
```

This is fairly easy to understand. We use the function atoi() to return the integer value represented by a string. Compile and run this program passing it four or five numbers as the arguments on the command line.

15

MESSING ABOUT WITH BITS

A great deal of real time programming concerns handling information at the bit level. In this chapter we look at some aspects of such operations. One problem is that C does not have a standard function for the display of binary information.

showbits

The function showbits() displays the bit contents of a byte. Have a look at Program 062, enter it, compile it and try to work out what it is doing. Then save the function showbits() in a file called showbits.c.

```
/ * * * * * * * * * * * * * * * * * * * * * * * * * * * * * * * * * * * * * * * * * * * * * *
* Program 062                                      *
* Demonstration of showbits                        *
* * * * * * * * * * * * * * * * * * * * * * * * * * * * * * * * * * * * * * * * * * * * * * /

main()
{
  int  num;

  num = 0;

  while ( 1 )
  {
  printf("\nEnter  a  number  ");
  scanf("%d",&num);
  printf("\n");
  if (num < 0) break;
  if (num > 255) continue;
  showbits(num);
  }
}
```

```
/******************************************************
 * function name   showbits                          *
 * arguments       single character variable var      *
 *                                                    *
 * output to stdout                                   *
 *                                                    *
 * The function takes a character variable which      *
 * is passed to it as an argument and displays        *
 * a printout of the bit pattern                      *
 ******************************************************/

showbits( char var )
{
  static unsigned char mask[8] = { 1, 2, 4, 8, 16, 32, 64, 128 };
  int bit;
  unsigned onezero;

  for ( bit = 7; bit >= 0; bit-- )
  {
   onezero = mask[bit] & var;
   printf("%c", onezero ? '1' : '0' );
  }
}
```

Looking at Memory

Program 063 shows an application of showbits() which although trivial could form the basis for a more useful function. This program allows you to obtain a binary display of memory.

```
/******************************************************
 * Program 063                                        *
 * Read memory in binary                              *
 ******************************************************/

# include <stdio.h>

main()
{
  char *ptr,d,c,k;
  int start,flag;

  printf("Enter start location ");
  scanf("%d",&start);
  printf("\n");
  ptr = start;
```

```
d = c = k = 0;

while ( d != 27 )
{
 if ( k == 0 ) printf("%d : ",ptr);
 /* If at the start of a line print value of pointer */

  c = *ptr;         /* Assign value pointed to by pointer to
                     * a character variable.
                     */

 showbits(c);      /* Display binary values of bits */
 printf(" ");
 flag = 0;

 while (!flag)
 {
  d = getch();
  if ( d == 27 ) flag = 1;   /* Exit loop if Esc is pressed */
  if ( d == 32 ) flag = 1;   /* Exit loop if Space is pressed */
 }

 k++;
 ptr++;

 if ( k == 6 )
 {
  k = 0;
  printf("\n");
 }
/* If six values have be printed set k to 0 to start new line */
 }
}

#include <showbits.c>
```

Although it is not a particularly useful or clever program, this does demonstrate both how to access memory directly using pointers and read the contents. Note that on compilation you may receive an error warning on the assignment of the integer variable start to the pointer.

Another fact in this which you might find useful is that we have included the showbits file at the end, not at the start. This is fairly common C programming practice, although you could (if you wanted to) put the file at the start. A general rule though is that only header files are put at the start of the program file and code files are always put at the end.

The reason for this is simple. Header files contain only declarations and defines. These may be wanted by the functions which come later. This means that you must put header files before you code. Why else would they be called header files? Code include files often need to make use of variables declared in the main code. In this case they must come after the main code. For this reason a rule has developed that all code include files are put at the end of the code.

A second important point, is that having them in this position makes debugging much easier. We look at this in Chapter 25.

The Bitwise AND Operator

The & symbol is the bitwise AND operator. In the bitwise AND operation the two values are compared bit by bit. If both bits in the values are one then the equivalent bit in the result will be set to one, otherwise it will be set to zero. Have a look at Program 064.

```
/********************************************
* Program 064                              *
* Demonstration of bitwise AND             *
********************************************/
main()
{
  char a,b,c;
  int fnum,snum;

  printf("Input a number up to 255 ");
  scanf("%d",&fnum);
  printf("\nInput a number up to 255 ");
  scanf("%d",&snum);

  a = fnum;
  b = snum;

  printf("\n\nFirst Number is    ");
  showbits(a);
  printf("\nSecond Number is   ");
  showbits(b);
  printf("\nThe AND result is ");

  c = a & b;
  showbits(c);
  printf("\n\n");
}

#include <showbits.c>
```

Testing Bits Set

It is possible to test if a specific bit is set using the & operator. If you have a single bit set in a mask variable and & this against the test variable, the value 0 will be returned if the bit is not set in the test variable. Consider the following illustration:

        test variable   10011001
        mask variable   00000100

        & result   00000000

This can be used within if tests by setting a mask variable to the appropriate value to test for the required bit. Consider Program 065.

```
/ * * * * * * * * * * * * * * * * * * * * * * * * * * * * * * * * * * * * * * * * * * * * * * * * * * *
*  Program   065                                             *
*   Demonstration  of  masking  using  &                     *
* * * * * * * * * * * * * * * * * * * * * * * * * * * * * * * * * * * * * * * * * * * * * * * * * * * * /

main ()
{
   int  val, i;
   static  char  mask[8]  =  {1,  2,  4,  8,  16,  32,  64,  128};
   char  a;

   val  =  0;
   while  ( val  != -1 )
   {
    printf("Enter  a  number  ");
    scanf("%d", &val);
    if ( val > 255 ) continue;
    a  =  val;
    for( i = 0;  i < 8;  i ++ )
    {
      if ( a & mask[i] )
          {
            printf("Bit  number  %d  is  set.\n", i);
          }
    }
   }
}
```

Compile and run this program and study how it works.

Switching Bits Off

The other use of the & operator is to switch bits off. In this case you have the bit you wish to switch off set to 0, with the rest of the bits set to 1.

The values used to switch specific bits off are:

bit number off	decimal value
0	254
1	253
2	251
3	247
4	239
5	223
6	191
7	127

Have a look at Program 066 which displays the bits of an input value then switches the required bit off if set.

```
/*************************************************
* Program 066                                   *
* Demonstration of switching bits off           *
*************************************************/

main()
{
  static unsigned char  omask[8]={254,253,251,247,239,223,191,127};
  char a;
  int val,bit;

  val = 0;
  while(1)
  {
   do
   {
    printf("Enter  a  number  ");
    scanf("%d",&val);
    if( val == -1 ) exit(0);
  } while ( val > 255 && val < 0 );

   do
   {
    printf("Which  bit  do  you  want  to  turn  off  ");
    scanf("%d",&bit);
  } while ( bit < 0 && bit > 7 );

  a = val;
  printf("Mask  value  selected  is   : %d\n",omask[bit]);
```

```
   printf("Current bit pattern is  : ");
   showbits(a);
   printf("\n");
   printf("Current mask pattern is : ");
   showbits(omask[bit]);
   printf("\n");
   a &= omask[bit];
   printf("Switched off pattern is : ");
   showbits(a);
   printf("\n\n\n");
   }
}


#include <showbits.c>
```

Notice in this example how we make use of a never ending loop while(1) which is always true, and escaping from the loop with the exit() function if a certain condition is met. This can often be a better way of handling tasks than putting the test in the while statement.

One area where this ability to switch bits off is very useful is in stripping word processor files. A number of word processors like Wordstar make use of setting the high bit on certain letters. This is apparent if you use the type command under MSDOS to view a Wordstar file. Program 067 will strip the high bits off a Wordstar format file leaving you with ASCII text.

The working of this program is fairly simple. A file is read in, one character at a time. The character is then ANDed with a mask which has been set to switch off the topmost bit. To do this we set mask to 127. The result of this is then written to another file.

A slightly more complicated program, but one which uses the same principle is Program 068. This enables you to display a Wordstar file to the screen one screenful at a time in ASCII format. You might like to consider combining both programs so that you have a tool to view a Wordstar file at the same time as you write a stripped copy.

```
/************************************************
* Program 067                                  *
* Program name   stripws.c                      *
*                                               *
* format stripws <inputfile> <outputfile>       *
*                                               *
* The program reads an input file character by  *
* character.  It strips the high bit off any    *
* character if set, and writes the character    *
* to the output file.                           *
************************************************/
```

142

```c
#include <stdio.h>

main(int argc, char *argv[])
{
        FILE *fp_in, *fp_out;
        /* Declare file pointers for input and output files. */

        char in_let, out_let, mask;
        int count = 0;

        mask = 127;  /* Set mask so only high bit is not set */
                     /* bit pattern is   01111111           */

        if ( argc != 3 )
        {
                puts("Usage stripws <inputfile> <outputfile>");
                exit (0);
        }
        /* If two files are not give as arguments, exit. */

        if ( ! strcmp(argv[1],argv[2]))
        {
                puts("Files must have different names. ");
                exit (0);
         }
          /* Check file names are different. */

        fp_in = fopen( argv[1],"r");
        if ( fp_in == 0 )
        {
                puts("Cannot open input file ");
                puts( argv[1] );
                exit(0);
        }

        fp_out = fopen( argv[2], "w");
        if ( fp_out == 0 )
        {
                puts("Cannot open output file ");
                puts( argv[2] );
                exit(0);
        }

        printf("Stripping file %s of high bits set.\n", argv[1]);

        puts("Each dot = 100 characters.");
```

143

```
            while ( (in_let = getc( fp_in )) != EOF )
            {
                    out_let = in_let & mask;
                    putc( out_let, fp_out );
                    count++;
                    if ( count >= 100 )
                    {
        count = 0;
                            putchar('.');
                    }
             }
            printf("\nStrip of file completed. Output in %s.\n", argv[2]);

            fcloseall();
}


/*************************************************
 * Program 068                                   *
 *                                               *
 * Program Name viewws.c                         *
 *                                               *
 * Usage   viewws <inputfile>                    *
 *                                               *
 * viewws reads an input file and displays it    *
 * one page at a time on the screen.             *
 *************************************************/

#include <stdio.h>

int line_count;        /* Declare line_count as global as it is
                        * increased in main() but reset in page().
                        */

main( int argc, char *argv[] )
{
        FILE *fp_in;
        char in_let, out_let, mask;
        int lets;

        mask = 127; /* Set bit pattern to 01111111 */

        if ( argc != 2 )
        {
                puts( " Usage :- viewws < filename > " );
                exit (0);
        }
```

144

```c
fp_in = fopen( argv[1],"r");

if ( fp_in == 0 )
{
        puts("Cannot open input file ");
        exit (0);
}

printf("%c[2J",27); /* ANSI Clear Screen Command */

line_count = 0;
lets = 0;

while  ( ( in_let = getc(fp_in) ) != EOF )
{
     out_let = in_let & mask; /* Switch off high bit */

     putchar( out_let );
     lets++;

     if ( out_let == '\n' )
     {
             line_count++;
             lets = 0;
     }

     if ( lets >= 80 )
     {
             printf("\n");
             line_count++;
             lets = 0;
     }

     if ( line_count == 23 ) page();
}

puts("End of file, press space bar to return to DOS ");

while ( ( in_let = getch() ) != 32 )
;

fcloseall();
```

```
/*************************************************
* function name   page()                        *
*                                                *
* arguments passed none                          *
*                                                *
* The function page prints the end of screen     *
* message then waits in a while loop for the     *
* space bar to be pressed.  When pressed the     *
* screen is cleared using the ANSI sequence      *
* and line_count is reset to 0.                  *
*************************************************/

page()
{
        char ch;

        printf("Press space bar for next screen.");

        while ( ( ch = getch() ) != 32 );

        printf("%c[2J",27);
        line_count = 0;
}
```

The Bitwise OR Operator

With the bitwise AND operator, both bits had to be one for the result to be one. With the bitwise OR if either of the bits is one then the result will be one. The symbol for the bitwise or is |.

Switching Bits On

The operator generally used to switch bits on is the bitwise OR operator |. Have a look at Program 069.

```
/*************************************************
* Program 069                                   *
* Demonstration of switching bits on            *
*************************************************/

main()
{
 static unsigned char imask[8] = { 1, 2, 4, 8, 16, 32, 64, 128 };
 char a;
 int val,bit;

 val = 0;
 while(1)
```

```
do
{
  printf("Enter  a  number  ");
  scanf("%d",&val);
  if( val == -1 )  exit(0);
} while ( val > 255 && val < 0 );

do
{
  printf("Which bit do you want to turn on  ");
  scanf("%d",&bit);
} while ( bit < 0 && bit > 7 );

a = val;
printf("Mask value selected is : %d/n",imask[bit];
printf("Current bit pattern is : ");
showbits(a);
printf("\n");
Printf("Current mask pattern is : ");
showbits(imask[bit]);
printf(""\n");
a |= imask[bit];
printf("Switched off pattern is : ");
showbits(a);
printf("\n\n\n");
}
}
```

Clearly, this is essentially the same as Program 066 that we used to switch bits off, but this time we have a different set of mask values and we are using the bitwise OR operator |.

The Bitwise XOR Operator

More complicated than the bitwise AND and the bitwise OR is the bitwise XOR or to give its full title, the exclusive-or operator. The symbol for this is the carat ^. The complication here is that it will result in the setting of the result bit if one or other of the operand bits is set.

To try and explain this more clearly, if we have two bits, one set to zero and the other to one then XOR will set the resultant bit. But if both had been one then XOR will not set the resultant bit.

See how this works on a byte set of bits.

first operand	00101100
second operand	10100110
XORed result	10001010

147

Toggling

A frequent use of the ^ operator is to toggle a bit. Consider Program 070.

```
/***********************************************
* Program 070                                  *
* Demonstration of toggling of bit             *
* using XOR bitwise function                   *
***********************************************/

main()
{
  char flag,mask;
  int i;
  flag = 1;
  mask = 1;

  for ( i = 0; i < 10; i++ )
  {
    printf("Current value of flag is "); showbits(flag);
    newline();
    flag ^= mask;
    printf("Toggled value of flag is "); showbits(flag);
    newline();
    if ( flag )
    {
      printf("This time round this is done.");
          printf("\nThe flag is set.\n\n\n");
    }
    else
    {
      printf("The flag is not set so do nothing\n\n\n");
    }
    delay();
  }
}

newline()
{
  printf("\n");
}

delay()
{
  long j;
  for ( j = 0; j < 100000; j++);
}
```

The Ones-complement Operator

The ~ symbol, the tilde, is the ones-complement operator. This is a unary operator as it affects only a single variable. What it does is change all the ones in a byte to zeros and all the zeros to ones.

So the number two has a binary value of 0000010. The ones-complement of two has a binary value of 1111101.

Have a look at Program 071 which shows this.

```
/*************************************************
* Program 071                                   *
* Demonstration of ones-complement              *
*************************************************/

main()
{
    unsigned char a;
    unsigned int val;

    while(1)
    {
    do
    {
     printf("Input a number between 0 and 255 ");
     scanf("%d",&val);
     if (val == 1000) exit(0);
     printf("\n");
    } while ( val < 0 || val > 255 );

    a = val;
    printf("The bits are "); showbits(a);
    printf("\n");

    a = ~a;     /* ones complement of a */

    printf("Now they are "); showbits(a);
    printf("\n\n\n");
    }
}
```

Clearing Zeroth Bit

One of the most common uses of the ones-complement is in conjunction with a bitwise AND to clear the zeroth bit. As the ~1 will have every bit set except the zeroth, you can always clear the zeroth bit no matter how many bytes a variable occupies, with:

```
result = num & (~1);
```

Note the use of brackets here. It is standard practice to include unary operations within brackets like this.

Shifts

There are two C operators for handling bitwise shifts, these are the left shift operator << and the right shift operator >>. Both operators require a positive value of the number of bits to be shifted. As an example:

```
<<2
```

will shift two bits to the left, whilst:

```
>>3
```

will shift three bits to the right.

Study Program 072 which illustrates their use.

```
/****************************************************
* Program 072                                      *
* Demonstration of bitwise shifts                  *
****************************************************/
main()
{
  unsigned char let,res;
  int i;

  let = 1;

  for ( i=1; i < 7; i++ )
  {
  res = let <<i;
  printf(" %d left shifted by ",let);
  printf("%d is %2d ",i,res);
  printf("which has the bit pattern. ");
  showbits(res);
  printf("\n");
  }
```

```
  for ( i=1; i < 7; i++)
  {
    let = res >>i;
    printf("%d right shifted by ",res);
    printf("%d is %2d ",i,let);
    printf("which has the bit pattern. ");
    showbits(let);
    printf("\n");
  }
}

#include <showbits.c>
```

16

SOME FURTHER FUNCTIONS

Getting Hold of Memory

When you run a C program, the program grabs hold of a certain amount of the memory in your computer. The exact way in which this memory is grabbed will vary with the type of compiler, operating system and computer you are using. Basically, one block of memory will be taken for the static variables in the program. Above this a block will be taken to hold the runtime code of the program. On top of this will be an area known as the runtime stack, which will hold those variables which are not held permanently in memory, that is, those declared as being auto rather than static. This actually means any variable other than an array, which is declared in a function and not explicitly declared as being a static variable.

So, all that memory is taken by the program. Above this you are liable to have a block of unused memory. This is known as free memory. You can 'grab' a section of this memory for your own use with the function malloc().

When called, you need to pass malloc() the number of bytes of memory that you want to use. If the memory is available it will return a void pointer to the start of that memory, otherwise it will return the null value.

Incidentally, notice that the pointer is of type void. The reason for this is simple. As you have to specify the memory in terms of a number of bytes, you use the type void which is a non- specific number of bytes type. With older compilers you will find that malloc() returns a pointer of type char.

Once you have your memory, what do you do with it when you have finished using it? (We look at how to use it later in this chapter, and in Chapters 19 and 20.) Well, you give it back. This is achieved by the use of the function free() to which you pass a pointer to the memory block. The block is then freed back to free memory.

There is another point which is quite important. In many systems the stack, which is where auto variables are stored, is held as part of free memory. You therefore need to make sure you do not take up all the free memory with a malloc(), but leave some clear for the stack. One way in which you can do this it to keep requesting and freeing memory with malloc() and free() increasing the size of bytes taken each time, until you get a NULL return, then take a lower figure.

Arrays Which Change Size

Until now we have dealt with arrays which have a fixed dimension. This can mean that a great deal of space is wasted. For instance, if you declare an array of twenty strings each of eighty characters, the total amount of memory needed to hold the array is 20 * 80 bytes, that is 1,600 bytes. If you have a case where only one of the strings needs the whole 80 characters and all the rest are between 10 and 20 characters in length, you will have considerable wasted memory.

An alternative situation, but in many ways worse, is when you have dimensioned an array too small. If you have allowed for a list of names to be entered with each name not more than 30 characters long (usually an adequate allowance) you have problems when you have to enter Ferdinand Michael Johannes Van De Slagharene. You may think that such events are unlikely, but there is one fundamental rule in computer programming. If you think an event is so unlikely that you do not have to cover for it: it is bound to turn up.

The answer to both these sorts of problems is to make use of dynamic arrays. Here you declare an array of pointers for the number of items you want to hold in the array. Then you place your items in memory, having acquired that memory with malloc() and address them via the pointers. Have a look at Program 073.

```
/ * * * * * * * * * * * * * * * * * * * * * * * * * * * * * * * * * * * * * * * * * * * *
*  Program 073                                        *
*  Demonstration of Dynamic Arrays                    *
* * * * * * * * * * * * * * * * * * * * * * * * * * * * * * * * * * * * * * * * * * * * /

#include  <stdio.h>
#include  <stdlib.h>

#define  MAX  80
#define  MXPTR  10

main()
{
    int  length,  num,  count;

    char  *ptr[MXPTR],  buffer[80];
```

```
for ( count = 0; count < MXPTR; count ++ )
{

  printf("Enter   name  %d  ",count);
  gets(buffer);
  length = strlen(buffer) + 1;

  if ( ( ptr[count] = malloc(length) ) == NULL )
  {
      puts("Out of  memory  space.");
      break;
    }

  strcpy( ptr[count],  buffer );
  }

num = -1;
puts ("To end name display enter 0 else enter number from 1 to 10");

while ( num )
{
  printf("Enter  number  of  name  you  want : ");
  scanf("%d",&count);
  getchar();
  if ( count == 0 ) break;
  if ( count < 1 || count > 10 ) continue;
  puts(ptr[count-1]);
  }
}
```

First, we define the maximum number of entries we are going to have in our array. This is done by defining MXPTR at 10. We then set up three integer variables, all of which are quite normal. This is followed by the character definitions. Here we declare the pointer to an array of pointers *ptr[] of type characters. We also have to declare a buffer. For this we use a standard character array called buffer[] of eighty characters. You will notice that the include files for this program have been extended. In addition to the normal stdio.h we now have stdlib.h. This is the standard library header which includes, amongst other things, the prototype for the function malloc().

The next part of the program takes the input of ten names. This is done inside a for loop. The name is inputted to buffer with the gets() function. It can be any length up to 80 characters. The whole point is to allow a buffer big enough to take whatever might come.

Next we establish the length of the name using the strlen() function and we add one to this. This is to allow for the terminating NULL at the end of the string which is not counted by strlen().

Our next step is to reserve memory to put the string into. This is done at the same time as we make a test to see if there is enough memory to store the string. The line:

```
if ( ( ptr[count] = malloc(length)) == NULL )
```

could have been written as:

```
ptr[count] = malloc(length);

if ( prt[count] == NULL)
```

and it might be easier to follow in that form. What we have done is make a call to malloc() for length bytes. If this call is successful it will return a pointer to the start of the reserved memory. If it is not successful, it will return NULL. If NULL is returned a message is printed to say that we have run out of memory and the break command takes us out of the loop.

If there is sufficient memory, the string is then copied into the reserved memory obtained by malloc(). This is done using the function strcpy.

In the second part of the program we set num to -1 then use this as the value in a while statement. This has the effect of setting up an indefinite loop, as the condition will always be true and no other operation is carried out on num. You should be able to follow the rest without problems. However, do not forget our friend the dummy getchar() to take care of the return character after the scanf(). The first time I tried this program I forgot to include it, and had to reset the computer to escape out of the program.

Also notice the use of the continue statement in the if test to check for valid numbers. This can be very useful for jumping back to the start of a while statement.

Have a look at the program, try it out, then amend it. See what happens when you do different things. How can you get out of entering names before you have put ten in? Try other modifications as well and see what effect they have.

There are a number of other uses for memory grabbed by malloc(). Experiment with putting data directly into memory and retrieving it. Have a look at Program 074.

Here, a block of memory is grabbed and text is stored in it on a character by character basis. An important point to note is that before the block of memory is used it is filled with NULL. This is done because there is no way that we can know what is in the memory.

```
/******************************************************
* Program 074                                        *
* Demonstration of using malloc()                    *
******************************************************/

#include <stdio.h>
#include <stdlib.h>

#define MAX 80
#define MX 500

main()
{
   int length, num, count;

   char ch,*ptr,*p2tr, buffer[80], *sptr;

   if (( ptr = malloc(MX)) == NULL )
   {
    puts("Insufficient Memory");
    return;
   }
   printf("Memory grabbed \n");
   sptr = ptr;

   ch = NULL;
   printf("Memory start %d ",ptr);
   for ( count = 0; count < MX; count ++)
   {
    *ptr = ch;
    ptr++;
   }
   printf("Memory filled with Null, Memory end %d \n",ptr);

   ptr = sptr;

   puts("Enter Text");
   buffer[0]=NULL;

   while( egets(buffer) )
   {
     count = 0;
     while( buffer[count] != NULL)
     {
      *ptr = buffer[count];
      ptr++;
      count++;
     }
   }
```

156

```
puts ("Printing.");
for ( p2tr = sptr; p2tr <= ptr; p2tr++ )
{
  ch = *p2tr;
  printf ("%c",ch);
}


}

/ * * * * * * * * * * * * * * * * * * * * * * * * * * * * * * * * * * * * * * * * *
* function name    egets ()                               *
*                                                         *
* arguments    address of character array                *
*                                                         *
* egets () takes the input of a string and places*
* in the buffer passed as argument.   It returns  *
* 0 if the ESC key has been pressed during input*
* * * * * * * * * * * * * * * * * * * * * * * * * * * * * * * * * * * * * * * * * /

egets( char buf[] )
{
        char let;
        int i;
        i = 0;


    do
      {
                let = getch();
                if ( let == 13 )
                                let = '\n';
                buf[i] = let;
                i = i + 1;
                if ( let == 27 )
                        return (0);

                putchar( let );
      } while ( let != '\n' );

        buf[i] = 0;
        return (1);
}
```

The function egets() which is used here provides you with a way around one of the problems with gets(). If you press the ESC key while putting input into gets() all the input before the ESC key depression will be ignored, but the value of the ESC will not be entered into the string. In many programs where you have string entry you may want to use ESC as a way out. This is a fairly standard feature of many text editing programs.

What egets() does is read the characters one by one from the keyboard into the array. If you press ESC the value 27 is detected and a return is made of the value zero. Otherwise, when you press RETURN the value one is returned.

Another point you should note is that we test for RETURN and then put '\n' in as the value of let. The reason for this is that the depression of the RETURN key gives the ASCII value 13. Under MSDOS the return does not automatically generate a line feed, so 13 is not equal to '\n'. The replacement is therefore undertaken so you get both a carriage return and a line feed. Note this reflects the situation with Turbo C under MSDOS on the Amstrad PC1640HD20. On other systems, with other operating systems and compilers, the situation may be different. You will have to check.

Forcing One Type into Another

One of the problems with type casting for variables is that often the variable you want is not in the form that you want it to be for a specific use. This is a common occurrence in graphic programming where you often need to assign a specific value to a pointer.

The way around this is to cast one variable onto another. This is a process by which a copy of a variable is assigned to a variable of a different type. The syntax for this operation is:

```
variable_type_a = (type) variable_type_b
```

where type is the type of the first variable. So if we have a character pointer ptr, and we wish to assign the value held in the integer variable num to it, the line would read:

```
ptr = (char *) num;
```

whilst to assign the value of num to a character called ch we would use:

```
ch = (char) num;
```

This last operation would only be strictly required if num was of a type float and not integer. Most compilers, but not all, will allow you to assign character values to integers and integers to character.

Here we have used the typedef command to define char_pointer to be a type of pointer to a character.

```
/****************************************************
 * Program 075                                      *
 * Demonstration of casting                         *
 *                                                  *
 * Program name   hexdump                           *
 *                                                  *
 * This program produces a dump of memory in        *
 * hexadecimal format.                              *
 ****************************************************/

#include <stdio.h>
#include <ctype.h>

#define CLS    printf("%c[2J",27)
#define SETCOLOR    printf("%c[44m%c[37m",27,27)
#define NORMAL      printf("%c[0m",27)
#define TRUE        1

unsigned char *start_ptr, *current_ptr, membuf[16];

main()
{
        notes();
        start();

        while ( TRUE )
                run();
}

/****************************************************
 *   notes()                                        *
 *                                                  *
 * The function notes() displays a screen of        *
 * help text.  Return to main program is by         *
 * pressing the ESC key which exits a loop          *
 ****************************************************/

notes()
{
        CLS;

        printf("\tThe program displays the contents of memory ");
        printf("in hexadecimal format \n");
        printf("\tand in ASCII. At the end of each page a menu ");
        printf("is displayed.\n\n");
        printf("\tThe choices are: \n\n");
```

159

```
        printf("\t\tG ................. goto specified location.\n\n");
        printf("\t\tB .................. go back one screen.\n\n");
        printf("\t\tF .................. go forward one screen.\n\n");
        printf("\t\tH ................. help, print this screen.\n\n");
        printf("\t\tESC ............... Escape to DOS.\n\n");
        SETCOLOR;
        printf("                     Press ESC to continue");
        printf("                                        ");
        NORMAL;
        printf("\n");

        while (  getch() != 27 )
            ;
}


/*****************************************************
* start()                                           *
*                                                   *
* The function start() takes the input of an        *
* integer value in hex or decimal and assigns       *
* this using the cast operator to the pointer       *
* start_ptr which is then assigned to the           *
* pointer current_ptr                               *
*****************************************************/

start()
{
        int val;
        char ans;

        CLS;
        printf("\n\n\tDo you wish to input start address ");
        printf("Hex or Decimal?  < H / D > ");

        do
        {
                ans = tolower( getch() );
                putchar(ans);
        } while ( (ans != 'h') && (ans != 'd') );

        if ( ans == 'h' )
        {
                printf("\n\n\nEnter start address in hex : ");
                scanf("%x",&val);
        }
        else
```

```c
        {
                printf("\n\n\nEnter start address in decimal : ");
                scanf("%x",&val);
        }

        start_ptr   = ( char *) val;
        current_ptr = start_ptr;
}


/******************************************************
*  run ()                                             *
*                                                     *
*  The function run() displays one  screen  at  a     *
*  time then waits for instructions  on  what         *
*  to do next.                                        *
******************************************************/

run ()
{
        int line, let, flag;
        char ch, ans;

        CLS;

        for ( line = 0; line < 16; line++ )
        {
                printf("%04x > ", current_ptr);

                for ( let = 0; let < 16; let++ )
                {
                        membuf[let] = *current_ptr;
                        printf("%2x ",membuf[let]);
                        current_ptr = current_ptr + 1;
                }

                printf("  |   ");

                for ( let = 0; let < 16; let++)
                {
                        if ( membuf[let] > 31 )
                                putchar(membuf[let]);
                        else
                                putchar('.');
                }

                printf("\n");
```

```
        }
        printf("\n\n\n\n");
        SETCOLOR;

        printf("       G(oto)      B(ackwards)   F(orwards)  ");
        printf("     H(elp)       ESC(ape to DOS)            ");
        NORMAL;

        flag = 1;
        while (flag)
        {
                ans = tolower(getch());

                switch (ans)
                {
                case 'g':
                        newstart();
                        flag = 0;
                        break;
                case 'b':
                        current_ptr = current_ptr - 512;
                        flag = 0;
                        break;
                case 'f':
                        flag = 0;
                        break;
                case 'h':
                        current_ptr = current_ptr - 256;
                        flag = 0;
                        notes();
                        break;
                case 27:
                        printf("\nConfirm you wish to return to DOS ?");
                        printf(" <Y/N> ");
                        ch = tolower(getch());
                        if ( ch == 'y' ) exit (0);
                        flag = 0;
                        current_ptr = current_ptr -256;
                        break;
                default:
                        ;
                }
        }
}
```

```
/******************************************************
*  newstart ()                                        *
*                                                     *
*  The function newstart () take the input of an      *
*  integer value in hex or decimal and assigns        *
*  this using the cast operator to the pointer        *
*  current_ptr                                        *
******************************************************/

newstart ()
{
        int  val;
        char ans;

        CLS;
        printf("\n\n\tDo you wish to input start address ");
        printf("Hex or Decimal?  < H / D > ");

        do
        {
                ans = tolower( getch() );

        } while ( ans != 'h' && ans != 'd' );

        if ( ans == 'h' )
        {
                printf("\n\n\nEnter new address in hex : ");
                scanf("%x",&val);
        }
        else
        {
                printf("\n\n\nEnter new address in decimal : ");
                scanf("%x",&val);
        }

        current_ptr    = ( char *) val;

}
```

Program 075 includes an illustration of the use of casting. The program also provides
a useful tool for looking at memory, and an illustration of one of the uses of pointers.
Examine the program and see how it works. You will find the detailed explanation of
some use.

First, there are the three code defines: CLS, SETCOLOR and NORMAL. These are
making use of the ANSI control codes to set screen operations. There are two ways in

which you can control the screen. In the first, you directly use C to address the hardware of your system. This method tends to be very efficient and gives you a great deal of flexibility. There is a problem, though, in that it tends to limit your application to very specific hardware. The second method which is often used is where you make use of the ANSI control code sequence to handle screen operations. You will find the approach is slower but it does produce more portable code.

The function main() in this program is very short. It calls up two functions which initialize the program and then enters an endless loop, escape from which comes from the function run(). You will notice that no variables are declared in main(). In this case all variables are either global and declared just before main(), or local to the operational functions.

The first of the operational functions is notes(). This informs you of what the program is actually doing and what keys to use. This function is invoked either at the start from main() or during operation from run().

After notes() you come to the function start(). This is where use is made of type casting. In this case we take the input of an address from which we want to read the memory. This can be taken in either decimal or hexadecimal format. The input is assigned to a variable val. This value is then assigned to the pointer *start_ptr. This is done in the statement:

```
start_ptr = ( char * ) val;
```

What we are doing here is that we are forcing the type of a character pointer onto the value held in val, when it is assigned to the character pointer start_ptr. In fact, as all pointers are integers anyway, you could have just done a direct assignment, but this would produce a warning at compilation time with Turbo C and some compilers will not allow it.

The function run() is fairly simple. It displays a 256 byte block of memory in hexadecimal and ASCII format, then waits for a keyed in command, the action to be taken on the key depression being decided in a switch-case statement. These are dealt with later in this chapter under Making Selections, but they fitted neatly into this program.

Another type cast is used to assign an integer value to a character pointer in the function newstart(). This is very similar to that done in start.

There are two points about this program for you to note. Although we assign an initial value to start_ptr this is not used other than for the assignment of that value to current_ptr. The reason for this is that it was intended to use this value so you would have an automatic return to start if you wanted it. In the final implementation of this program this is achieved by pressing the letter 's' which will take you back to the first screen. This is not implemented in this version. Try adding it.

The other facility you might like to try adding is a way in which you can edit memory. This might mean that you will need to read on further first, but it is something to come back and attempt when you feel ready.

Creating New Types

It is often convenient to be able to have a type description of a special class of types. This can be done with typedef. For instance, if we are using a number of arrays to hold strings all of 80 characters we might want to declare a type called strings:

```
typedef  char  STRINGS[80];
```

We can now declare a set of strings with:

```
STRINGS  name,road,town,county,country;
```

which is the same as:

```
CHAR  name[80],road[80],town[80],county[80],country[80];
```

Another important point is that many compilers will not accept char * in a cast statement. The only way to get a character pointer is to make use of the typedef to declare a character and then put that in the cast statement. Even worse, some compilers insist that every type declaration in the cast statement must be a declared type.

Making Selections

A fairly common requirement in programming is to carry out a task in accordance with a value of a variable. A typical example is where there is a choice of actions to be taken, and the choice made is reflected in the value of a variable returned. In such circumstances C provides us with an easy means of handling the selection using the switch case statement.

The statement consists of two parts. First, the declaration of the switch, that is the value upon which the test is to be made, and then a list of cases stating which action should be taken if the value matches the value in that case. The general structure is shown below:

```
switch ( choice )
{
  case 'a':
       action;
       break;
  case 'b':
       action;
       break;
```

```
    case 'c':
        action;
        break;
    default:
        action;
}
```

Look at Program 076.

This is a very simple offer of a menu type choice and then the use of the switch case statement to effect the selection. It well illustrates the basics of using the statement.

```
/****************************************************
 * Program 076                                      *
 * Demo of Switch Case                              *
 ****************************************************/

#include  <stdio.h>

main()
{
  int  num;
  char  ch;

  printf("Please  make  your  selection  \n\n");
  printf("1  -  a\n\n2  -  b\n\n3  -  c\n\n");

  num = 0;
  while  (  (  num  <  1  )  ||  (  num  >  3)  )
   {
     num = getch()  -  '0';
   }

  switch  (num)
   {
     case  1:
        ch = 'a';
        break;
     case  2:
        ch = 'b';
        break;
     case  3:
        ch = 'c';
        break;
     default:
        ch = 'z';
   }

  printf("%c\n\n",ch);
}
```

Often, you may want one of two or three selections to trigger an action. This is quite possible in a switch case statement by stacking the cases. Consider the following:

```
case 'Y':
case 'y':
case 'J':
case 'j':
acceptance_action;
break;
case 'N':
case 'n':
rejection_action;
break;
```

Clearly, there are no instructions for 'Y', 'y' or 'J'. If any of these are true the selection will drop down to the first set of instructions following them, in this case the set following 'j'. The selection of 'N' will result in the instructions following 'n' being carried out.

Such set ups are very useful for user proofing programs. The illustration above comes from a program at a point where it is asking for the input of Y for yes. A British user might enter Y or y, this program, though, is also in use in Northern Europe, so allowance is made for the input of J or j which are commonly used to give a positive response.

You will find a fuller example of using the switch_case statement in the memory read program, 075, earlier in this chapter. Go back to it and have another look.

Jumping Around

It is sometimes useful to be able to jump to somewhere else in a program. In fact, properly used, a jump can greatly increase the effectiveness of a program.

What you need to be able to jump around inside a program is a command to tell the program where to jump to and somewhere to indicate that location. This is done using LABELS and the command goto.

Look at Program 077

```
/ *****************************************************
* Program 077                                         *
* Demo of Goto                                         *
***************************************************** /

main()
{
  char ch;
  int num,flag;

  printf("Make Selection \n\n");

  printf("1 - a\n\n2 - b\n\n3 - c\n\n");
```

```
START:
flag = 0;
num = getch() - '0';

switch (num)
{
  case 1:
        ch = 'a';
        break;
  case 2:
        ch = 'b';
        break;
  case 3:
        ch = 'c';
        break;
  default:
        flag = -1;
}
if (flag) goto START;
printf("%c",ch);
}
```

This basically does the same as Program 076 in demonstrating the switch case, except here we are using a flag to indicate if none of the acceptable options has been selected, and a jump to go back to the start of the selection procedure.

The label START: indicates to the program where it should jump to. Note that the label is terminated with a colon. A label may come either before or after the goto, but the label and the goto must be contained in the same function.

Although Program 077 is a useful illustration of how the goto command works, it is a bad example of its use. The main use of gotos (many would claim the only legitimate use of them) is to escape from deep inside a series of nested loops. Here a goto can provide a way out in the event of a major error. The basic structure would be something like:

```
for(.........)
{
    for(.........)
    {
        do
        {
            while(.........)
            {
                if(problems)
                    goto WAYOUT;
            }
        } while (........);
    }
}

    WAYOUT:
```

In a case like this the goto would escape you from within four levels of loop. The use of a break would only take you up to the next level. However it should be noted that in situations like this it might be better to use exit() or return to provide a clean escape, although this may not always be possible.

Another point to consider is restructuring the code to avoid the deep levels of loops.

There are many software engineers and academic computer programmers who will say that you should never use gotos. Experience suggests that such people have had little experience of having to write software in the real world, or if they have, are working in a very software friendly environment.

It is valid to say the use of gotos should be avoided as much as possible, but there are times when it is the only acceptable means of solving a problem. The situation where this is quite common is in real time software which is operating under tight time controls. Here, real time software does not refer to much of the financial and banking software which is often described as real time. In such software, response times of over a second are often quite acceptable. What is meant by real time is software which has to respond within a time period of less than one tenth of a second.

When faced with this situation, you often find that the time taken to escape from the depths of a complex loop structure is more than acceptable. In these circumstances you have to revert to using gotos. If you need to use them, do so with care, and only after you have established that there is no acceptable alternative.

17

MIXED DATA TYPES

An array can hold a collection of variables under one name. The only problem is that they all have to be of the same type. Often, you need to hold together several variables of different types . For example, in an employee record the information you want to store is:

Name	String
Age	Integer
Male/Female	Character

Here we have three different items which are all connected. They can be held together in a structure.

A structure is essentially a special type of array which can hold several diverse variables. A typical example of the use of a structure is where the holding of information about people is required. Here the basic information is name and age. This gives us two different types of variable which have to be used. The name will be an array of characters, and the age an integer.

If we want to make this into a structure, the first task is to give the compiler a definition of the 'pattern' that the structure is going to hold. The pattern is a description of the individual members of the structure. So in this case we would declare a pattern for a structure called people as follows:

```
struct people {
    char  name[80];
    int   age;
            };
```

In this we are telling the compiler that it will recognize a type of structure called people. This structure will consist of two variables. The first member is a character array called name and the second member is an integer called age.

At this stage we now have to declare our structure before we can make use of it. So far the only task to have been done is to give C the details of how it is made. To declare a structure with the pattern given in people the declaration would be:

```
struct people member;
```

In this illustration we are telling the compiler to make a structure of the type (or pattern) people and give it the name member. It is then possible to address the individual variables within the structure by their structure member names. In this example we have two, the first is member.name and the second is member.age.

If we had declared a structure called family with the pattern people, using:

```
struct people family;
```

The names would be family.name and family.age. So, in referring to any member of a structure the first part of the variable name is the name under which the structure is declared followed by a full stop, the second part the name for the element (or member) of the structure.

Program 078 illustrates the above points.

```
/ ************************************************
 * Program 078                                  *
 * Demo of Structure                            *
 ************************************************/

#include <stdio.h>

struct people {
        char       name[80];
        int        age;
               };
main()
{
  struct people member;

  puts("Please enter members name");
  gets(member.name);
  puts("Please enter members age ");
  scanf("%d",&member.age);
  getchar();
  printf("\n\n\nThe member is %d years ",member.age);
  printf("of age and the name is ");
  puts(member.name);

}
```

In Program 078 a structure is set up with the pattern people. This pattern is then used to declare the structure member. The rest of the program is fairly simple. The input of the member's name is obtained using gets() with the variable name member name being passed to it to give the address of the array.

Quite often with structures you will only be using them in one section of code, or they will be global. In such cases it seems a rather long-winded way to go about things to set up the pattern, then declare a structure. You can do it in one move, using the form:

```
struct {
        [member list];
              } name1, name2, name...;
```

Where all the structures are being declared at once there is no need for a pattern name. Taking Program 078 it can be rewritten using the above form as shown in Program 079.

```
/*************************************************
* Program 079                                   *
* Demo of Structure                             *
*************************************************/

#include <stdio.h>

struct {
        char        name[80];
        int         age;
        } member;

main()
{

  puts("Please enter members name");
  gets(member.name);
  puts("Please enter members age ");
  scanf("%d",&member.age);
  getchar();
  printf("\n\n\nThe member is %d years ",member.age);
  printf("of age and the name is ");
  puts(member.name);


}
```

One area of inconsistency amongst compilers is the ability to pass structures as parameters to functions. Some compilers allow this and will accept the code shown in Program 080.

```
/*************************************************
* Program 080                                   *
* Passing structures to functions               *
*************************************************/

#include <stdio.h>

struct people{
        char name[80];
        int  age;
              };
```

```
main()
{
  struct people employee;

  printf("Enter employee's name ");
  gets(employee.name);
  printf("\n\nEnter employee's age ");
  scanf("%d",employee.age);
              ↑&

  puts("Employee's name is ");
  puts(employee.name);
  puts("Employee's age is ");
  printf("%d\n",employee.age);

  retire(employee);
}

retire(struct people detail)
{
  int ret;
  ret = 65 - detail.age;

  printf("%s will retire in %d years\n\n",detail.name,ret);
}
```

Other compilers will not accept structures as parameters to functions. In such cases (which seem to cover most compilers at present) you have to pass details of a structure to a function by way of a pointer to that structure.

Whilst with the above method you worked on a copy of the structure, in the case of passing a pointer you will be working on the structure elements directly. This difference must be kept in mind.

When you have to address the members of a structure using a pointer a new form of addressing has to be used. This is the directed to address form ->.

Have a look at Program 081.

```
/****************************************************
* Program 081                                       *
* Demo passing structures to functions              *
* using pointers                                    *
****************************************************/

#include <stdio.h>

struct people{
        char name[80];
        int  age;
             };

main()
```

```
  {
    struct  people  employ;

    printf("Enter  employee's  name  ");
    gets(employ.name);
    printf("\nEnter  employee's  age  ");
    scanf("%d",&employ.age);
    getchar();
    printf("\n\n");
    printf("Employee  %s  is  %d\n",employ.name,employ.age);
    retire(&employ);
  }

retire(struct  people  *detail)
  {
    int  ret,cage;
    cage  =  detail->age;
    ret  =  65  -  cage;

    printf("The  employee  %s  ",detail->name);
    printf("will  retire  in  %d  years.\n\n",ret);
}
```

Here the address of the structure employ is passed to the function retire. Within the function the structure members are addressed by the pointer to the structure detail.

Of course, it is not often that you want to deal with only one item of the type held in a structure. For instance, in the above cases you might want to keep a record of all employees in the firm. This can be done within an array of structures. Have a look at the version of the same program shown in Program 082.

```
/***************************************************
* Program  082                                    *
* Demo  of  arrays  of  structures                *
***************************************************/

#include  <stdio.h>

struct  people{
        char  name[80];
        int   age;
            };

main()
  {
    struct  people  employ[100];
    int  count,check;

    for  (count=0;  count  <  100;  count  ++  )
    {
      puts("Do  you  want  to  enter  another  record");
```

174

```
   if ( !OK() ) break;
     else
         {
           printf("Enter employee's name ");
           gets(employ[count].name);
           printf("\nEnter employee's age ");
           scanf("%d",&employ[count].age);
           getchar();
           printf("\n\n");

           printf("Employee %s is
           %d\n",employ[count].name,employ[count].age);
         }
 }
 for ( check = 0; check < count; check++ )
   {
     retire(&employ[check]);
   }
 }

retire(detail)
struct people *detail;
 {
    int ret,cage;
    cage = detail->age;
    ret = 65 - cage;

    printf("The employee %s ",detail->name);
    printf("will retire in %d years.\n\n",ret);
  }

 OK()
 {
 char ch;
 int num,flag;
 num = -1;
 flag = 0;

 while(!flag)
  {
    ch = getch();
    switch (ch)
    {
      case 'y':
      case 'Y':
        flag = -1;
        num = -1;
        break;
      case 'n':
      case 'N':
```

```
            flag = -1;
            num = 0;
            break;
          default:
            flag = 0;
      }
   }
 return (num);
 }
```

Here we declare the structure employ to be an array using the form:

```
structure people employ[10];
```

This declaration declares an array of structures with the pattern as specified by people, which has ten members and will be called employ. From here the operation of the program is similar to the previous examples, except that the input is handled inside a loop and we have the function OK(), which tests for a Yes or No answer.

Getting Values into Unions

A data type which allows you to enter a value of any type appears to be useful at times but it does not seem to be used very much by C programmers. The union is such a data type.

At first sight a union looks very much like a structure. It is set up with a pattern like a structure, as shown in this declaration:

```
union date {
     char word[4];
     int  num;
     };
```

The difference between a union and a structure is that a union only allows you to hold one value at a time. The above example can hold either a three letter word like "JAN","DEC" or "AUG" or a number like 1, 12 or 8. It does not matter which you select, they are both held in the same area of memory.

This is where unions offer some advantage over structures. If we wanted to allow a structure which could hold the date either in numeric or character form, it would have to be set up with a pattern similar to the one above. In such a case it would take four bytes of memory for the word and two for the integer. This would mean that the minimum size of such a structure would be six bytes.

A union reserves space for the largest element in the union. In this case, the word needing four bytes. This means that two bytes of memory can be saved. If you were working with a large number of such unions, say in an array, this could result in a sizable saving in memory use.

The problem with unions is that you still have to specify the correct member of the union to receive the correct type of data. You cannot put general input into the union and expect it to sort out the storage for you.

Bitfields

Bitfields are a special type of structure whose members are fields made up of one or more bits. If that seems complicated, do not despair, in fact bitfields are the programmer's life-saver if it comes down to messing around with bits. They enable you to avoid most of the complications of having to work with bitwise operators.

Bitfields are described in the Kernighan and Ritchie description of C, but many compilers leave them out. There are complications to their implementation so leaving them out is an easy solution. Turbo C does provide full support to bitfields in keeping with the ANSI standards.

Consider the following definition of a bitfield:

```
struct bitmap {
                unsigned    bit0  :       1;
                unsigned    bit1  :       1;
                unsigned    bit2  :       1;
                unsigned    bit3  :       1;
                unsigned    nib1  :       4;
                unsigned    nib2  :       4;
                unsigned    nib3  :       4;
                } flags,nibbles;
```

In this we have defined a structure which will take up sixteen bytes. Note that the form of this declaration is like that of a normal structure except for the use of the colon as a field separator. This informs the compiler it is handling a bitfield structure.

In this bitfield we have defined four bits as individual bits, these will be the bits 0, 1, 2 and 3. The remaining twelve bits of the structure are split into three nibbles of 4 bits each. Note that all have been specified as being of type unsigned. Turbo C will support both unsigned and ints, the latter being stored in twos complement form.

Two important points to consider are the storage order of the bitfields and the effect of using int rather than unsigned.

First, the storage order. Turbo C stores bitfields from the low bit up. So the first bit declared in a structure definition is the zeroth bit in the low order byte of a two byte int. Bit 8 in the structure definition is the zeroth bit in the high order byte. Incidentally,

Turbo C follows ANSI in only allowing bitfields up to the size of an int, that is sixteen bits, two bytes. Not all compilers follow this form of storage and problems may be expected if you are moving between compilers and hardware.

Second, is a concern when you declare a single bit to be of type signed int. Have a look at the following declaration:

```
struct    bits{
                int       n1    :      1;
                int       n2    :      1;
           };
```

Here we have defined a bitfield consisting of two bits. Both have been declared as type int. This means they are signed. A single bit can only hold one of two values, 0 and 1. In a signed value the two complements system is used, so if the left-most bit is 1, then the value is negative. So when you declare a single bit to be of type int, that is signed, it can only hold 0 or -1.

Four bits, normally called a nibble, can hold up to the value 31. In practice, though, they are normally used for holding the values 1 to 9 in BCD (Binary Coded Decimal) format. This is very useful in many forms of hardware interfacing.

So much for the theory, let us look at a very simple example of using bitfields shown in Program 083. We go back to the question of C having no binary output functions. The function, disbits(), can be used in place of showbits().

```
/ * * * * * * * * * * * * * * * * * * * * * * * * * * * * * * * * * * * * * * * * * * * * *
* Program 083                                         *
* disbits,    demonstration of bitfields              *
* * * * * * * * * * * * * * * * * * * * * * * * * * * * * * * * * * * * * * * * * * * * * * /

#include  <stdio.h>

            struct bitmap {
                              unsigned n0 :  1;
                              unsigned n1 :  1;
                              unsigned n2 :  1;
                              unsigned n3 :  1;
                              unsigned n4 :  1;
                              unsigned n5 :  1;
                              unsigned n6 :  1;
                              unsigned n7 :  1;
                            } allbit;

main()
{
```

```
        int  num;
        char  let;

        do
        {
              printf("Input  a  number  from  0  to  255");
              scanf("%d",&num);
        } while ( ( num < 0 )  ||  ( num > 255 ) );

        let = (char) num;

        disbits(char);

}

void disbits( char a )
{
        struct  bitmap  *r;        /*  pointer  to  structure  */

        r = &a;                    /*  make  it  point  to  value  */

        printf("%d",r->n7);
        printf("%d",r->n6);
        printf("%d",r->n5);
        printf("%d",r->n4);
        printf("%d",r->n3);
        printf("%d",r->n2);
        printf("%d",r->n1);
        printf("%d",r->n0);

}
```

What we are doing here is making a pointer to a specific type of structure point to the address of a variable of a different type. This will give a warning message when you compile, then, use the bitfields to read off the values of the appropriate bits. Note that we are addressing via pointers.

18

CODE MACROS

A very useful and most powerful aspect of C is the ability to define macros with arguments. Such macros enable simple functions to be stated as macros. In fact, if you are prepared to put some work into your definitions, quite complex functions can be stated as macros.

The use of code macros has the effect of eliminating the overheads which are part of making function calls. These include the call to the function, the passing of arguments, and the handling of return values.

If a program has to frequently undertake a specific type of operation, considerable savings on speed can be made by using code macros for such functions rather than function calls. This is one of the ways that Turbo C obtains its high execution speeds; many of the more common functions like getc() are defined as macros and expanded to in-line code.

There is a price to pay for such savings in speed in that you get a larger amount of code in the end. Incidentally, if with Turbo C you want to use the function getc() rather than the macro, you can do so by removing the macro from the header file. If you do this it is advisable to rename the header file so you have one copy with the macros in and one without. The result of this will be smaller code, but you must expect your programs to be slower.

A fairly common type of function is one to find the largest of two numbers. This can be done with the function:

```
largest(int  a,  int  b)
{
    int  ret;
    ret = (a > b) ? a : b;
    return (ret);
}
```

A call to such a function requires the actual function call, the passing of the arguments, evaluation of the expression and the passing of the return value. You could enter the expression in the main body of the code. There is nothing technically wrong with this, but it necessitates extra typing and in the case of complex expressions, increases the difficulty of reading the code.

A more effective approach is to declare the expression as a macro with arguments. The use of such code macros has the effect on expansion of entering the function in the code, whilst reducing the typing for you and keeping the code legibility. In the current example we would define such a macro in the form:

```
#define  Largest(a,b)        (a>b)?a:b
```

When entering our code we would use entries like:

```
val  =  Largest(num1,num2);
```

During compilation the in-line replacement will be carried out so that the above line will be replaced with:

```
val  =  (num1>num2)?num1:num2;
```

One important point is that the code macro does not include any type information. A simple substitution takes place of variable names for arguments. Any types are therefore according to the declarations of the variables used. This can present problems if you are not careful, but it can also be an advantage, especially where you want to use the same expression on a range of variable types.

Define statements are terminated by the newline character. Where you are trying to define very complex expressions this can cause problems. The way round this is to use the backslash '\' to escape the newline. Study the following:

```
#define    Swap_if_big(a,b);      if ( a > b ) \
                                  { int c;\
                                    c = a; a = b; b = c; }
```

Code macros of this type can become quite complex and can be difficult to debug. However, they can make a major contribution to software efficiency, if used with care. One point to note is that we have included the termination semi-colon in the definition. The reason for this is that we do not want a terminating semi-colon after the closing } of the expanded expression. By including it in the definition we remove it on the expansion.

19

MEMORY MANAGEMENT

Without doubt one of the most powerful aspects of the C language is the ability to manage memory from within your program, to grab hold of chunks of free memory, use them for storing data and then to release them. The flexibility given to the programmer's handling of data by the ability to handle memory allocation directly is enormous. It also means that the subject of memory management has many complex aspects to it. We do not intend to go deeply into such aspects for two reasons: first, they are beyond the scope of a book which is intended to be a basic tutorial, but more importantly, 95% of all C programmers will never have to use them. Should you need in depth information on memory management from within C, look at some of the books given in Appendix 8, the Bibliography.

It is important to understand the concepts behind the memory management functions in C. This is especially so in relation to Chapter 20 on the Linked List where these functions are used as the basis for constructing such lists. First, a glance at memory.

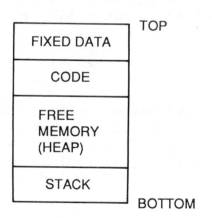

Figure 19.1

When a program is compiled, certain memory allocations will take place. These will vary according to a number of factors. In the case of Turbo C, the memory model you are compiling under is significant, and with other compilers different reasons will play a part. Basically, the memory is divided into four areas. At the very top of memory the fixed data is held, below this is the program code. There is then a gap. At the bottom of memory is the area used to hold variables, this is called the stack. Between the top of the stack and the bottom of the code section is an area of free memory called the heap.

Figure 19.1. is just a diagrammatic representation of the basic idea. It is not a representation of the memory allocation under Turbo C. The actual method of allocation is much more complicated and if you are interested, details are given in the Turbo C documentation. This illustration will serve our current purpose.

As explained above, in the middle is this free memory called the heap. What you need is a method of getting your hands on this memory in a form you can use. C supports a set of function calls which are called memory allocation functions. These allow you to grab hold of blocks of memory, and release them as and when required.

Before going on to look at these calls we briefly consider the difference between Turbo C and classic C in respect to memory allocation calls. All memory allocation calls which allocate memory, return pointers to the start of a block of memory. That block of memory may be of any size. The problem here is that all pointers have to have a type, but there is in classic C no type for a pointer which points to a block of memory. However, there is a type for a pointer which points to a single byte of memory, the type char. So the classic C approach has been to give the pointers the type char. This worked, but it could cause problems. For example, if you wanted to store a structure in a block of memory, you had to allocate the address pointed to by the char pointer to a pointer pointing to a type struct. This would involve casting the pointer.

In Turbo C, advantage has been taken of the new ANSI type void. As pointers of type void are generic (that is they have no specific type) they can be assigned to any type of pointer without casting. Therefore, in Turbo C all memory allocation functions return a pointer of type void. This makes programming using memory allocation much easier in Turbo C than it was in classic C, although it can pose some portability problems when you move code over from classic C to Turbo C.

malloc()

The most basic of the memory allocation functions is malloc(). Its name stands for memory allocation. To use it you pass to the function a value of type unsigned int which tells the function how many bytes you want to grab. If the function is successful, that is if there is memory to grab, it will return a pointer to the address of the start of the block grabbed. Should the function fail, usually due to insufficient memory, then it will return a zero.

As the function is returning a type other than int, it must be made known to the calling function. The way to do this under Turbo C is to include one of the two header files in which it is prototyped, these are stdlib.h and alloc.h. If you are not using Turbo C you will have to declare the function in the calling function, or give it a global declaration, normally as being of type char *, though you should refer to your documentation.

Now have a look at the Program 084 which provides a basic demonstration of malloc().

```
/ ************************************************
* Program   084                                *
* Demonstration of malloc()                    *
************************************************ /

#include  <stdio.h>
#include  <stdlib.h>

main ()
{
        void *ptr;         /* pointer to receive the address from
                            * malloc().  If  using  another  compiler
                            * than Turbo C, this will probably have
                            * to be of type char.
                            */

        int  num;

        while  (TRUE)      /* Endless Loop */
        {
                printf("Enter the number of bytes to grab : ");
                scanf("%d",&num);

                if(num <= 0 ) exit(0);      /* get out of program */

                if (( ptr = malloc(num) ) == 0 )
                {
                        printf("\nAll the memory has been grabbed.\n");
                        exit(0);
                }

                printf("\n%d bytes grabbed at location %d.\n",num,ptr);
        }
}
```

This program will keep on grabbing memory until you either enter the value zero or below for the number of bytes to be grabbed, or it runs out of free memory.

Running out of free memory is a problem when you are grabbing memory for data storage. If, during the run of a program, a number of requests are made for space in memory you are quite liable to run out unless some of the space already used is released. The way this is done is to use the free() function.

free()

The releasing of memory can be accomplished by using the function free. This function is passed a pointer pointing to the address of a block of memory grabbed with one of the memory allocation routines. It then releases that block of memory so it can be used again.

coreleft()

Before we can consider how free works, we need a way of looking at how much memory there is. Turbo C supports a function which does this and that is coreleft(). This is not a standard function and you will not find it on other compilers. If you are working with another compiler, or if you are writing a program which you want to transport to other compilers, you will have to write your own function to report the size of memory left.

The coreleft function is simple to use. Nothing is passed to it and it returns either an unsigned int or an unsigned long, depending on the memory model used at compile time. (See your Turbo C documentation for details on memory model). If you are running under Turbo C, enter and run Program 085 which will demonstrate not only coreleft() but also malloc() and free().

```
/********************************************************
 * Program 085                                         *
 * Demonstration of coreleft, malloc & free            *
 ********************************************************/

#include <alloc.h>

main()
{
    unsigned long size;
    void *ptr;

    while ( TRUE )                   /* Endless loop */
    {
        printf("\nEnter number of bytes to be grabbed ");
        scanf("%d",size);

        if ( size <= 0 ) exit (0);   /* way out of loop */
```

```
    printf("\nMemory available before malloc() is ");
    printf("%d\n",corefree());
    ptr = malloc(size);

    printf("\nMemory available after malloc() is ");
    printf("%d\n",corefree());

    printf("\nMemory available after free() is ");
    free(ptr);
    printf("%d\n",corefree());
    }
}
```

calloc()

An alternative memory allocation function to malloc(), and one which is much more used is calloc(). The name stands for calculated allocation, which gives a clue to what calloc() does.

Basically, it works like malloc() but unlike malloc() it needs to have two arguments passed to it. The first is the number of units for which memory must be made available, and the second is the size of each unit. This is very useful if you want to store, say, two hundred structures of a certain type. All you need to do is pass calloc() the number two hundred and the size of the structure and it will go ahead and work out how much memory you require and grab it for you.

At this point you may be about to panic at the thought of trying to work out the size of any specific item. Don't worry, C has an answer for you.

sizeof

First, before anyone becomes confused, sizeof is a keyword and not a function, although it looks like a function in code. The usage of sizeof is:

```
variable = sizeof ( item );
```

where variable is a variable to which the size is to be assigned and item is an object which you want to know the size of.

Program 086 illustrates the basics of sizeof.

```
/ * * * * * * * * * * * * * * * * * * * * * * * * * * * * * * * * * * * * * * * * * *
* Program 086                                                *
* Demonstration of sizeof                                    *
* * * * * * * * * * * * * * * * * * * * * * * * * * * * * * * * * * * * * * * * * * /

main()
{
            struct test {
                    int num1, num2, num3;
                    char  name[20],street[20];
                       } fitest;

            int  number;

            number = sizeof ( fitest );

            printf("The size is %d bytes \n",number);

}
```

Here we are using sizeof to find the size of the structure fitest. Notice how we have left a space between the keyword sizeof and the first bracket. This makes no difference to the compiler, but does make it clear to the person looking at the code that this is not a function.

Using calloc()

Having obtained a means to find the size of objects we can now have a look at a way in which calloc() can be used. Look at the following code fragment.

```
#include <stdio.h>
#include <alloc.h>

void *mem_start;

main()
{
        int num;
        printf("Enter number of data items :");
        scanf("%d",&num);
        getchar();

        mem_start = calloc( num, sizeof( long ) );
```

This is from the start of a statistics program. Before the start of a run we do not know how many data items are to be entered. The number is therefore input and memory is obtained using calloc. You will notice also that in this code use has been made of sizeof on the type long. This might seem strange as long has a set size under Turbo C. It does not, however, have the same size on all systems. By using sizeof in the calloc() call to give the size of long, maximum portability is obtained across different systems.

If you are writing software which you want to be portable across a wide range of systems and compilers it is often preferable to make use of calloc() than malloc(). For instance if you wanted to obtain enough memory to hold one thousand integers, this could be done under Turbo C on a MSDOS system with the code fragment:

```
start_mem = malloc( 2000 );
```

an integer taking two bytes on such a system. If this code was now moved to a compiler and system where integers took four bytes, as on some Unix systems, you would only have space for five hundred integers. This could result in problems. However, these could be avoided by making use of calloc() and grabbing the memory required with:

```
start_mem = calloc( 1000, sizeof( int ) );
```

Now it does not matter what type of system the code is moved to the correct amount of space to hold one thousand integers is always grabbed.

20

LINKED LIST

One of the problems which faces many programmers is how to cope when you have a quantity of data to handle but do not know the scope or extent of that data prior to the program being run. A data structure which is often used to deal with this problem is the linked list.

Figure 20.1 shows the basic structure of a one way linked list.

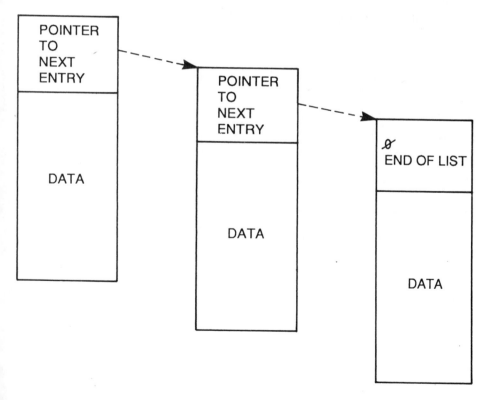

Figure 20.1

A linked list is a set of data elements which are linked together. The location of only one element in the list is known to the program. Other elements are accessed by reference to information on their location which is held in the list.

The simplest form of the linked list is the one way. In this, each list element consists of two parts: a data element which holds the data contained in that element, and a pointer which gives the address of the next element in the list.

In such a list the program only needs to know the location of either the first or the last member in the list depending on whether the pointers point forwards or backwards. From there it can look at the pointers in each element to find the next element in the list.

The simplest use of this list is where you know the basic nature of the entries which will be made in the data element, but do not know the size of them or the number. In such a list each new entry will be added to the last entry. No provision needs to be made for deletion of entries or for insertion of entries into positions other than at the end of the list.

An illustration of this is given in Program 087.

```
/**************************************************
 * Program 087                                    *
 * Demonstration of basic one way linked list     *
 **************************************************/

#include <stdio.h>
#include <stdlib.h>
#define   TRUE  1

/* Prototypes */

int  menu(void);
void  add(void),list(void),get_out(void);

typedef struct a {
                struct a *next;      /* pointer to next
                                      * record in list
                                      */
                char     *string;    /* pointer to data */
              } record;

/* Defining a type called record which will be used to form basis
 * for list
 */

record *start;            /* pointer to first element */
int elements = 0;         /* number of elements */
```

```
main()
{
        int select;


        while (TRUE);
        {
            select = menu();

            switch ( select )
            {
                    case 1:
                        add();
                        break;
                    case 2:
                        list();
                        break;
                    case 3:
                        get_out();
                        break;
                    default:
            }
        }
}

void add()
{
        record *current;      /* pointer to current element */

        char buffer[225];     /* buffer to hold data input */
        int len;

        while (TRUE)          /* endless loop started */
        {
            puts("Enter data item, RETURN to finish ");
            gets(buffer);

            if(buffer[0]==0) return;      /* escape from loop */

            if ( !elements )        /* This is the first entry */
            {

                    len = strlen(buffer);  /* get length of data */
                    current = malloc( sizeof (record) );

                    /* set start pointer to first record */

                    start = current;
```

```
        current->string = malloc(len);
        /* get memory to hold data */

        strcpy(current->string,buffer);
        /* copy contents of buffer into reserved
         * memory.
         */

        current->next = (record *) 0;
        /* this is last record so points nowhere */

        elements++;
        /* increase count of elements */

    }

    else          /* not the first record */
    {
        len = strlen(buffer);
        current = start;
        /* set current to first element */

        while ( current->next != 0 )  /* while not last
                                       * record
                                       */
        {
            current = current->next;
            /* move forward one record */
        }

        /* At end of list make new record */
        current->next = malloc(sizeof (record) );
        current = current->next;
        /* move forward to new record */

        current->next = 0;
        /* this is last record set pointer to null */

        current->string = malloc(lent);
        /* make space for data and set pointer */

        strcpy(current->string,  buffer);
        /* copy data into element */

        elements++;
        /*i increase count */
    }
  }
}
```

```
void get_out()
{
exit(0);
}

int menu()
{
        int val;
        char let;

        puts("Add new entries to list ............ <1> \n");
        puts("List entries in list ............... <2> \n");
        puts("Exit this program .................. <3> \n");
        puts("\nPlease make your selection ");

        let = NULL;

        while( let < '1' || let > '3' )
                let = getch();

        val = let - '0';

        return (val);
}
```

This is not a very sophisticated program but it does show the basics of putting together a linked list type of data structure.

Such a program could easily be expanded to include facilities to insert or delete elements from the middle of the list. Think about what would be needed to delete a record.

> Find Element
> Find out which element it points to.
> Find out which element points to it.
>
> Make the element which points to it, now point to next.
> Release memory used.

The following fragment of code can be used when you know the number of the element you want to delete:

```
int delete( int num )
{
        record *current,last;
        int i;
        current = start;
```

```
if ( num == 1 )  /* first record to be deleted */
{
    start = current->next;

    free(current->string;     /* release data memory */
    free(current)             /* release structure mem */

}
else
{
    for( i = 1; i < num; i++)
    {
        last = current;
        current = current->next;
    }
    last->next = current->next;
    free(current->string);
    free(current);
}
}
```

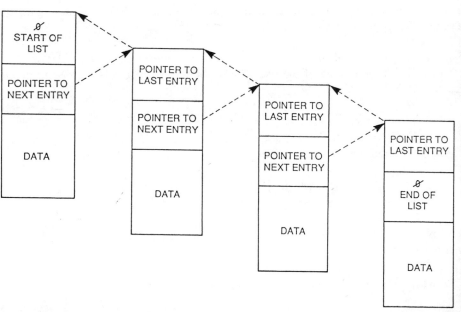

Figure 20.2

Adjust the simple list program to add this, then try writing your own routine to insert an entry at a specific spot.

One of the difficulties with one way linked lists is that you are constantly having to keep track of where the last record is if you want to do anything more than just add onto the end. If this information was included in the element, life would be simpler, especially when it comes to sorting data.

This is what is done in the two way linked list. Figure 20.2 shows how it works. Each element contains two pointers: one which points to the next element, and one which points to the last. Having this information can make complex data moving operations much easier.

The telephone number program shown in Program 088 uses a two way linked list together with a basic search system.

```
/***************************************************
* Program 088                                     *
* Two way linked list                             *
***************************************************/

#include <stdio.h>
#include <alloc.h>

#define TRUE 1
#define FALSE 0

#define CLS printf("%c[2J",27)   /*ANSI sequence to clear screen*/

/***************************************************
* Define structure type to hold entry data        *
***************************************************/

typedef struct     a {
                   struct a *next;     /* Next Entry in List */
                   struct a *last;     /* Last Entry in List */
                   char    name[30];   /* Name Entry */
                   char    nums[30];   /* String to hold number */
                      } entry_type;

/***************************************************
*           Globals                               *
***************************************************/

char filename[] = "Telnums.dat";

entry_type *start_entry, *last_entry, *current;

int edit_flag,entries;
```

```
FILE *fp;


main()
{
        int select;

        edit_flag = FALSE;
        entries = 0;

        load_file();

        while ( select = menu() )
        {
                switch ( select )
                {
                case 1:
                                view();
                                break;
                case 2:
                                add();
                                break;
                case 3:
                                search();
                                break;
                }
        }

        if ( edit_flag ) save_file();
}

/***************************************************
 * load_file() opens a the data file.  If no file*
 * is present it checks to see if one should be   *
 * created.  If not the program is exited.        *
 ***************************************************/

load_file()
{
        char name_buf[30], num_buf[30];

        fp = fopen( filename, "r");   /* Open file to read */

        if ( fp == 0 )    /* File cannot be opened. */
        {
            CLS;
            puts("Cannot open file.");
            puts("Do you want to start a new file, Y / N ?");

            if ( ok() == FALSE ) exit(0);
```

```
                /* Negative response.  Do not proceed */

                entries = 0;
                return;
        }

        /* File is opened, read file. */

        while ( fgets( name_buf, 30, fp ) != NULL )
        {
            fgets( num_buf, 30, fp );
            current = malloc( sizeof( entry ) );
            strcpy( current->name, name_buf );
            strcpy( current->nums, num_buf );


            if ( entries == 0 )
            {
                    start_entry = current;
                    current->last = 0;
                    current->next = 0;
                    last_entry = current;
            }
            else
            {
                    current->last = last_entry;
                    last_entry->next = current;
                    current->next = 0;
                    last_entry = current;
            }

                entries++;
        }
        fclose( fp );
}

/*****************************************************
* menu() displays a menu and obtains a choice.      *
* This is returned to the calling function.         *
*****************************************************/

int menu()
{
        int select;
        char let = 0;

        CLS;
        puts("Please select one of the following :");
        puts("\n\n\tView Contents of File..... 1 ");
        puts("\n\n\tAdd entries to File....... 2 ");
```

```c
        puts("\n\n\tSearch for entry in File.. 3 ");
        puts("\n\n\tExit from program........ 0 ");


        while ( ( let < '0' ) || ( let > '3' ) )
        {
        let = getch();
        }
        return ( let - '0' );
}

/****************************************************
* ok() returns either TRUE of FALSE according to*
* whether the Y or N key is pressed.            *
****************************************************/

int ok()
{
        char let;

        while( TRUE )
        {
                let = toupper(getch());

                if( let == 'Y' ) return ( TRUE );
                else
                        if ( let == 'N' ) return ( FALSE );
        }
}

/****************************************************
* view() displays the file starting at the first *
* entry.  Movement through the file is by press- *
* F for forward, B for back.  Records may be     *
* deleted by pressing D. X to exit.              *
****************************************************/

int view()
{
        char let;
        int count = 0;
        current = start_entry;

        while( TRUE )
        {
                entry_type *prev_entry;
                CLS;
                printf("\tEntry Number %d \n\n", count );
                printf("\tName     : %s\n", current->name);
                printf("\tNumber : %s\n\n\n", current->nums);
```

```
        printf("  <B>ack,    <F>orward, <D>elete,  e<X>it ");


        while( TRUE )
        {
                let = toupper(getch());

                if( let == 'F' && current->next != 0 )
                {
                     current = current->next;
                     count++
                     break;
                }

                if( let == 'B' && current->last != 0 )
                {
                     current = current->last;
                     count--;
                     break;
                }

                if( let == 'D' )
                {
                     puts( "Confirm Delete this entry Y/N" );
                     if ( ok() == TRUE )
                     {
                           prev_entry = current->last;
                           prev_entry->next=current->next;
                           prev_entry = current->next;
                           prev_entry->last = current >last;
                           free( current );
                           current =    start_entry;
                           count = 0;
                           entries--;
                           edit_flag = TRUE;
                           break;
                     }
                }

                if ( let == 'X' ) return;
        }

    }
}


/******************************************************
* add() adds an entry to the list.                    *
******************************************************/
```

```
add()
{
        char  name_buf[30],num_buf[30];

        current = malloc( sizeof(entry_type) );

        while( TRUE )
        {
                CLS;
                printf("\n\n\tEnter  name    :");
                gets(name_buf);
                printf("\n\n\tEnter  number:");
                gets(num_buf);

                printf("\n\n\t Confirm Entry :\n");
                printf("\t%s\n",name_buf);
                printf("\t%s\n",num_buf);

                if ( ok() ) break;
        }
        strcpy( current->name,  name_buf);
        strcpy( current->nums,  num_buf);


        if ( entries == 0 )
        {
                start_entry = current;
                last_entry = current;
                current->next = 0;
                current->last = 0;
        }
        else
        {
                last_entry->next = current;
                current->next = 0;
                current->last = last_entry;
                last_entry = current;
        }
        entries++;
        edit_flag = TRUE;
}


/***************************************************
* search() carries out a search of the list for  *
* a pattern.  A match can be made on either       *
* the name field or the number field.             *
***************************************************/
```

```
search()
{
        char object[30], let;

        CLS;
        printf("Enter pattern to be searched for : ");
        gets( object );

        current = start_entry;

        do
        {
                if ( strstr(current->name,object)
                || strstr(current->nums,object) )
                {
                    CLS;
                    printf("\n\n\t%s\n",current->name);
                    printf("\n\n\t%s\n",current->nums);
                    printf("\n\n\n");
                    printf("Press <C> to continue, or <X> to exit.");

                    while( TRUE )
                    {
                            let = toupper( getch() );
                            if ( let == 'X' ) return;
                            if ( let == 'C' ) break;
                    }
                }
                current = current->next;
        } while ( current );

}

/***********************************************************
* save_file() saves the file if edit_flag is set. *
***********************************************************/

save_file()
{
        if ( edit_flag == 0 ) return;
        /* Data has not be changed so do not save. */

        CLS;
        puts("\n\tData has been amended.");
        puts("\n\tConfirm you want new data saved, Y/N ?");

        if ( ok() == 0 ) return;
        /* Not ok to save, return to main. */

        fp = fopen( filename, "w"); /* open file to write. */
```

```
        current = start_entry;   /* set to start of list. */

        while( current )
        {
                fprintf(fp,"%s\n%s\n",current->name, current->nums);
                /* Newline added for fgets() on load. */

                current = current->next;
        }

        fclose( fp);
}
```

Program 088 is a simple demonstration of a two way linked list. In the view() function, movement is made through the list by using the pointers to the next or previous element in the list.

The structure for the list is defined as a type with the typedef of entry_type. This is a structure which contains two pointers to structures of its own type. One of these is used to point back to the previous entry in the list and the other to point forward to the next entry in the list. To keep track of the list three pieces of information are required: the start of the list, the end of the list, and the current position in the list. For this reason three global pointers of type entry_type are declared, start_entry, last_entry and current.

The function main() is quite simple, being a basic controlling function making use of a selection generated in a menu() function. This should present no problems to your understanding.

The list itself is constructed in two functions, load_file() and add(). Of these load_file() is the first called when the program is run. A call is made to open the file in read only mode. If this is successful a non-zero value will be returned to the file pointer fp. A test is, therefore, made to see if fp is equal to zero. This would mean that the file cannot be opened. A check is made to see if you want to start a new file.

If the file can be opened, it is read into memory, with the linked list being constructed. Notice that if the variable entries has the value zero, then you are dealing with the first element in the list. In such a case start_entry is set to current. As each entry is made in the list the pointer current- >last is made to point to the previous entry in the list, whilst current->next is set to zero, as the current entry will be the last entry in the list.

Of course, the first time the program is run there will not be a file to read in. In such cases the whole list will be constructed in the function add(). So here, again, you use the test to see if the entry is the first entry in the list. The setting of the pointers follows the pattern used in load_file().

Use of these forward and backward looking pointers is demonstrated in the function view(). Here you move forward or back through the file by reading the pointers. One point to note is that the delete procedure in this function does not work properly. If you delete the first or last element in the list it will leave the pointers start_entry and last_entry, pointing at the wrong values. You should try and write your own additions to the code to correct this.

It is possible to have more than two links to a data element in a list. Three ways is not uncommon. In such lists you have pointers which point to the records on each side of the element and a pointer which points to another list containing data related to that element. This type of structure is often used when you have a secondary list in respect to data elements. You can have this structure also in one way linked lists.

In the program CROSSREF our main list is of occurrences of identifiers used in a C program. The secondary lists are of line numbers where these occur. This gives us a one way linked list, which points to another set of one way linked lists.

```
/*****************************************************
* Crossref.c                                        *
*                                                   *
* M. Larner & N. G. Backhurst                       *
*                                                   *
* The program reads a C source file and extracts*
* a list of all variable names, function names      *
* and occurrences.  These are then sorted and a     *
* print out made giving occurrence.                 *
*****************************************************/

#include <stdio.h>
#include <stdlib.h>
#include <ctype.h>

/*****************************************************
*              definitions                          *
*****************************************************/

#define        BOOL            int
#define        DQUOTE          '"'
#define        SQUOTE          '\''
#define        SLASH           '/'
#define        ASTERISK        '*'
#define        EQUALS          0
#define        FALSE           0
#define        TRUE            1

#define        MAXWORDSIZE     32
#define        MAXSTRLEN       255
```

```c
/*************************************************
*              Type Defs                        *
*************************************************/

typedef struct a {
                  char    *prog_line; /* program line */
                  struct a *next; /* next line */
                  }   program_type;

typedef struct b {

                  int   line_num;
                  struct b *link;   /* link to next entry */
                  }   occur_type, *occur_ptr;

typedef struct c {
                  char    *token; /* pointer to token */
                  occur_ptr   line_list; /* list
                  of line numbers */
                  struct c *next;
                  } token_type,  *token_ptr;

/*************************************************
*           Globals                             *
*************************************************/

token_type *start_token;
program_type    *start_prog;
int  comment_flag, line_number;

main( int argc, char *argv[] )
{
      if ( argc < 2 )
      {
            puts("Usage : crossref < sourcefile >");
            exit (0);
      }

      read_file ( argv[1] );
      process_file();
}

/*************************************************
* read_file, reads the source file into memory  *
*************************************************/
```

```
read_file( char *filename )
{
        FILE *fp;
        program_type *current_line, *last_line;
        char  buf[MAXSTRLEN],*tmp;

        fp = fopen( filename, "r" );

        if ( fp == 0 )
        {
                puts("Cannot open input file to read.");
                exit (0);
        }

        start_prog = 0;

        while ( ( fgets( buf,MAXSTRLEN, fp )) != NULL )
        {
                current_line = malloc( sizeof ( program_type ) );
                if ( start_prog == 0 )
                        start_prog = current_line;
                else
                        last_line->next = current_line;
                current_line->next = 0;
                tmp = malloc( strlen( buf ) + 1 );
                strcpy( tmp, buf );
                current_line->prog_line = tmp;
                last_line = current_line;
        }
}


/*****************************************************
* process_file searches file for tokens and places*
* them in the token list.                          *
*****************************************************/

process_file()
{
        program_type *current, *last;

        char  buf[MAXSTRLEN];

        start_token = 0;
        comment_flag = 0;
        current = start_prog;
```

```
        line_number = 1;

        puts("Start Processing");
        while ( current != 0 )
        {
                strcpy ( buf, current->prog_line );
                get_token( buf );
                last = current;
                current = last->next;
                line_number++;
        }
        puts("End Processing");
        sort();
        results();
}


/*****************************************************
*  get_token reads the in memory file line by      *
*  line checking each word.  If a valid word is    *
*  not inside comments or string delimitors        *
*  it is entered as an occurrence in the entry     *
*  list.                                            *
*****************************************************/

get_token( char buf[] )
{
        char  word[MAXWORDSIZE],let;
        int   num,cur_char,q_flag,sq_flag;

        cur_char = num = q_flag = sq_flag = 0;

        printf("%03d > %s",line_number,buf);
        while ( buf[ cur_char ] != 0 )
        {
                let = buf[ cur_char ];

                if ( comment_flag )
                {
                        if ( let == ASTERISK && buf[ cur_char + 1 ] == SLASH )
                                comment_flag = FALSE;
                        cur_char++;
                        continue;
                }

                if ( q_flag )
                {
```

```
            if ( let == DQUOTE )
                    q_flag = FALSE;
            cur_char++;
            continue;
    }

    if ( sq_flag )
    {
            if ( let == SQUOTE )
                    sq_flag = FALSE;
            cur_char++;
            continue;
    }

    if ( valid_first_let ( let ) )
    {
            while ( check_let( let ) )
            {
                    word[num++] = let;
                    let = buf[ ++cur_char];
            }
            word[num]=0;
            place_entry(word);
            num = 0;
    }

    if ( let == SLASH  &&  buf[ cur_char + 1 ] == ASTERISK )
    {
            comment_flag = TRUE;
    }

    if ( let == DQUOTE  &&   sq_flag == FALSE )
    {
            q_flag = TRUE;
    }

    if ( let == SQUOTE  &&   q_flag == FALSE )
    {
            sq_flag = TRUE;
    }
    cur_char++;
    }
}
```

```
/*****************************************************
 * valid_first_let checks to see if the a           *
 * character is one which can be the valid first    *
 * letter of a C token.                             *
 *****************************************************/

valid_first_let( char let )
{
        return ( ( isalpha( let ) || let == '_' ) ? TRUE : FALSE );
}


/*****************************************************
 * check_let checks to see that a character in a    *
 * token is a valid character for a C token.        *
 *****************************************************/

check_let( char let )
{
        return ( ( isalnum( let ) || let == '_' ) ? TRUE : FALSE );
}


/*****************************************************
 * place_entry makes an entry for the occurrence    *
 * of the token in the list.  If it is the first    *
 * time the word has occurred a new entry is made.  *
 * If not an addition is made to the line number    *
 * list.                                            *
 *****************************************************/

place_entry( char word[] )
{
        token_type *this_token, *last_token;
        occur_type *this_entry, *last_entry;

        this_token = start_token;


        if ( this_token == 0 )
        {

                this_token = malloc( sizeof( token_type ));
                this_token->token = malloc( strlen( word ) );
                strcpy( this_token->token, word );
                this_entry = malloc( sizeof( occur_type ));
                this_token->line_list = this_entry;
                this_entry->line_num = line_number;
```

```
                this_entry->link = 0;
                this_token->next = 0;
                start_token = this_token;
                return;
        }

        while ( this_token != 0 )
        {

                if ( ! strcmp( this_token->token, word ))
                {

                        this_entry = this_token->line_list;

                        while( this_entry != 0 )
                        {
                                last_entry = this_entry;
                                this_entry = last_entry->link;
                        }
                        this_entry = malloc( sizeof( occur_type ) );
                        this_entry->line_num = line_number;
                        this_entry->link = 0;
                        last_entry->link = this_entry;

                        return;
                }

                last_token = this_token;
                this_token = last_token->next;
        }

        this_token = malloc( sizeof( token_type ));
        this_token->token = malloc( strlen( word ) );
        strcpy( this_token->token, word );
        this_entry = malloc( sizeof( occur_type ));
        this_token->line_list = this_entry;
        this_entry->line_num = line_number;
        this_entry->link = 0;
        this_token->next = 0;
        last_token->next = this_token;
}

/*****************************************************
* results displays each occurrence of a word  in  *
* the program context.                            *
*****************************************************/

results()
{
```

```
            program_type *current, *last;
            token_type *this_token, *last_token;
            occur_type *this_entry, *last_entry;
            int i;

            this_token = start_token;

            while( this_token )
            {
                    printf("\n\n\n-----   %s  -----\n\n",this_token->token);

                    this_entry = this_token->line_list;

                ,   do
                    {

                        current = start_prog;
                        for( i = 1; i < this_entry->line_num;i++ )
                        {
                        last = current;
                        current = last->next;
                        }
                        printf("%03d > %s",this_entry->line_num, current->prog_line);
                        last_entry = this_entry;
                        this_entry = last_entry->link;
                    }while( this_entry );
                    last_token = this_token;
                    this_token = last_token->next;
            }
}


/************************************************
* sorts the token list into alphabetical order  *
* using a simple bubble sort.                    *
************************************************/

sort()
{
        token_type *this_token,*next_token,*ex_token;
        int  sort_flag,test;

        ex_token = malloc( sizeof( token_type ) );

        do
        {
                sort_flag = FALSE;
```

```
        this_token  =  start_token;
        next_token  =  this_token->next;

        while ( next_token )
        {
                test = strcmp( this_token->token, next_token->token );

                if ( test > 0 )
                {
                        ex_token->token    =  this_token->token;
                        ex_token->line_list = this_token->line_list;

                        this_token->token    =  next_token->token;
                        this_token->line_list = next_token->line_list;

                        next_token->token    =  ex_token->token;
                        next_token->line_list = ex_token->line_list;

                        sort_flag  =  TRUE;
                }
                this_token  =  next_token;
                next_token  =  this_token->next;
        }

    } while ( sort_flag );
}
```

At first sight this program may appear complicated, but if you break it down it is not
nearly as bad. There are two separate linked list structures in this program. The first is
a simple one consisting of a list containing the lines of a C program which has been
read into memory. The second is more complicated. Figure 20.3 shows what we have.

You will notice that there is a one way linked list of structures. These structures are of
a type which contains a pointer to a C token and a pointer to a secondary linked list.
This secondary linked list is made up of structures which contain the line number of an
occurrence of a C token and the pointer to the next occurrence.

Exactly what this program does is explained below, followed by an in-depth look at
each section. The program reads an input file which is a C source file. This is then
processed to extract from it a list of all valid C tokens in input file. A C token is
either a command or an identifier. A record is kept of each occurrence of a token and a
list of such occurrences is produced for you at the end.

The output of this program can be seen in Chapter 25 on Debugging, but at present we
will just analyse how it works.

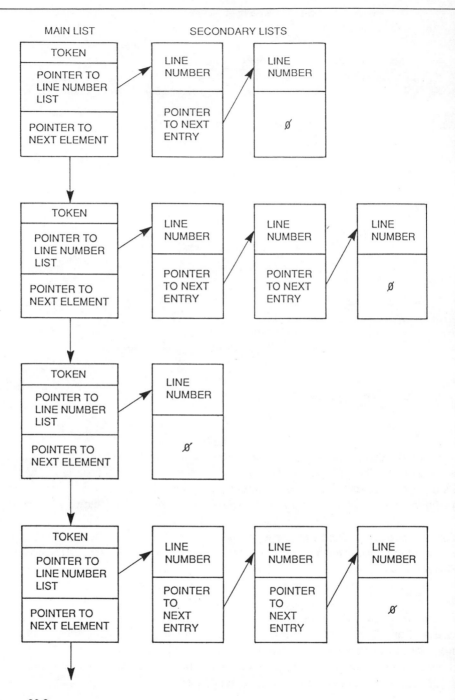

MAIN LIST SECONDARY LISTS

Figure 20.3

We start with the include files. Three files are used: the standard stdio.h together with stdlib.h because we are using the memory allocation command malloc, and ctype.h to provide the type testing macros isalpha and isalnum. This is followed by the defines which are fairly normal. One point to note is the use of the backslash in the definition of SQUOTE. This is used to escape the special meaning of the single quote sign.

We next come to the definition of some types. This is where the basic structures of your linked list are defined.

The first one is a definition of a type program_type. This provides the base for the list to hold the program lines. The structure consists of two elements. The first is a pointer of type character which you will use to point to the string held in memory. The second is a pointer to a structure of its own type which will be used to point to the next element in your list.

The second definition is of a structure to hold the occurrences of a token. Here you have an integer to hold the line number and a pointer to the next structure in the list.

Our final type definition is again of a structure to hold each unique token found. There are three elements to this structure. First, a pointer to a string where the token itself is stored. Then there is a pointer to a list composed of the structures occur_type. This will therefore be the list of line numbers. Finally, there is a pointer to the next structure in the list.

There are four variables which are declared as global. These are the pointer to the first element in the token list, and a pointer to the first element in the program list. There is also a flag to indicate the status of a comment and a variable holding the current line number.

Nearly every function will need to know either the location of the start of the program list or the token list, and often both. It makes a great deal of sense to declare these as global. To do otherwise would have required a great deal of parameter passing.

It would have been possible to handle the comment flag and line number variable as locals without too much difficulty. However, having them as globals makes life much easier. It also opens the way for a couple of extensions of the program.

The function main() is short. You should be able to follow what it is doing with no difficulty.

Read file is the first of the 'working' functions. It opens the file which has been passed on the command line argument and copies the contents of that file into memory. Note though that no check is made to see that the file is actually a C source code file. You might like to add this to the function.

Before any reading is done start_prog is set to zero. You then enter a while loop. This loop is controlled by the return value of the fgets(), which is reading a string from the file pointed to by fp, into a buffer buf up to a maximum of MAXSTRLEN characters. If the end of a file is reached, fgets() will return NULL. So our test is while fgets() is not equal to NULL.

The first task we have to do is grab a block of memory to put our list structure into. This is done in the line:

```
current_line = malloc( sizeof ( program_type ) );
```

Next, we have to test to see if this is the first entry in the list. If it is, start_prog will be equal to zero. In this case we make the start_prog pointer point to the current_line with:

```
start_prog = current_line;
```

If the start_prog pointer is not equal to zero it means that there are already lines in the list. In this case we have to make the last entry point to the current line. This is done with:

```
last_line->next = current_line;
```

Once this stage has been completed we have a list element which has been linked into the list. Now we have to set the current entry in the list to indicate that this is the last entry so far. This is done with:

```
current_line->next = 0;
```

Our next problem is to link the program line into the list element. This is done in two stages. First, we have to put the program line into an area of memory which has been grabbed. To do this we first have to grab a block of memory.

```
tmp = malloc( strlen(buf) + 1 );
```

grabs our block of memory. Notice that we have had to use strlen(buf) + 1. The reason for this is that strlen() does not count the terminating zero of the string, only the characters in the string. You have to add one to allow space for the zero.

Having grabbed the memory to hold the string, it is now moved into that memory with the strcpy() function and the pointer in the list structure linked with it. This is done in:

```
strcpy( tmp, buf);
current_line->prog_line = tmp;
```

We have now added a new element to the list and linked a memory buffer containing a program line to that element. Before we can go on to make the next entry we have to make a new last entry, which will be the current entry. This is done with:

```
last_line = current_line;
```

At that point the process can be repeated adding more and more elements until the file is read.

The next function in the program is the process_file() function. You will find this fairly easy to follow. It works its way through the program line list passing each line to the get_token() function. When all lines have been processed the sort() function is called to put the tokens into alphabetical order and the results() function is called to output the resulting lists.

In the next function get_token() most of the work is done, and you should study this function with care. There is nothing particularly complicated in it, but there are a few points which should be noted.

First, the flags q_flag and sq_flag are for string elements contained within quotes or single quotes and defined in this function. The flag for comments, comment_flag, is global and set to zero in process_file(). The reason for this is quite simple. You can have a comment which spreads over a number of lines. Any quoted string must be terminated within the line, otherwise the compiler will not accept the code. Therefore, you do not have to allow for strings covering more than one line of code.

The calls to valid_first_let and check_let are quite simple. If a token is not being processed and the letter is a valid first letter of a token, then the process goes into a loop reading the other letters of the token until a letter is found which is not a valid token element.

There is a weak point here in that the version of the code given here does not allow for the -> and . symbols in structures. Therefore, current.name and current->next would be processed as the tokens current, name and next. You might like to look at ways of amending the code to get round this.

At first sight the function place_entry() can look offputting. In fact, it is relatively simple. The first if test is to see if this is the first entry in the list. If it is, the start of a new list is created and a return is made to the calling function. If it is not, we then go onto the while loop which is nothing more than a search through the current list to find if there is a match.

It is useful to note here that the test is made using the not operator '!'. strcmp() will return a zero if both strings are the same, that is, if a match has been found. We are, therefore, interested in the operation being carried out only if the value is zero. This could also have been written, and the code might have been easier to read, as:

```
if ( strcmp( this_token->token, word ) == 0 )
```

If a match is made, that means the token already exists in the list so the current line number is added to the list of line numbers for that token. We then return to the calling process.

If no match is made, then a new entry has to be created before the function is terminated and return made to the calling process.

The results() function is fairly simple. We work our way through the token list, printing out each token. After each token has been printed we work our way through the line list for that token, each line being printed to show the context of the token's occurrence.

The final function is sort(). This is a very simple bubble sort but quick enough. It is in sorting that the use of pointers can do much work. All that is necessary here to change the position of a token in the list is to swap four pointers. This is much easier than the copying and swapping of strings and array elements which would have been necessary in other languages.

This program is used in Chapter 25 on debugging. Although a very useful tool, it could do with some improvements. One which might be worth considering is the way we have to do a for loop to find the line in the program list to print it out in the result() function. Would it not be better to keep both the line number and a pointer to that line in the program list, within the line occurrence list? This is something you might like to have a go at adding yourself.

21

LOW LEVEL INTERFACE

No matter how powerful a language is there are times when you want to deal directly with the system. You need to be able to address the system at a lower level.

Turbo C supports three ways of gaining access to the low level functions of the system. These are pseudo-variables, in- line assembly, and the interrupt functions.

Essentially, these subjects are for advanced programming, so we do not go into any depth in this chapter. Also, everything in the chapter is specific to Turbo C.

DOS and BIOS Calls

It is possible to access various facilities on your system by directly instructing the hardware to carry out certain actions. This is not generally advisable as any software written making use of hardware specific functions will work only on the system for which it was written. Even when you are dealing with PC compatibles, they are only compatible at the operating system level and often differ considerably when it comes to the hardware.

Under MSDOS and PCDOS there is an interface to the hardware which is constant, and of which we can make use. This consists of two parts: the Disk Operating System (DOS) and the BIOS, which handles the interface to the hardware.

DOS and BIOS offer to us a number of services which we can use to manipulate the system. These services are invoked by sending a software generated interrupt signal to the system. Then, according to the instructions within the system, certain actions will be carried out.

Details of the DOS and BIOS calls can be found in the *MSDOS Technical Reference Manual* and Norton's *Programmer's Guide to the IBM PC*. If you are thinking of making use of DOS and BIOS calls I recommend that you obtain both these books.

When you make a call to any of the DOS or BIOS services, you have to provide a set of information to that service. This information is passed to the service by way of processor registers. If you do not know what processor registers are, you probably should not be trying to work your way through this chapter.

Essentially, a processor register is a special area in the microprocessor which is used by the microprocessor to store values which it is manipulating. Most of these registers have special uses, but many can also be used for general purposes. The general purpose registers are the four pairs AX, BX, CX, and DX. Figure 21.1 shows these registers:

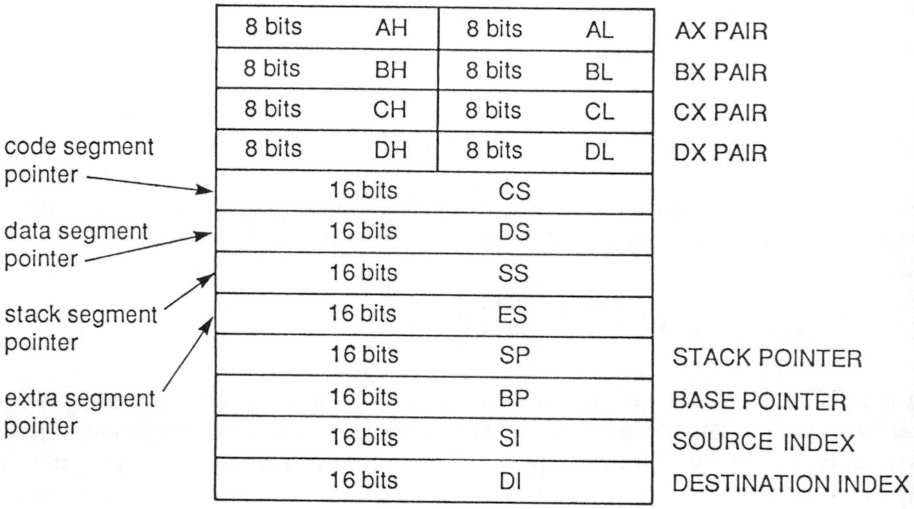

8 bits	AH	8 bits	AL	AX PAIR
8 bits	BH	8 bits	BL	BX PAIR
8 bits	CH	8 bits	CL	CX PAIR
8 bits	DH	8 bits	DL	DX PAIR
16 bits		CS		
16 bits		DS		
16 bits		SS		
16 bits		ES		
16 bits		SP		STACK POINTER
16 bits		BP		BASE POINTER
16 bits		SI		SOURCE INDEX
16 bits		DI		DESTINATION INDEX

code segment pointer ⟶ CS
data segment pointer ⟶ DS
stack segment pointer ⟶ SS
extra segment pointer ⟶ ES

Figure 21.1

As you can see, each of these registers is made up of two registers: a low register and a high register, so in the case of AX we have the pair AH and AL. In addition to the eight registers which make up the X pairs shown above, there are another eight registers which are used for specific purposes.

If we want to make use of a DOS or BIOS call we have to put some values into the registers and then send an interrupt signal to the system.

Turbo C provides several ways in which you can do this, and some actions are so common that it provides library functions to deal with those specific cases so you do not need to worry about all the fiddling about with loading values into registers and generating interrupts. An example of this would be absread() and abswrite() which make calls to DOS interrupts, but you need no knowledge of these to make use of the functions. However, Turbo C does give you a direct way of manipulating the register contents.

Pseudo-variables

Turbo C supports a set of identifiers which correspond to the registers of the processors. These are known as the pseudo- variables.

You can make use of these variables just as if they were a normal variable of type unsigned int or char. The difference is that if you assign a value to one of these variables it will be put into the associated register in the processor. Note an important point here: do not expect to put a value into a pseudo-variable then come back later in the program and use that value. The registers are used by the processor and their contents are changing. The values given by the pseudo-variables are those currently in the associated registers.

Another important point is the type of a pseudo-variable. The registers are made up of two types: the sixteen bit registers: AX, BX, CX, DX, CS, SS, ES, SP, BP, DI, SI and the eight bit registers: AL, AH, BL, BH, CL, CH, DL and DH. As an integer takes up sixteen bits, the sixteen bit registers are of type int. The eight bit registers are of type char as this only takes eight bits.

The pseudo-variables have the same identifier as the register to which it refers but preceded by an underscore. So if you wanted to load the value 10 into the register AL you would use:

```
_AL = 10;
```

A complete list of the pseudo-variables, their type and size is given in Table 21.1.

How can we make use of this? Let us consider a fairly simple example, that of drawing a line in graphics mode on the screen. Access to the video can be obtained through a set of BIOS services known as the BIOS Video Services. These are invoked by giving an interrupt 16 (Hex 10).

To be able to draw a line on the screen we need to complete two tasks. First, set the computer into graphics mode, then plot a series of pixels on the screen.

The PC supports a number of video modes, for more details see the *Programmer's Guide to the IBM PC*. The one we will be using is the medium resolution graphics mode 4. This will give us a graphics screen of 320 x 200 pixels.

Table 21.1   List of the pseudo-variables

Identifier	Register	Size	Type
_AX	AX	16 bits	unsigned int
_AL	AL	8 bits	unsigned char
_AH	AH	8 bits	unsigned char
_BX	BX	16 bits	unsigned int
_BL	BL	8 bits	unsigned char
_BH	BH	8 bits	unsigned char
_CX	CX	16 bits	unsigned int
_CL	CL	8 bits	unsigned char
_CH	CH	8 bits	unsigned char
_DX	DX	16 bits	unsigned int
_DL	DL	8 bits	unsigned char
_DH	DH	8 bits	unsigned char
_CS	CS	16 bits	unsigned int
_DS	DS	16 bits	unsigned int
_SS	SS	16 bits	unsigned int
_ES	ES	16 bits	unsigned int
_SP	SP	16 bits	unsigned int
_BP	BP	16 bits	unsigned int
_DI	DI	16 bits	unsigned int
_SI	SI	16 bits	unsigned int

To invoke this mode we have to call up the BIOS Video Services and request service zero, Set Video Mode. We also have to tell the service which video mode we want. To do this we have to load the number of the service we want into the register AH and the mode we want into the register AL. Then we use the Turbo C function geninterrupt() to generate interrupt number 16 to invoke the services. So our procedure would be:

```
_AH = 0;        /* Set Video Mode */
_AL = 4;        /* Number of Video Mode wanted */

geninterrupt(16);    /* BIOS Video Service */
```

We can therefore write a function called set_video() as follows:

```
set_video(int i)
{
_AH = 0;
_AL = i;
geninterrupt(16);
}
```

Note that in this case we are passing the value of the video mode we require to the function. This makes it more flexible.

Now we can set the screen, next we want to draw a line. A line is a series of dots joined together, so what we need to do is first plot a single pixel on the screen. Again, this can be done using one of the video services, in this case service 12, Write Pixel Dot. To do this we have to pass three items to the service, the x co-ordinate of the pixel, the y co-ordinate of the pixel and finally the colour. The x co-ordinate is put in the register DL, this can never be more than 200 so it can always be stored in an eight bit register. The y co-ordinate can go as high as 640 in some graphics modes, so this needs to be stored in a sixteen bit register. For this, use is made of the CX register pair. Finally, the colour is stored in the AL register with the service request being made in the AH.

Note that service requests are always made in the AH register for all BIOS and DOS services.

Our routine to plot a single pixel is:

```
_AH  =  service_number;
_AL  =  colour;
_DL  =  x_co_ordinate;
_CX  =  y_co_ordinate;
```

then give the interrupt 16. This is done in the following routine called dot(). To keep it simple we are only passing the x and y co-ordinates and having a default colour setting of four. You may want to try amending this later so you can send your own colour setting to it.

```
dot( char x_co,  int y_co)
{
      _AH  =  12;
      _AL  =  4;
      _DL  =  x_co;
      _CX  =  y_co;
      geninterrupt(16);
}
```

As the x co-ordinate is being assigned to an eight bit register, to be on the safe side, we are passing this as a character variable.

As a line is a series of dots, where the plotting points are amended between each plot, this can be done by calling dot() from within a loop and changing the co-ordinates on each call. Look at Program 089.

```
/*****************************************************
* Program 089                                       *
* Drawing a line                                    *
*****************************************************/

#include  <stdio.h>
#include  <dos.h>

main()
{
     int  i,j;

     i = 50;

     set_video(4);          /* set video to graphics mode 4 */

     for ( j = 0; j < 320; j++ )
          dot( i,  j);

     getch()
}


set_video(int  i)
{
     _AH = 0;               /* Select service 0, set video mode */
     _AL = i;               /* Select mode required */
     geninterrupt(16);      /* Invoke Bios Video Services */
}


dot( char  x_co,  int  y_co)
{
     _AH = 12;              /* Select service 12, write pixel */
     _AL = 5;               /* Select colour required */
     _DL = x_co;            /* Set x co-ordinate */
     _CX = y_co;            /* Set y co-ordinate */
     geninterrupt(16);      /* Invoke Bios Video Service */
}
```

This program is fairly simple and self explanatory. We are plotting a series of pixels from 50,0 to 50,320. You will notice the empty getch() function at the end of the main() function. This causes the program to wait for a key to be pressed before exiting. Thus you can see your graphics without any disturbance from the text generated by the C environment.

If you are trying out any graphics, it is sensible to put a getch() at any point where you might want to wait while you look at the screen.

A final point about the above examples is that the programs were originally tried on an IBM AT compatible with a colour monitor and colour graphics adapter worked without any problems. But when the programs were moved over to another compatible which was supposed to have the same configuration, another colour had to be selected in order to obtain any display. So if you find you have problems try changing your colours.

There is much more which can be done using the pseudo-variables, but it is outside the scope of this tutorial. You can use them to find out the status of any register at any specific time. An example of this is given in the Turbo C User's Guide in Chapter 9 on Advanced Programming in Turbo C.

In-line Assembly Language

A feature of Turbo C is that it supports an extensive in-line assembly language. To use this you must have a copy of the Microsoft Macro Assembler (MASM) version 3.0 or later. The reason for this is that when you make use of the in-line assembly language, the compiler generates an assembly file, then invokes MASM to produce the object file.

Also to use it you need to have a good knowledge of assembly language and the 8086 instruction set.

Given the two facts above the in-line assembly language is well and truly outside the scope of this book and we will not be covering it to any extent here. If you do need details about it, you should refer to Chapter 9 of the Turbo C User Guide.

If you are going to use in-line assembly you must start the compiler with the -B option set. See the User Guide for details.

The keyword asm is used for in-line assembly. This tells the compiler that what is on that line is assembly code and will be treated by the compiler as such. The format for using asm is:

```
asm <opcode> <operands> <; or newline>
```

Note that with in-line assembly either a semi-colon or a newline can be used to terminate a line of code, so both the following are legal:

```
asm     mov   ah,10

asm     mov   al,1;
```

You can have more than one assembly instruction on the line:

```
asm push bp;     asm mov bp,sp;
```

provided that each entry is ended with a semi-colon.

A word of warning here about the semi-colon. Experienced assembly programmers (and if you are going to use in-line assembly you need to be experienced) will be used to placing the semi-colon to indicate the start of comments. This is not the case with in-line assembly. Comments must be included in the normal C comment fields. This is indicated below:

```
asm   mov   ah,11;     /* BIOS Video Service 11 Set Colour */
```

In-line assembly can make use of C variables just like normal C code. Have a look at the following version of set_video() :

```
void set_video( int mode )
{
        if( ( mode < 0 ) || ( mode > 15 ) )
                return ;

        asm mov   ah,0;      /* Service 0, set video mode */
        asm mov   al,mode;   /* Load mode selected into al */
        asm int   16;        /* Interrupt 16, video services */
}
```

For details of the opcodes, string instructions and jump instructions which may be used as part of the in-line assembler you should refer to Chapter 9 of the User's Guide.

The Interrupt Functions

There is a set of functions in Turbo C which allows you to generate interrupts and pass data to the processor in the correct registers. These are designed to give you access to MSDOS and BIOS calls.

In the first part of this chapter, under psuedo-variables, we have looked at the simplest of these, geninterrupt() which allows us to generate any specific interrupt.

The main one used for giving MSDOS system calls is bdos() or its related function bdosptr(), which are covered in the Reference Guide.
bdos() allows you to call up directly a MSDOS system call; you can find details of such calls in the MSDOS Programmer's Reference Manual. To use them you must have a fairly good knowledge of the working of MSDOS. Also, many of the functions for which you might want to call MSDOS can be accessed with greater ease through one of the special functions provided in the Turbo C library. If you think you need to make a direct call to MSDOS (say to read a specific disk sector) have a good read through the Turbo C Reference Guide. There you will probably find a function which will do what you want, for example, absread().

There are a number of tasks which you cannot do using the existing functions. In addition to bdos() there is a set of functions to handle interrupt generation, these all start with int and include int86(), int86x(), intdos(), intdosx(), and intr(). We are not going to look at all these as they are covered in the Turbo C Reference Guide, but we will examine the use of intr() which gives some indication of how to use the others, although they mostly work with a union rather than a structure.

One element that all these functions have in common is that before you can use them you must include dos.h in your program. They are all prototyped in that file. It also contains the definitions of the structures REGPACK and SREG and the union REG, which are used by the interrupt functions.

intr() makes use of the structure REGPACK. This has the following form:

```
struct  REGPACK
{
        unsigned  r_ax,  r_bx,  r_cx,  r_dx;
        unsigned  r_bp,  r_si,  r_di,  r_ds,  r_es,  r_flags;
}
```

When invoked, intr() copies the values held in the structure and loads them into the registers, it then issues the required interrupt after which it places the resultant register values back into the structure. To do this it needs to be passed two arguments: the first is the interrupt value it should issue and the second is the address of the structure, so it has the form:

```
void intr( int  interrupt_value,  struct  REGPACK *preg );
```

Have a look at how this has been used in Program 090.

```
/ * * * * * * * * * * * * * * * * * * * * * * * * * * * * * * * * * * * * * * *
* Program 090                                             *
* Sketch Master                                           *
* * * * * * * * * * * * * * * * * * * * * * * * * * * * * * * * * * * * * * * /
#include  <dos.h>
#include  <stdio.h>
#include  <ctype.h>

main()
{
        int  i,j,c;
        char  let;

        vidset();               /* Set video to graphics mode 4 */

        c = 1;                  /* Set colour to one */

        i = 100;
```

```c
        j = 160;                /* Set x, y, co-ordinates for start */

        dot(i,j);               /* Start with dot in middle. */

        while ( 1 )             /* Start endless loop */
        {
                let = toupper(getch()); /* Get key depression */

                if( isdigit(let))   /* test for number key */
                {
                        c = let - '0'; /* set colour to number */
                }
                else
                switch (let)
                {
                                case 'U':       /* UP */
                                        i--;
                                        break;
                                case 'N';       /* DOWN */
                                        i++;
                                        break;
                                case 'H':       /* LEFT */
                                        j--;
                                        break;
                                case 'J':       /* RIGHT */
                                        j++;
                                        break;
                                case 'I':       /* Right up diag */
                                        j++;
                                        i--;
                                        break;
                                case 'M':       /* Right down diag */
                                        j++;
                                        i++;
                                        break;
                                case 'B':       /* Left down diag */
                                        j--;
                                        i++;
                                        break;
                                case 'Y':       /* Left up diag */
                                        j--;
                                        i--;
                                        break;
                                case 'Q':       /* Quit */
                                        exit(0);
                                default:
```

```
                        break;
            }

            /* Take measure for going off screen */

            if ( i < 0 ) i = 200;
            if ( i > 200 ) i = 0;
            if ( j < 0 ) j = 320;
            if ( j > 320 ) j = 0;

            dot(i,j,c)        /* Make dot on screen */
      }
}

dot( int x, int y, int col )
{
            struct REGPACK treg;      /* Structure for the
                                       * registers. In dos.h
                                       */

            int k = 0x0C00;           /* Set K with high to 12 and low
bytes
                               * set to 0
                               */

            k += col;        /* Add col to k so setting low byte
                             * to col;
                             */

            treg.r_dx = x;   /* load dx with column number */
            treg.r_cx = y;   /* load cx with row number */
            treg.r_ax = k;   /* load ah with service number 0
                             * and al with colour, col.
                             */

            intr(16,&treg);         /* invoke interrupt 16 */
}

vidset()
{
            struct REGPACK treg;
            treg.r_ax = 0x0004;     /* Service 0 in high byte and
                                     *  mode 4 in low byte.
                                     */
            intr(16,&treg);
}
```

This works quite well to give you a way of drawing lines on the screen using the U,N,H,J,Y,I,M,B, keys together with the number keys for the colours. Incidentally, you only have four colours.

The one problem you will have noticed with this is that you can only load values into the pair registers, you cannot access AL or AH directly. So, if you need to put a value into AH and another into AL it can be complicated. The easiest way to do this is to turn the value to be held in the upper register, eg AH into hex, so 10 would be 0x0A, then add two zeros to the end. This would give you 0x0A00 which would put the value 10 into the upper byte. Now assign that to a variable and add the number you want in the lower register to it. Provided the second number is below 255 it will go into the lower byte of the pair, and you can now assign the value to the double register.

The Extended Code Keys

A small matter, but one which can cause problems is the code values returned by some of the keys on PCs. You will notice that in the above program example we have used the normal alpha keys for movement, not the cursor keys.

The reason for this is that it was easier to write the program this way. The cursor keys return what is known as an extended key code value. This means that they have no ASCII value.

Whenever a key is pressed an integer value is returned to the system. If the lower eight bits are set then these are the ASCII value of the key pressed. This is taken as a normal key value. However, if the lower eight bits are zero, then the key is one of the special keys, ie the cursor or function keys. In such cases the upper eight bits contain the value. This cannot normally be read directly with the functions like getch().

The following code fragment is from a commercial program. It enables you to read the value for cursor and function keys.

```
read( char *ch )
{
        char a,b;
        _AH = 0;                    /* Load AH with service required. */

        geninterrupt(0x16);    /* Call bios keyboard services */

        b = _AL;                    /* Read values */
        a = _AH;

        if ( b == 0 )
        {
                *ch = a;
                return ( -1 );
        }
```

```
        else
        {
                *ch = b;
                return (0);
        }
}
```

This function is quite useful as it will either return a 0 with the ASCII character placed in the character variable pointed to by the argument passed, or it will return -1 with the extended code of the key pressed placed in the character variable, in the case of a special key.

Turbo C also supports a function, bioskey() which gives you direct access to the keyboard biosfunction. This is a very powerful function and well worth some study. Look it up in the Turbo C Reference Guide. However, although it is a powerful and useful function, it does not always behave quite as you would expect. You can have some unexpected results from using this call, so treat it with care.

22

RAW I/O

The subject of raw I/O is rather a questionable one when it comes to working under most operating systems. C was developed alongside Unix, and under Unix the raw I/O routines provide direct access to the Unix operating system I/O handling routines. As a result of this, they generally provide you with a much faster form of file access than you have with the normal buffered I/O routines looked at earlier.

Once you move out of the Unix environment this advantage does not generally apply. Practical experience indicates that for most work you can safely leave raw I/O operations well and truly alone. As such operations are not without a degree of risk at times, this might be an advantage.

There are times when raw I/O has a role to play. This is especially the case when you have to send a value to a file which would normally be considered a terminating value.

Files to be accessed in a raw I/O mode are opened using either the function open() or the function creat(). The former is used to open an already existing file, and the latter to create and open a new file, or to open an existing file for overwriting.

The call to the open function takes the form of:

```
fd = open( pathname, access [,permissions] );
```

where fd is an integer file descriptor, pathname is a pointer to a character string and access is an integer value, which is usually expressed in a symbolic form which defines the type of access to the file. The optional parameter permissions allow variations to be imposed on the type of access. However, there are a number of problems here in that they are not supported by versions of MS-DOS below 3.

The open function is prototyped in the header file 'io.h'. This file should be included. You must also include 'fcntl.h'. This is the file which contains the symbolic forms for the access values.

The access value is composed of bitwise ORing symbolic values of the Read/Write flags and the Access type flags.

Table 22.1   The Read/Write flags

Symbolic	Description	Hex Value
O_RDONLY	Open for reading only	0x0001;
O_WRONLY	Open for writing only	0x0002;
O_RDWR	Open for reading or writing	0x0004;

The Access type flags

Symbolic	Description	Hex Value
O_APPEND	All writes to append to end.	0x0800
O_CREAT	If file does not exist create it with the permissions set.	0x0100
O_TRUNC	Truncate file to length 0.	0x0200
O_BINARY	Open in binary mode.	0x8000
O_TEXT	Open in text mode.	0x4000

There are two additional flags available O_NDELAY and O_EXCL which are provided only for Unix compatibility and are not used under MSDOS.

With Turbo C under MSDOS 3.x and higher, there is a set of additional values which can be given to cover file locking. They are:

O_NOINHERIT   This means that the file is not to be passed to any child program.

O_DENYALL   This allows no other access to the file while it is open with the current handle.

O_DENYWRITE   This allows only reads to be done from other file opens to this file.

O_DENYREAD   This allows only writes to be done from other file opens to this file.

O_DENYNONE   With this all access rights are allowed to the file by all other opens.

Although they are not of much importance for normal, single user, single tasking MSDOS working, this is changing. With the arrival of full network support under

MSDOS 4 and the new multi-tasking systems these options are going to be used increasingly.

Another concern with the open() function is its portability. There tends to be a variation in the way it works between compilers, especially when code is being moved between operating systems.

To output to a file opened with open() or one of the other calls for raw I/O (create, open, dup, dup2 or fcntl) use is made of the function write(). The format for using this function is:

```
write( file_descriptor,  buffer,  number_of_bytes );
```

where the file_descriptor is an integer value returned by the call which opened the file for access, buffer is a pointer to the address of a buffer, and number_of_bytes is an integer telling the call how many bytes to write from the buffer.

Write behaves slightly differently according to how the file has been opened. If the file has been opened in text mode, that is O_TEXT set, a translation will take place of the linefeed character to the carriage return and linefeed pair. However, if O_BINARY was set, no such translation will be made.

The complementary function to write() is read(). The form of this is:

```
read( file_descriptor,  buffer,  number_of_bytes );
```

This will read the number of bytes specified from the file indicated by the file_descriptor into the buffer pointed to by buffer. Again, there is a difference in operation according to whether a file is opened in text mode or not. If it is in text mode read() removes carriage returns as they are read, and it will report any occurrence of the Ctrl-Z character as an end of file.

Another basic function in this set of raw file access functions is lseek(). This is to the raw I/O functions what fseek() is to the standard access functions. It allows you to position the pointer within the file. The format for this call is:

```
lseek( file_descriptor, offset,   whence );
```

where file_descriptor is an integer returned by the call which opens the file. Offset is a long integer giving the offset to move to and whence is an integer value which indicates from where the offset is to be calculated.

The lseek() function is often used along with the function tell(). This has the form of:

```
offset = tell( file_descriptor );
```

Table 22.2 The Symbolic values for whence

Symbolic Name	Offset calculated:	Value
SEEK_SET	from file beginning	0
SEEK_CUR	from current position	1
SEEK_END	from end-of-file	2

where offset is a long integer, and file_descriptor is a file handle returned by the opening call. The value returned by tell, which in this example is assigned to offset, is the current offset of the pointer within the file referred to by file_descriptor.

The use of the above basic raw I/O with the exception of write() can be seen in Program 091. This is a common use for raw I/O, handling a hex dump of a file. The problem here is that if you are looking at a binary input you may well get the Ctrl-Z value as a valid element in the file. With the standard buffered input this would be taken as an EOF marker. With the open() set to a binary read this problem is avoided using the raw I/O.

```
/***************************************************
* Program 091                                     *
*                                                 *
* Hex Dump of file using raw file I/O calls       *
***************************************************/

/*   Include files */

#include <stdio.h>
#include <io.h>
#include <stdlib.h>
#include <ctype.h>
#include <fcntl.h>
#include <errno.h>

/*    Definitions  */

#define   BUFSIZE       256
#define   TRUE          1
#define   FALSE         0

/*     Code Macros     */

#define   CLS           printf("%c[2J",27);
#define   PUT_CUR(x,y)  printf("%c[%d;%dH",27,x,y);
```

```
/*      Globals          */

long    offset;
int     file_des;
char    buf[BUFSIZE];

main( int argc, char *argv[] )
{
        if ( argc < 2 )      /* Not enough arguments */
        {
                puts("Usage   fdump < filename >");
                exit (0);
        }

        file_open( argv[1] );
        file_show();
}


/********************************************************
* file_open, opens a file using raw I/O access      *
* in the case of an error the program is exited      *
********************************************************/

file_open( char *filename )
{
    int access;

    access = O_RDONLY | O_BINARY;  /* Set access to read only in
                                    * binary file mode.
                                    */

    file_des = open( filename, access );

    if ( file_des < 0 )              /* Error opening file */
    {
            switch ( errno )   /* Reports error */
            {
                    case ENOENT:
                        puts("Path or file name not found");
                        break;
                    case EMFILE:
                        puts("Too many open files.");
                        break;
                    case EACCES:
                        puts("Permission denied.");
                        break;
                    case EINVACC:
                        puts("Invalid access code.");
                        break;
                    default:
```

```
                        puts("Unspecified file access failure.");
            }
            puts("Unable to open file.  Exiting.");
            exit(0);
      }
}

/********************************************************
 * file_show displays the contents of the file    *
 * on screen using hex and ascii.  The file is     *
 * read into a buffer with file_read and movement*
 * forward or back is done with file_move.         *
 ********************************************************/

file_show()
{
      int  exit_flag;

      exit_flag = FALSE;
      offset = 0;

      while ( ! exit_flag )
      {
            file_read();
            screen_show();
            exit_flag = file_move();
      }
}

/********************************************************
 * file_read, reads a buffer from the current     *
 * pointer position and puts it in buf            *
 ********************************************************/

file_read()
{
      int  e_num;

      e_num = read( file_des, buf, BUFSIZE );

      if( e_num == 0 )
      {
            PUT_CUR(23,2);
            puts("At end of file. Press key to continue.");
            getch();
      }

      if( e_num < 0 )
      {
            puts("File reading error. Exiting.");
```

```
                exit(0);
        }
}


/*************************************************
 * screen_show displays the contents of buf on   *
 * the screen.                                    *
 *************************************************/

screen_show()
{
        int    line_num, i, j, buf_off;
        unsigned char ch;


        line_num = offset;
        CLS;

        for ( i = 0; i < 16; i++ )
        {

                printf("%04x > ",line_num);

                for ( j = 0; j < 16; j++ )
                {
                        buf_off = ( i * 16 ) + j ;
                        ch = buf[ buf_off ];
                        printf("%02x ",ch);
                }

                printf("   |   ");

                for ( j = 0; j < 16; j++ )
                {
                        buf_off = ( i * 16 ) + j ;
                        ch = buf[ buf_off ];

                        if ( isprint( ch ) )
                                printf("%c",ch);
                        else
                                printf(".");
                }
                printf("\n");
                line_num += 16;
        }
}
```

```
/*******************************************
* file_move moves the pointer forward or back in*
* the file according to keys pressed.  If q is   *
* pressed the exit_flag is set.                  *
*******************************************/

file_move()
{
        long tmp;
        char key;

        PUT_CUR( 24,1 );
        printf(" F - forward.   B - back. Q - exit. ");

        offset = tell( file_des ); /* Get current position of file ptr */

        while( TRUE )
        {
                key = toupper( getch() );

                switch ( key )
                {
                        case 'F':
                                return (0);
                        case 'B':
                                tmp = 512;
                                if ( ( offset - tmp ) < 0 )
                                        break;
                                else
                                        lseek( file_des, -tmp, SEEK_CUR );
                                return (0);
                        case 'Q':
                                return (1);
                        default:
                }
        }
}
```

Raw I/O can be useful, but is best avoided unless necessary. There are times when it can be too high a level. If you want to write software to repair damaged disk sectors, a much lower level of access is required.

With many versions of C this would require you to write your own assembler routines making use of the MSDOS interrupts 25 and 26 hex. Fortunately, with Turbo C life is much easier. You are provided with two functions absread() and abswrite() which give you direct access to disk sectors for reading and writing.

The format of absread() is:

```
absread( drive, number_of_sectors, sector_num, buffer );
```

where drive is an integer giving the drive number, 0 = A, 1 = B, and so on. The next integer number_of_sectors gives the number of sectors to be read. This is followed by an integer giving the sector number from which to start the read, and finally there is a pointer to a buffer where the data read will be stored.

The format for abswrite is basically the same:

```
abswrite( drive, number_of_sectors, sector_num, buffer );
```

where buffer contains the data to be written back to the disk.

Program 092 gives a basic disk sector editor. It reads a sector and displays the result on the screen. You can then edit a sector, either in Hex or ASCII. This is a basic program and it is advisable to do some work on it to improve the interface. One suggestion is to only display half a buffer at a time and use the side by side display we had in the hex dump Program 091. Be careful, though. Direct writing of disk sectors is the easiest way to ruin your computer's health. Make sure you are working on a scrap floppy disk. Do not try anything on your hard disk, or even with a valuable floppy, until you are certain that everything is working as it should.

```
/********************************************
 * Program 092                              *
 *                                          *
 * Disk sector editor                       *
 *                                          *
 * Warning, use of this program could seriously *
 * damage your disk data if you are not careful. *
 ********************************************/

/*            Include Files                 */

#include <stdio.h>
#include <stdlib.h>
#include <errno.h>
#include <dos.h>
#include <ctype.h>

/*            Definitions                   */

#define TRUE        1
#define FALSE       0
#define SECTSIZE        512    /* Size of MSDOS sector */

/*            Code Macros Ansi Code          */

#define CLS                 printf("%c[2J",27)
```

```c
#define  PUT_CUR(x,y)          printf("%c[%d;%dH",27,x,y)

/*           Globals                          */
char  sec_buf[SECTSIZE];
int   drive, num_of_sects, sector;

main()
{
      warning();
      get_start();

      pro_buffer();
}

/*****************************************************
* warning displays a warning about editing disk  *
* sectors.                                        *
*****************************************************/

warning()
{
      CLS;
      puts("Editing Disk Sectors can have unexpected results.  Do not ");
      puts("edit a disk sector unless you are certain you know what you ");
      puts("are doing.");

      printf("\n\nDo you want to continue. Y/N ? ");

      if ( ok() )
            return;
      else
            exit (0);
}

/*****************************************************
* ok returns TRUE if Y is pressed and FALSE if   *
* N is pressed.                                   *
*****************************************************/

int  ok()
{
      char let;

      while ( TRUE )
      {
            let = toupper( getch() );
            if ( let == 'Y' )
                  return (TRUE);
            if ( let == 'N' )
                  return (FALSE);
      }
}
```

```
/*****************************************************
 * get_start gets the initial setting for the      *
 * drive and sector on which to work.              *
 *****************************************************/

get_start()
{
        char let;

        CLS;

        /* Set number of sectors to 1 */
        num_of_sects = 1;

        /* Obtain disk designation to work on. */


        while ( TRUE )
        {
                printf("\n\n\tWhich disk do you wish to work on A, B, or C ");

                do
                {
                        let = toupper( getch() );
                } while ( let < 'A' || let > 'C' );

                drive = let - 'A';

                printf("\n\n\tEnter sector to start from. ");

                scanf("%d",&sector);

                printf("\n\n\n");
                printf("\tDrive  = %c\n\n",let);
                printf("\tSector = %d\n\n",sector);
                printf("\tIs this correct Y/N ? ");

                if ( ok() )
                        return;
                else
                        CLS;
        }
}


/*****************************************************
 * pro_buffer holds the main control loop           *
 * this is exited by a q selection from the edit   *
 * menu.                                           *
 *****************************************************/
```

```
pro_buffer()
{
        int exit_flag = FALSE;

        while( ! exit_flag )
        {
                read_sector(); /* Refresh in memory image
                                * of sector even if loaded
                                * so that all changes are
                                * shown.
                                */
                show_sector();

                exit_flag = edit_sector();
        }
}


/**************************************************
* read_sector reads the selected sector from the*
* disk into memory.                             *
**************************************************/

read_sector()
{
    if ( absread( drive, num_of_sects, sector, sec_buf ) >= 0 )
            return;
    else
    {
            puts("Error on sector read, exiting. ");
            exit (0);
    }
}


/**************************************************
* show_sector displays the contents of the      *
* sector on the screen.  The top 16 lines are   *
* the sector in hex, the bottom 8 in ASCII.     *
**************************************************/

show_sector()
{
        int line, i, j;
        unsigned char ch;
        CLS;
        line = 0;

        for ( i = 0; i < 16; i++)
        {
                printf("%04x > ",line );
```

```
                for ( j = 0;  j < 32;  j++,  line++ )
                {
                        ch = sec_buf[ line ];
                        printf("%02x",ch);
                }
                printf("\n");
        }
        line = 0;
        for ( i = 0;  i < 8;  i++)
        {
                printf("%04x > ",line );
                for ( j= 0;  j < 64;  j++,  line++ )
                {
                        ch = sec_buf[ line ];
                        if ( isprint( ch ) )
                                printf("%c",ch);
                        else
                                printf(".");
                }
                printf("\n");
        }
}


/**************************************************
 * edit_sector allows the user to select which    *
 * form of edit to undertake if required and to   *
 * move forward or back one sector.  Q exits.      *
 **************************************************/

edit_sector()
{
        int edit_flag, key,  key_flag;
        char let;

        edit_flag = FALSE;
        PUT_CUR(25,1);
        printf("<F>orward, <B>ack, <H>ex edit, <A>scii edit, <Q>uit.  ");
        printf(" current  sector = %d ",sector);

        key_flag = 0;
        while ( ! key_flag )
        {
                key = toupper(getch());

                switch ( key )
                {
                        case 'F':
                                sector++;
                                key_flag = TRUE;
                                break;
```

```
                    case 'B':
                            if( sector > 0 )
                                    sector--;
                            key_flag = TRUE;
                            break;
                    case 'H':
                            hex_edit();
                            edit_flag = TRUE;
                            key_flag = TRUE;
                            break;
                    case 'A':
                            ascii_edit();
                            edit_flag = TRUE;
                            key_flag = TRUE;
                            break;
                    case 'Q':
                            key_flag = TRUE;
                            return ( 1 );
                    default:
            }
}

        if ( edit_flag )      /* If there has been an edit. Save? */
                save_buf();
        return (0);
}

/*****************************************************
* hex_edit undertakes the edit of the hex dump.  *
* position is controlled by cursor keys.         *
*****************************************************/

hex_edit()
{
        char let;
        int line, col, s_off, val, exit_flag, key;

            s_off = 8;        /* Allow for offset at start of each
                               * line of hex display.
                               */
        let = 0;

        PUT_CUR(25,1);
                printf("%c[K",27);     /* Erase to end of line */

        PUT_CUR(25,1);

        printf("Cursor keys to move round screen, F10 to exit.");

        exit_flag = FALSE;
        line = 0;
```

243

```
col = 0;

while ( ! exit_flag )
{
        int ln, cl, pos;   /* local to loop. */

        /* Calculate values for cursor positioning.
         * you have to allow for the offsets.
         */

        ln = line + 1;
        cl = s_off + ( col * 2 );

        /* Calculate the position in the buffer
         * represented by the cursor.
         */

        pos = ( line * 32 ) + col;

        PUT_CUR(ln,cl);

        key = read_key( &let );   /* read_key will return -1
                                   * if function or cursor key
                                   * pressed.
                                   */

        if ( key )                /* Function or curso key. */
        {
              switch ( let )
              {
                    case 68:
                          exit_flag = TRUE;
                          break;
                    case 80:
                          line++;
                          if ( line > 15)
                                line = 0;
                          break;
                    case 72:
                          line--;
                          if ( line < 0 )
                                line = 15;
                          break;
                    case 75:
                          col--;
                          if ( col < 0 )
                                col = 31;
                          break;
                    case 77:
                          col++;
```

```c
                        if ( col > 32 )
                                col = 0;
                        break;
                default:
        }
}


else                    /* ASCII key pressed. */
{
        if( !isxdigit( let ) )       /* Test for Hex */
                continue;
        {
                        /* Take inputted letter
                         * and convert to hex num value.
                         * Then get next letter of pair.
                         */

                int hold, h1, h2;
                let = toupper( let );
                printf("%c",let);

                if( let >= '0' && let <= '9' )
                        h1 = let - '0';
                else
                        h1 = 10 + ( let - 'A' );

                while( !isxdigit( let =
                        getch() ));

                let = toupper( let );
                printf("%c",let);
                if ( let >= '0' && let <= '9' )
                        h2 = let - '0';
                else
                        h2 = 10 + ( let - 'A' );

                hold = ( h1 * 16 ) + h2;

                /* Display location and value */
                PUT_CUR(25,70);
                printf("%02X    %d",hold,pos);

                /* Move to next position. */

                col++;
                if( col > 31 )
                {
                        line++;
                        col = 0;
                }
```

```
                            if( line > 15 )
                                    line = 0;

                            sec_buf[pos] = hold;


                    }
                }
            }
}

/***************************************************
* ascii_edit uses the same basic system as hex   *
* edit, but the edit is on the ASCII display     *
***************************************************/

ascii_edit()
{
        char let;
        int line; col, s_off, l_off, val, exit_flag, key;
        s_off = 8;
        l_off = 17;
        let = 0;

        PUT_CUR(25,1);
                printf("%c[K",27);      /* Erase to end of line */

        PUT_CUR(25,1);

        printf("Cursor keys to move round screen, F10 to exit.");

        exit_flag = FALSE;
        line = 0;
        col = 0;

        while ( ! exit_flag )
        {
                int ln, cl, pos;

                ln = line + l_off;
                cl = s_off + ( col );
                pos = ( line * 64 ) + col;

                PUT_CUR(ln,cl);

                key = read_key( &let );

                if ( key )
                {
                        switch ( let )
                        {
```

```
                        case  68:
                                exit_flag = TRUE;
                                break;
                        case  80:
                                line++;
                                if ( line > 7)
                                        line = 0;
                                break;
                        case  72:
                                line--;
                                if ( line < 0 )
                                        line = 7;
                                break;
                        case  75:
                                col--;
                                if ( col < 0 )
                                        col = 63;
                                break;
                        case  77:
                                col++;
                                if ( col > 63 )
                                        col = 0;
                                break;
                        default:
                }
        }


                else
                {
                        if( !isprint(let) )
                                continue;
                        printf("%c",let);
                        sec_buf[pos] = let;
                        col++;
                        if ( col > 63 )
                        {
                                line++;
                                col = 0;
                        }
                        if ( line > 7 )
                                line = 0;
                }
        }
}

/************************************************
* save_buf checks to see if the buffer should be*
* saved back to sector.  If it should a abswrite*
* is performed.                                 *
*************************************************/
```

```
save_buf()
{
      PUT_CUR(25,1);
      printf("%c[K",27); /* Clear to end of line */
      printf("Save Edited Buffer Y/N");
      if( !ok() )
         return;
      abswrite(drive,num_of_sects,sector,sec_buf);
}


/****************************************************
* read_key, reads the keyboard using a direct     *
* call to dos. If a normal key is pressed that    *
* value is passed to the character pointed to      *
* by the pointer passed and the zero value         *
* is returned. If an extended key is pressed       *
* the -1 is returned and the key value is passed*
****************************************************/

read_key( char *ch )
{
      char a,b;
      _AH = 0;                   /* Request for service. */
      geninterrupt(0x16);

      b = _AL;
      a = _AH;

      if ( b == 0 )          /* Low bits zero so extended key */
      {
            *ch = a;
            return ( -1 );
      }
      else           /* Low bits not zero so ascii key */
      {
            *ch = b;
            return (0);
      }
}
```

As a final reminder, raw I/O is powerful but, dangerous. Use it with care. It is well worth thoroughly reading your documentation just to find out what is possible. Also, read some of the more advanced C books before trying anything but the simplest raw I/O operations.

23

CONDITIONAL COMPILATION

One of the problems in writing software is that customers are never happy with what you have. Usually, they want something slightly different, not much different, just a bit. Also, you are liable to find yourself making minor changes to code just to account for differences in hardware between systems.

One aspect of C which can be very useful for dealing with instances like this is conditional compilation. This is a set of preprocessor directives which cause certain tasks to be done, or not done, at compilation time.

You already know the preprocessor directives #define and #include. The others you need to know to carry out conditional compilation are:

`#ifdef    SYMBOL`	If SYMBOL has been defined the following code is included.
`#ifndef   SYMBOL`	If SYMBOL has not been defined the following code is included.
`#if  (expression)`	If the expression is true the following code is included.
`#endif`	Conclude the preceding #if, #ifdef or #ifndef.
`#else`	Else for #ifs.
`#undef    SYMBOL`	Undefine previously defined SYMBOL.

What do we mean by conditional compilation? Basically, it means putting a series of tests in your code which tells the compiler which code should be compiled and which left out. Look at the following example:

```
#define DEBUG

#ifdef DEBUG
        puts("At start of code.");
#endif


    . . . . . . . . . . . . . . . . .
    main code body
    . . . . . . . . . . . . . . . . .

#ifdef DEBUG
        puts("At the end of code.");
#endif
```

Here we have defined DEBUG. When the code is compiled the debug statements will be included. Later, when we have found all the bugs we can compile without the debug statements, without having to go through all the code to remove them, just undefine DEBUG.

This sort of usage is fairly common for conditional compilation, especially with verbose and non-verbose versions of a program.

Another interesting use for this is where code is being produced for different countries. For example code may be intended for customers in England or in Holland. Most of this code is written just for that one program. There are, however, a large number of standard routines which can be included. Typical instances are those for Y/N responses.

There is a difference in Yes/No responses between the two countries. This can be overcome with a standard ok() function which includes the printing of the <Y/N>? at the end of the query line and which adjusts for country.

```
ok()
{
        char let,match;

#ifdef HOLLAND
        printf(" <J/N> ");
        match = 'J';
#else
        printf(" <Y/N> ");
        match = 'Y';
#endif

        while ( 1 )
        {
                let = toupper(getch());
```

```
            if ( let == match )
                    return (1);
            if ( let == 'N' )
                    return (0);
        }
    }
```

With this function if HOLLAND is defined at the start of the program, the J/N will be printed, and a yes match made on J, not on Y.

The use of the #if preprocessor is more complicated. Here, the directive evaluates a constant expression which is in the brackets following it. Subsequent inclusion of code will depend on the value of that test. If the evaluation results in zero, the test is false and the code is skipped. If it is any other value, the test is true and the code is included in the compilation. A basic outline example of this is given below:

```
#define MESLEN 256

#if ( MESLEN < 255 )

            code to include.

#else

            code to include.

#endif
```

This outline came from a program where two different include files had to be used according to the message protocols being employed. The difference between which protocol was being used was the size of message they would accept. So the selection was made on message length.

A final important point about the #ifs. Each one must have its own #endif. It does not matter if there are other #ifs in-between, but you must make sure that you have an #endif for each. So be careful.

Defining Out Code.

In Chapter 3, the use of comments for cutting out code was discussed. This technique is often used during debugging, especially to make sure that certain elements are constant.

The problem is that if you have comments inside the block of code you wish to comment out, recourse has to be made to the nested comment option at compile time to allow comments inside comments. Such use is not considered good practice. Furthermore, many debugging tools will not accept nested comments.

Another way for cutting out a block of code is to use the #ifdef preprocessor directive with a default symbol OUT which is not defined. So, to cut out a block of code you would use the following technique:

```
        if ( max < 10 )
        {
#ifdef OUT
        printf("\nPlease enter new value for size [default
10]");
        scanf("%s" &val);
        max = atoi(val);
        if ( max >= 10 )
          return (max);
        else
#endif
        return (10);
        }
```

This is an illustration from a program which required debugging. It was necessary to check that a routine which called the above code fragment was working correctly. To do this the value input had to be constant. By defining out the section which allowed the value of max to be varied, its value was set constantly to 10, the default return value in the code. This made debugging easier.

MODULARITY

One of the advantages of C which is often put forward is its structured nature. In this, it is often compared to Pascal. In this chapter we look at the modular nature of C, how you can use this, and some problems it can cause.

Chapter 1 discussed the basic structure of C and explained that any C program was made up of a number of functions. There is one function you have to have: the function main(). This is the entry point for the C program.

In Figure 24.1 you will see a diagrammatic representation of a C program which displays the basic modularity found in most programs.

At the top you have the entry point function main(). In anything larger than a small program it is unusual for any processing to take place in main(). Normally, from main() you will call a number of control functions which handle different parts of the program. Most programs consist of two or more distinct parts which are fairly independent of each other in an operational sense, but may be linked by their use of common data.

This can be seen if you consider the example of an interpreter for a Computer Based Training language. Here you will have two distinct parts, the program input section and the program running section. The following code fragment is from the main () function of such a language called L-taal, which shows the way that the control functions for the various elements of the language are invoked.

```
main()
{
      int select;
      current = start = last = (prog_line *) 0;
      error = match_flag = 0;
      return_point = stack_point = -1; /* must point to position
                                        * below the empty cell
                                        */

      while ( TRUE )                   /* Endless Loop */
      {
```

```
        CLS;
        select = menu();
        switch (select)
        {
                case 1:
                        new();
                case 2:
                        add();
                        break;
                case 3:
                        edit();
                        break;
                case 4:
                        run();
                        break;
                case 5:
                        list();
                        break;
                case 6:
                        load();
                        break;
                case 7:
                        save();
                        break;
                case 8:
                        get_out();
                        break;
                default:
                        puts("No valid selection");
        }
        if ( error )
        {
                rep_error(error);
        }
    }
}
```

After the initializing, some common variables main() enters an endless loop. First, it calls a control function menu() which handles the selection of operations. Then, according to the selection made, it invokes the appropriate control function.

According to the size and complexity of the program, the control functions may (or may not) carry out processing. Generally, they do some, but it is only limited. Most of the processing will be done by a lower level of functions called process functions.

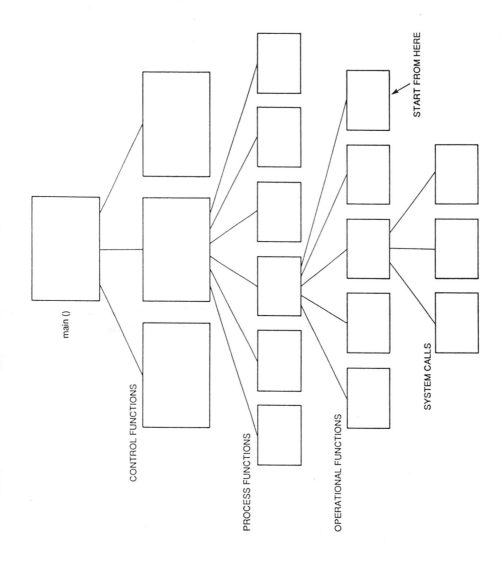

main ()

CONTROL FUNCTIONS

PROCESS FUNCTIONS

OPERATIONAL FUNCTIONS

SYSTEM CALLS

START FROM HERE

Figure 24.1

255

These process functions often call even lower levels of functions known as operational functions. The difference between a process function and an operational function is that a process function will carry out a number of operations on data, whilst an operational function will only carry out one operation. Consider the following code fragments:

```
get_entry[ int offset]
{
    char let, row, col;

    while ( TRUE )
    {
        let = getch();
        if ( isnum( let ) )
            break;
    }

    row = (offset / 32) + 5;
    col = (offset % 32) + 10;

    put_cur( row, col);
    printf("%c",let);
    buf[ offset] = let;
}
```

This function get_entry() is completing three tasks. It is obtaining a valid entry, then calculating a display position and displaying it, and finally assigning it. It could be re-written as:

```
get_entry(int offset)
{
        buf[offset]  = valid_entry();
        show_entry( offset );
}

char  valid_entry()
{
    char let;

    while ( TRUE )
    {
        if ( isnum( let = getch() )
                return ( let );
    }
}

show_entry( int offset )
{
    int row, col;
```

```
    row = ( offset /32 ) + 5;
    col = ( offset %32 ) + 10;

    put_cur( row, col);
    printf("%c", buf[offset] );
}
```

In this second set, get_entry() is a process function. It is handling the process of getting an entry. The two functions valid_entry() and show_entry() are operational functions. Each is carrying out one of the operations required by get_entry(). Each operational function is only doing one clearly defined job.

This single activity status has two advantages. First, it makes testing and debugging a function far easier. For more on this see Chapter 25. Second, as a number of tasks are liable to be common to different processes, you can use the same operational function to support a number of process functions.

In fact, some operational functions are so common in programs that you will find yourself writing the same function in nearly every program you create. An example of this is the put_cur() function called in the above programs. Numerous programs which have to access display output on the screen use this function.

Rather than having to re-write the function every time, it can be included as part of a #include file. For example a file called screen.c can contain a series of screen functions for common use. These are clear screen, position cursor, and clear to end of line.

Using the #include preprocessor directive to include standard files like this can have major benefits in software development. First, less time has to be taken entering code. Once you have typed a set of standard functions, all you need do is include them. Second, as they are already tested and working it reduces the amount of debugging which has to be done. One reason for this is that it cuts down the chance of a typographical error as a function is entered.

There is a price to pay for a high degree of modularity in a program: that is the overhead in calling functions. This was briefly mentioned at the start of this book, but a quick recap is worthwhile here. Every time a function is called, a jump has to be made to that function. Parameters have to be passed and return locations recorded. All this takes time.

If you are working in a time sensitive environment, essentially real time programming, this could cause a problem. In such cases you have to include the process as in-line code. This may not be a good structured approach to programming. However, what matters is that the program works.

Far too often when you look at C code, or code in any other highly structured language, you find that modularity has been carried to excess. For a start, there is no point is calling a function which itself just contains a single system call. The overhead on making such a call is not worthwhile.

There are two problems with having to write in-line code, where that code fragment has to be repeated a number of times. The first is the amount of time taken in entering code. The second is that with each entry the chances of a mistake being made are increased.

One way around this is to make use of code macros. Do not be put off by the fact that a macro may take more than one line to write. This is no problem as you can use the backslash to escape the carriage return. Also remember that you can define variables as local within a code macro. Look at the following definition:

```
#define Sort_Exchange( x, y )     { int h;\
                                   if ( x < y )\
                                   { h = x;  x = y;  y = h;}  }
```

You can place the macro in your code as and where required. This will save you considerable of typing and thus reduce the risk of mistakes.

Such code macros do have the advantage that they are faster in execution than function calls. There is, though, a price to pay for this speed. As was said earlier in the book, they result in more code being generated. This means that your executable code will be larger. That is the final tradeoff which faces you when programming in C: size versus speed. Generally, if you program for speed there will be some loss of efficiency in program size, and *vice versa*.

DEBUGGING AND TESTING C

One of the problems with C is that the rules for debugging other languages do not apply to it all that well. It is a price that we pay for the power of C. In discarding the protection which languages like Pascal provide, we have to accept the problems this can bring.

Often, novices to C can underestimate this difference. They presume that because of the similarity between C and Pascal in being highly structured languages, techniques which work in Pascal are also applicable to C. Sometimes they are, but sometimes they can be completely misleading.

What is important about debugging is that essentially it is a search and destroy operation. First, the bug has to be found, then it has to be fixed.

Testing

Before you can even start looking for a bug you have to know that it is there. The first thing you have to do is test your software. Here an interesting point is raised. What is the purpose of testing?

Many, if not most, software authors consider that the aim of testing is to show that the software is running correctly. That is one, and certainly the predominant school of thought. There is, however, another somewhat academic approach that has a different answer. It says that the purpose of a software test is to show the presence of bugs.

The argument for this idea is long, involved and rather outside the scope of this book. The basic point of view is quite simple. It states:

-   Any complex piece of software will contain bugs.

-   The more complex software is the more bugs it is liable to contain.

- It is impossible to write a series of tests for anything more than the simplest piece of software which can demonstrate that it has absolutely no bugs in it.

- It therefore follows that the only thing you can be certain of proving by any test is that a bug does exist.

- It therefore makes sense to design test to detect bugs, not to show that the software is performing correctly, as when all bugs are detected the software will be performing correctly anyway.

Whether you agree with this argument or not, there is one interesting point in it: the statement that it is impossible to write a series of tests for anything more than the simplest piece of software which can demonstrate that it has absolutely no bugs in it. It follows that you can write a test for a simple piece of software which can show it has no bugs in it. Consider the following example:

```
add( int a, int b)
{
      if ( a < 0 || a > 100 ) return (0);
      if ( b < 0 || b > 100 ) return (0);
      return ( a + b );
}
```

This is a very simple piece of code to test. If you can write all your functions so that they are this simple then you can test all your functions with very easy tests.

To do this, you have to break all your functions down into their component parts and write each part as a separate function. This is a very good approach to programming in theory, but it is not always practical. This was discussed in Chapter 24 on modularity.

This testing and proving of the very small blocks of a program is the approach to testing known as bottom up testing. You start at the lowest level of a program and work your way up testing each level as you go.

Although bottom up testing is efficient in proving that the individual functions in a program are working correctly and that no bugs are found in them, it is not very good at testing program design. To do this you need to reverse the process and test from the top down.

Top down testing is fairly complicated and you are best advised to read one of the specialist books on testing to fully understand it. The following is a brief description of how it works.

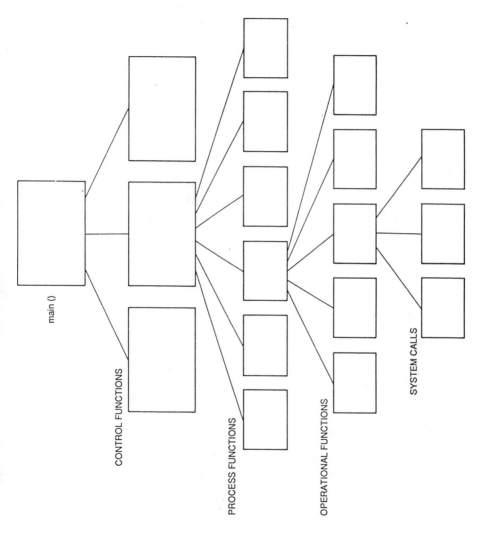

main ()

CONTROL FUNCTIONS

PROCESS FUNCTIONS

OPERATIONAL FUNCTIONS

SYSTEM CALLS

Figure 25.1

261

First, the top-level of control functions is tested, substituting the lower level functions with stub-functions which provide just enough support to allow the higher level function to run.

For instance, if you have a main() function which calls a function called menu() that returns a value from zero to eight according to a selection which is made, menu() would be replaced with a stub. This stub function would not print up and display a menu, or request an input. It would just return a preset value.

Once the top level control has been tested you then move down a level and test the next level of functions.

There are both advantages and disadvantages to top down testing. Really, they are outside the scope of this book. The main advantage is that such a testing approach does show up weaknesses in the structure of a program.

Debugging

One of the problems with discussing testing and debugging is that it is often referred to as two separate activities. In theory, this may be the case. Operationally, they are tightly interleaved. So let us go on to debugging.

First, a very simple piece of advice. If you have a bug, do not sit there reading the code. It is very rare that you will spot a bug just by reading through the code time after time. What you have to do is go out and hunt it down with all the tools at your disposal.

Frequent Mistakes

First let us consider a few of the common mistakes that are made in C. Even the most advanced programmers tend to make these mistakes, not just the novice.

Missing semi-colon

Probably the most common mistake is the missing semi-colon. Here you are fortunate in that the compiler will give you a warning that a semi-colon is missing. The problem is that the error message that you get will not always refer to the line on which the error exists.

```
main()
{
        int i;

        printf("Starting Loop")

        for (i = 0; i < 5; i++ )
                printf("Inside Loop");
}
```

The piece of test code above, when compiled with Turbo C, will produce an error message on the line:

```
for ( i = 0; i < 5; i+= )
```

stating that there is a missing semi-colon. In fact, there is, but not on this line. The mistake is on the previous line:

```
printf("Starting Loop")
```

which should be:

```
printf("Starting Loop");
```

This type of occurrence where the compile message actually refers to an error on the previous line is fairly common. What is happening is that the compiler parses, that is scans, the line. As there is no semi-colon it continues onto the next line. There it comes across a C construct which it knows, the for. However, as far as the compiler is concerned, the for cannot legally be here in what it considers to be the centre of a line. It therefore reports an error.

Excess semi-colon

A far more difficult problem with semi-colons concerns putting one where it should not be. You become so used to putting semi- colons at the end of a line that, you start to put them everywhere. This can lead at times to very unexpected results. Consider the following code fragment.

```
main()
{
        int i;

        printf("Starting Loop");

        for (i = 0; i < 5; i++ );
                printf("Inside Loop");
}
```

The output intended from this code was:

```
Starting Loop
Inside Loop
Inside Loop
Inside Loop
Inside Loop
Inside Loop
```

What we will actually get in this case is:

```
Starting Loop
Inside Loop
```

The reason for this difference is that there is a semi-colon at the end of the for statement. As a result we have an empty or do nothing loop. Such loops are valid C code so will not produce an error and at times can be useful.

```
for ( i = 0, j = max; i < 23; i++, max += change );
```

The above is a perfectly valid piece of C code which exists inside an empty loop. What we want to do here increases the value of max. There is no way, therefore, that a compiler can sort out the occurrences of empty loops which are valid and those which are not valid.

There are only two statements which can produce an empty loop. The for and the while statements. It is advisable to look through your code for every such statement and check that it is not an empty loop created by mistake.

One way you can do this is by means of the CROSSREF program we looked at in Chapter 20 on the linked list. This produces a listing of all C tokens, sorted in alphabetical order, and a list of the lines where they occur. One set of these lines will contain all the fors and the other all the whiles.

Another good idea is never to put a semi-colon on the same line as a for or while. If you want an empty loop, place it on the following line:

```
for ( i = 0, j = max; i < 23; i++, max += change )
;
```

This has two effects. It shows clearly that you had intended the loop to be empty. It also makes it easier to write a program which will look for instances of a semi-colon on a line with for or while. There are a number of programs around in both commercial and public domains which will do this. You might like to get one, or better still, have a go at writing your own.

Missing braces

Braces, that is the curly brackets used to hold compound statements, are another common source of problems. These come basically in two forms. First, the none use of braces.

One of the problems with C is that braces are not always required in certain positions. For instance, both:

```
if ( num < max )
        another_go();
```

and:

```
if ( num < max )
{
        another_go();
}
```

are perfectly valid code. If though, there is to be more than one line of code relevant to a test, then it must be within braces. So:

```
while( num < max )
{
        another_go();
        set_score();
}
```

is correct. Unfortunately, if you write the above and leave out the braces you still get valid code, but not what you intended:

```
while( num < max )
        another_go();
        set_score();
```

In the first piece, so long as num is less than max the function another_go() will be invoked followed by the invocation of set_score(). In the second set of code, so long as num is less than max the function another_go() will be invoked. Only this time set_score() will not be invoked until num is greater than max.

You should really take care when dealing with these statements which impose a test and carry out actions. One way followed by many programmers is always to use braces, even if you are only having one line connected with the test statement. So you would have:

```
while( ( let = getch() ) != 'q' )
{
play_game();
}
```

Although the compiler will not report errors when a pair of braces is missing, what it will report is when one brace is missing. The problem is that it will not tell you which of a pair is missing and it can often be hard to find out. You can obtain some help here with one of the public domain programs.

Missing comment closure

A rather difficult problem at times is the missed comment close. If you fail to close a comment correctly the compiler will continue to regard the code as a comment until it finds a valid comment close. This may comment out a large part of your program.

The basic answer here is to be careful. It is possible to modify the code for CROSSREF so that it just prints out comment lines. This can be useful, as if you get a printout of comment lines and find code in the middle, you know something is wrong.

Program 093 gives you a variation on CROSSREF which does this.
However, it does need some cleaning up to handle line feeds, so you will need to do some work on it.

```
/****************************************************
 * Program 093                                      *
 * This program shows those characters between      *
 * comment delimitators.                            *
 ****************************************************/

#include <stdio.h>
#include <stdlib.h>
#include <ctype.h>

/****************************************************
 *               definitions                        *
 ****************************************************/

#define         BOOL            int
#define         DQUOTE          '"'
#define         SQUOTE          '\''
#define         SLASH           '/'
#define         ASTERISK        '*'
#define         EQUALS          0
#define         FALSE           0
#define         TRUE            1

#define         MAXWORDSIZE     32
#define         MAXSTRLEN       255

/****************************************************
 *               Type Defs                          *
 ****************************************************/

typedef struct a {
                char    *prog_line;     /* program line */
                struct a *next;         /* next line */
                } program_type;
```

266

```
/****************************************************
*              Globals                              *
****************************************************/

program_type   *start_prog;
int comment_flag, line_number;

main( int argc, char *argv[] )
{
        if ( argc < 2 )
        {
                puts("Usage : comref < sourcefile >");
                exit (0);
        }

        read_file ( argv[1] );
        process_file();
}

/****************************************************
* read_file, reads the source file into memory    *
****************************************************/

read_file( char *filename )
{
        FILE *fp;
        program_type *current_line, *last_line;
        char  buf[MAXSTRLEN],*tmp;

        fp = fopen( filename, "r" );

        if ( fp == 0 )
        {
                puts("Cannot open input file to read.");
                exit (0);
        }

        start_prog = 0;

        while ( ( fgets( buf,MAXSTRLEN, fp )) != NULL )
        {
                current_line = malloc( sizeof ( program_type ) );
                if ( start_prog == 0 )
                        start_prog = current_line;
                else
                        last_line->next = current_line;
                current_line->next = 0;
                tmp = malloc( strlen( buf ) + 1 );
                strcpy( tmp, buf );
                current_line->prog_line = tmp;
                last_line = current_line;
        }
}
```

```
/*****************************************************
* process_file searches comments                    *
*****************************************************/

process_file()
{
        program_type *current, *last;

        char buf[MAXSTRLEN];

        comment_flag = 0;
        current = start_prog;
        line_number = 1;

        puts("Start Processing");
        while ( current != 0 )
        {
                strcpy ( buf, current->prog_line );
                get_comment( buf );
                last = current;
                current = last->next;
                line_number++;
        }
}
puts("End Processing");
}

/*****************************************************
* get_comment reads the in memory file line by      *
* line checking for comments. Characters inside      *
* comments are printed                               *
*****************************************************/

get_comment( char buf[] )
{
        char word[MAXWORDSIZE],let;
        int  num,cur_char,q_flag,sq_flag;

        cur_char = num = q_flag = sq_flag = 0;

        while ( buf[ cur_char ] != 0 )
        {
                let = buf[ cur_char ];

                if ( comment_flag )
                {
                        if ( let == ASTERISK && buf[ cur_char + 1 ] == SlASH )
                                comment_flag = FALSE;
                        cur_char++;
                        putchar(let);
                        continue;
                }

                if ( q_flag )
                {
                        if ( let == DQUOTE )
```

```
                q_flag  =  FALSE;
          cur_char++;
          continue;
     }

     if ( sq_flag )
     {
          if ( let  ==  SQUOTE )
                sq_flag  =  FALSE;
          cur_char++;
          continue;
     }

     if ( let  ==  SLASH  &&  buf[ cur_char + 1]  ==  ASTERISK )
     {
          comment_flag  =  TRUE;
          putchar(let);
     }

     if ( let  ==  DQUOTE   &&   sq_flag  ==  FALSE )
     {
          q_flag  =  TRUE;
     }

     if ( let  ==  SQUOTE   &&   q_flag  ==  FALSE )
     {
          sq_flag  =  TRUE;
     }
     cur_char++;
   }
}
```

Assignment – equality mix

A mistake which is far more common than most C programmers like to admit comes
directly from the power of C. This is where an assignment is made in place of a test
for equality.

The C test for equality is == whilst the assignment is =. Unfortunately, it is very easy
to enter:

```
if ( A = B )
```

when what you meant was:

```
if ( A == B )
```

In many languages this would not matter. The assignment in a test situation would be
thrown out by the compiler. In C, though, it is a valid statement. What you are
saying is:

assign the value of B to A
if the resultant value of A is other than zero then
the test is TRUE.

There are times when such assignments are useful in programming. With Turbo C you have an advantage over many other Cs. The compiler will generally warn you when it finds a suspicious assignment of this type. Do not rely on it, though.

Pointer initialization

When a pointer is declared it does not point to anything useful. Before you can make use of a pointer you must assign an address to it.

This might seem fairly obvious. Nonetheless, it is surprising how often problems with programs come about because they are trying to make use of an un-initialized pointer. One of the most common causes of this is when the use of a pointer is subject to a conditional test. Turbo C is quite helpful here in giving warnings of possible use before initialization. Such warnings should be studied carefully.

Error Detection

There are essentially three types of error: syntax errors, program errors, and the horror of horrors, latent errors. Within these three types there is a wide variety.

Syntax errors

Of all the errors, syntax are the easiest for you to find. In fact, you do not need to find them as the compiler will. Unfortunately, it will not always tell you where the error is, or even the correct type of error.

We looked at one of the reasons for this earlier in this chapter when we discussed missing semi-colons. Another compiler trick is to report an error different from the one which exists. This usually happens when you have an error in one part of the code which still produces acceptable code, but makes some of the following code invalid.

If you find that you get a syntax error reported by the compiler but despite your best efforts can find nothing wrong with the code where it is reported, look again at the earlier code. One thing well worth checking in these circumstances is that you have not commented out a section of code.

Program errors

These are far more serious as they will go undetected by the compiler, although with the Turbo C compiler you may get some warnings of suspect code. This is the case with one of the most common causes of program errors: the incorrect use of assignment and equality operators.

Fortunately, a program error will show up in the fact that the program will not run correctly. In such cases you have work your way through the program and try to find out why it is not working in the way you expected.

Code expansion

If you cannot find any obvious reason in the code why you are not getting the results you anticipated, it might be worth expanding out the code. This means obtaining a full listing of the code with all the include files included and all the defined macros expanded. You can do this by running your source code through the C preprocessor. Unfortunately, you will probably find that this is not well documented in your manuals.

The method given below is the one I use with Turbo C.

- Set up a temporary directory below the Turbo C main directory.

- Copy over to that directory my source code, all include files and the Turbo C file CPP.EXE.

- Enter the command CPP <sourcefile>.

This will result in a file with an I suffix to it. You can print this out and have a full listing of your code with all your macros expanded.

As an example in one program would not work and no fault was apparent in it. It was not until the source was expanded out that an included macro was found which was not doing as expected. This was the cause of the problem.

Lints

Turbo C is fairly good compared with many compilers in providing warnings on possible incorrect usage. In the traditional Unix background to C we did not have such help, so a tool known as a lint was developed.

A lint is a very sophisticated syntax analyzer which will go through your source code and report errors and give warnings. The range of these warnings is often far more extensive than those produced by the standard compilers.

Unfortunately, all the lints which I have access to at present running under MSDOS, will not accept Turbo C and other ANSI C standard source code. This, no doubt, will change in the near future.

With its effective warning reporting system, Turbo C offers you most of what you will get from a lint, but not quite all. The benefit of a lint for the Turbo C user is possibly marginal. However, if you are using a compiler which does not have an extensive warning system you may be well off obtaining a lint. There are a number in the public domain, or a very good commercially distributed one called PC-Lint(TM).

Cross referencers

Cross referencers provide you with a list of C tokens and information about where these are used. They are often useful when you know that something is getting the wrong value, but you are not certain where that value is coming from.

There are a number available in the public domain, mostly called XREF. These generally produce a list of tokens and line numbers. The version given in Chapter 20, CROSSREF, provides a context printout of the line containing the variable. A sample of part of the output of this program is given here when it has been run on Program 088.

```
-----   CLS   -----

006 >   #define CLS  printf("%c[2J",27)
074 >                   CLS;
125 >           CLS;
176 >                   CLS;
240 >                   CLS;
284 >           CLS;
294 >                       CLS;
321 >           CLS;


-----   FALSE   -----

004 >   #define FALSE  0
036 >           edit_flag = FALSE;
078 >               if ( ok() == FALSE ) exit(0);
156 >                   if ( let == 'N' ) return ( FALSE );


-----   FILE   -----

029 >   FILE *fp;


-----   NULL   -----

087 >               while ( fgets( name_buf, 30, fp ) != NULL )
```

```
-----    TRUE    -----

003 >   #define  TRUE  1
150 >           while(  TRUE  )
154 >               if(  let  ==  'Y'  )  return  (  TRUE  );
173 >           while(  TRUE  )
184 >             while(  TRUE  )
205 >                       if  (  ok()  ==  TRUE  )
215 >                           edit_flag  =  TRUE;
```

The full output of CROSSREF is much longer. The above, though, shows the type of information which programs of this type provide. If you found a problem with a program and suspected that it might be related to a specific variable, by using a cross-referencing program you could quickly find all the lines of code containing that variable.

There is a problem with both XREF and CROSSREF in that they ignore strings. If you have a message which appears at the wrong time it is often useful to be able to find out where it is coming from. Program 094 provides you with a basic utility to do this.

```
/*****************************************************
* Program 094                                      *
* strfind.c                                         *
*                                                   *
* Prints out a list of strings with line number.*
* usage strfind <sourcfile>                         *
*****************************************************/

#include <stdio.h>

#define DQUOTE '"'
#define BSLASH '\\'

main( int argc, char *argv[] )
{
        FILE *fp;
        char buf[256],last,this;
        int blet;
        int line_num = 0;

        if ( argc < 2 )
        {
                puts( "Usage strfind <sourcefile> " );
                exit(0);
        }

        if ( ! ( fp = fopen( argv[1], "r" ) ) )
```

```
        {
                puts("Cannot  open  source  file.");
                exit(0);
        }

        while( fgets( buf, 256, fp ) != NULL )
        {
                line_num++;
                last = this = blet = 0;

                while( (this = buf[blet++]) != 0 )
                {
                        if( this == DQUOTE && last != BSLASH )
                        {
                                printf("%03d > %s",line_num,buf);
                                break;
                        }
                        last = this;
                }
        }
}
```

Both CROSSREF and STRFIND are very basic utilities when it comes to this type of work. There are a number of commercial programs which provide a higher degree of functionality. One which I recommend is a program called VICAR, from Iansyst Ltd.

Call listers

Another type of utility program which can be very useful in debugging program errors is a call lister. These programs provide you with a list of all functions called from a specific function.

It is common to find that the cause of program error is either a function not being called when you would expect it to be, or a function being called from the wrong place.

There are a number of these programs available in the public domain, one of the most widely known being CALLS.

Personally, one of the best programs I have found in this field is TREE DIAGRAMMER from Albedaran Laboratories in California. If you are going to do any extensive work, it is well worth aquiring this.

Code tidies

There are a number of programs around to tidy up your source code and provide you with a well laid out printout. This can be an invaluable aid when you are looking for a program bug. It is all too easy for them to hide in a badly laid out piece of code.

One of the most commonly used is a public domain program called CPRINT. There are a number of versions of this and generally they provide quite an easy to read output.

SOURCE PRINT from Albedaran Laboratories goes further, providing you with graphical guides to levels of nesting and including indexing and cross referencing utilities. If you are doing large amounts of C coding this utility is very useful.

Latent bugs

Without doubt this is the most serious bug facing the C programmer, mainly because it is the type of bug which is most difficult to find.

A latent bug is one which will not manifest until certain conditions apply, and usually this means the one set of data for which you did not test the software.

Once you identify the condition which will cause the latent bug to appear, it is fairly easy to track down and correct. The problem lies in detecting them.

There are two basic rules here. First, carry out thorough testing. Do not just test functions with the values they are supposed to receive, but also with all possible values which might be sent to them.

The second rule is to follow the programming practice known as defensive coding. This means keeping the data interaction to a minimum. If possible, at the lowest level each function should carry out one task and one task only. That task should affect only one item of data. By doing this it is far easier to check the effect of each function on the data it is handling and to ensure that a change to one data item is not causing an unwanted result in another.

Appendix 1

C CODE LAYOUT

There are many different ideas about how C code should be laid out. The essential point is to find a style which suits you and to stick to it.

Some readers probably want a firm guideline for C code layout. The following is one which I have given as a standard for a number of commercial programming operations. It works.

I do not claim that this is the one and only correct way to lay out C code. There are many others. It is not even the way followed in this book. Also, I do not recommend that you take it as it stands. Coding standards have to be worked out for the situation in which they are being used. Have the following standard as a base and write your own version which suits your own requirements.

1. Each source file should start with an Identification Descriptor. This will have the following structure.

   - Begin Comment (/*)
   - Space
   - Title (The Program Identification Name + Source File Name)
   - Subtitle (Detail of program structure this program belongs to)
   - Space
   - Classification
   - Year
   - Programmer
   - Owner
   - Status (See below)
   - Date
   - Functional/Structural Description in brief
   - Portability synopsis
   - Space
   - End Comment */
   - Space

   The program status can be one of the following:

Outline
Draft
Prototype
Test   Alpha, Beta, etc.
Release

An example of a program identification block would be:

```
/*

Editor          l-edit.c
L-Taal Editor module.

Copyright: released for non-commercial purposes.

1985            Interspike Ltd
                N. G. Backhurst & R. Stuurman

Prototype.

Version 2.00 This is the first C version written

31st November 1985

The module will take the input from the keyboard and assign it to
the program structure.  All command and option input will be
validated before acceptance.  The command and action lines are
stored in two buffers, com_buff & act_buff.  Once the input has
been completed and verified, the contents of the buffers are
written into a structure of type prog_struct, space being
obtained for this using malloc, and the pointers of the preceding
and following line structures are adjusted to include the new
line in the program structure.


The screen handling functions (SCR_) are all system dependent.
All other functions are portable.

*/
```

2. Tabs are used for program indentation; the standard level of tabbing being three
   spaces.

3. A brace is generally on a line by itself.

- The lowest level of braces appear on the left margin.

- Comments may appear on lines containing a brace, but only after the brace and
  there should be two tabs between the brace and the comment marker.

- Braces are indented to the same depth as the statement that invoked the block that they frame.

- In variable initializations, the opening brace may be placed on the same line as the equal sign, but the closing brace must have the same indentation as the opening one.

- No statement may appear on the same line as a brace.

4. A block begins with a left brace and ends with a right brace. Its contents are indented an extra level to indicate the nesting depth.

- Whenever a block is longer than 24 lines (a standard CRT page) a comment should follow the closing brace to indicate the block that the brace closes.

   This applies to whole functions as well as regular blocks.

   This rule should also be used with shorter blocks when block nesting makes the code complex and these comments improve the readability.

- The opening and closing braces of a block are always indented identically.

- The case/default labels of a switch statement are always indented a level, like statements in a block. The statements that follow these labels are always indented an extra level to improve readability.

- Regular labels (destinations for gotos) are always placed at the left margin regardless of nesting. Such labels should be commented saying where the gotos which refer to them are situated.

- The null block {} should be avoided. It is better to use the null statement.

- If a single statement is used instead of a block, it is indented a single level, just as if it were surrounded by braces.

   Null statements (that is just a ";") are indented in the same way as regular statements.

   The null statement is always on a line by itself.

```
while ( name[j++] != NULL )
;
```

5. White space is added in expressions and assignments to improve readability.

- Relational operators are delimited by single spaces:

```
a > b;               c != x;
```

- Binary operators (for example, +, -, /) and assignment operators are delimited by white space.

```
a  =  x - j;              a  *=  2;
```

- Unary operators are not separated by space from their operands.

```
i++;               -j;
```

- Parentheses are added to improve readability in complex expressions, even if they are not required to produce correct evaluation.

```
a  =  ( j * k ) + ( l / q ) - 5 ;
```

- The return statement will always have parentheses surrounding its expression.

```
return  (answer);
```

With many Cs this is compulsory anyway.

- No white space is placed between a function name and the parentheses of its argument list.

```
get_screen_square(tleft,tright,bleft,bright);
```

- A single white space is place between a keyword and its parenthesized argument.

```
for (i = 0, j = strlen(word); i < j ; i++, j--)
```

- Parentheses should be adjacent to the arguments they enclose.

- A comma is bound to the argument that precedes it and should be followed by a single space.

6. Operators such as "->" and "." (used in structure references) directly bind to their arguments with no intervening spaces.

- Comments are added liberally to make the program read easily.

- If the comment is outside a function it should be surrounded by a comment box.

```
/***************************************************************
*   get_name takes the input from the keyboard and places  *
*   it in the buffer name.  A check is made to ensure that*
*   the first character is an upper case letter and only   *
*   letters are accepted in the input.                     *
***************************************************************/

get_name(name)
```

- Where the comment in a comment box relates to a specific function there should be one line between the closing line of the comment box and the header line of the function. Where the comment in the comment box does not relate to any specific function, the comment box should be separated from the main body of the program by at least four blank lines above and below.

- If a comment in a function takes more than one line the start and end token should be lined up with a star at the start of each comment line. The whole comment should be indented across from the main body of the program.

```
if ( !get_scr(tl,tr,bl,br) )
return ( clear );                  /* Test if the screen
                                    * is clear.  If it is
                                    * return to the screen
                                    * update routine.
                                    */

else
    if (confirm_clear() != YES )
        escape_update();
    else
        return ( clear );     /* If the screen is not
                               * clear, check if safe
                               * to clear.  If it is,
                               * return to screen
                               * update routine, if
                               * not, escape the update
                               * procedure.
                               */
```

- Where a comment fits on a single line, the start and end tokens should be placed on the same line.

```
n = ( j < 10 ) ? 10 : j ; /* Keep n >= 10 */
```

- Even if the compiler will allow it, do not nest comments.

7. Variables should always be declared, even if the version of C you are using has default variables. Always explain the purpose of your variables other than minor counting variables.

- Declare the variables in logical groups, and include a comment on the same line as the declaration to describe the function of the variable.

- Avoid numerous declarations on a single line.

- Explain complex pointer declarations.

- Variable names are always lower case only.

- External variable declarations must be indented a single level for greater readability.

- If you have a number of declarations on one line or many, put them into alphabetic order.

8. Constants created with #define are always upper case. Macros created with #define will have the first character upper case and the rest lower case.

Appendix 2

ANSI SCREEN CONTROL CODES

The following set of C functions carry out various screen operations using ANSI Screen Control Codes. For these to be used you must include device = ANSI.SYS in your config.sys file.

```
/****************************************************
* move_up() moves the cursor up by the number     *
* of lines specified in lines.  If the cursor      *
* reaches top of screen, or is at the top of       *
* screen no changes are made.                      *
****************************************************/

move_up( int lines )
{
    printf("%c[%dA",27,lines);
}


/****************************************************
* move_dn() move the cursor down by the number     *
* of lines specified in lines.  If the cursor       *
* reaches the bottom of screen, or is at the        *
* bottom of screen no changes are made.             *
****************************************************/

move_dn( int lines )
{
    printf("%c[%dB",27,lines);
}


/****************************************************
* move_rt() moves the cursor to the right unless   *
* it is at the rightmost position on the screen.   *
* The number of columns to move is specified by    *
* cols.                                            *
****************************************************/
```

```
move_rt( int cols )
{
    printf("%c[%dC",27,cols);
}

/*****************************************************
* move_lt() moves the cursor to the right unless *
* it is at the leftmost position on the screen.  *
* The number of columns to move is specified by  *
* cols.                                          *
*****************************************************/

move_lt( int cols )
{
    printf("%c[%dD",27,cols);
}

/*****************************************************
* put_cur() places the cursor at the row and    *
* column specified.                              *
*****************************************************/

put_cur(int row, int col )
{
    printf("%c[%d;%dH",27,row,col);
}

/*****************************************************
* cls() clears the screen and returns the cursor *
* to the home position.                          *
*****************************************************/

cls()
{
    printf("%c[2J",27);
}

/*****************************************************
* set_screen() sets the screen mode.  This is set *
* up for the AMSTRAD PC1640, but should be correct*
* for most true compatibles.                     *
* Mode         Description                       *
*   0          40 x 25 Black & White            *
*   1          40 x 25 Colour                   *
*   2          80 x 25 Black & White            *
*   3          80 x 25 Colour                   *
*   4          320 x 200 Colour                 *
*   5          320 x 200 Black & White          *
*   6          630 x 200 Black & White          *
*   7          wrap at end of line              *
*****************************************************/
```

```
set_screen( int mode )
{
    printf("%c[=%dh",mode);
}


/****************************************************
* save_cur() saves the current cursor position    *
* to be restored later.                            *
****************************************************/

save_cur( void )
{
    printf("%c[s",27);
}


/****************************************************
* rest_cur() restores   the cursor at a previously*
* saved position.                                  *
****************************************************/

rest_cur( void )
{
    printf("%c[u",27);
}
```

The above functions cover the most used ANSI control sequences. There are others; for details you should refer to your system documentation.

Appendix 3

FUNCTIONS

This appendix contains a number of functions which you might find useful. Each is provided with a small driver function main() for development and testing purposes. You will need to adapt the functions for the situation in which you will be using them. This is especially true with the functions which are being passed arrays of integers. There is no reason why these cannot be passed arrays of type float or double, it is just that for a basic version I always write using integers. This makes basic debugging much easier.

```c
/*****************************************************
* compound_interest() returns the amount of        *
* compound interest on the principle, over a        *
* number of time periods, at a rate per time        *
* period.  The return value is of type float.       *
*****************************************************/

#include <stdio.h>

float compound_interest( int principle, int time, float rate);

main()
{
        int principle, time;
        float rate, interest;

        printf("\nEnter principle : ");
        scanf("%d",&principle);
        getchar();
        printf("\nEnter rate : ");
        scanf("%f",&rate);
        getchar();
        printf("\nEnter time : ");
        scanf("%d",&time);
        getchar();
        printf("\n\nPrincible %d, Time %d, Rate %f ",principle, time, rate);
```

```
        interest = compound_interest(principle,time,rate);

            printf("\n\nInterest due is %f\n",interest);
}

float compound_interest( int principle, int time, float rate )
{
        int i;
        float interest, total;
        total = ( float ) principle;

        for ( i = 0; i < time; i++ )
        {
                total *= ( 1 + (rate / 100) );
        }

        interest = total - principle;
        return ( interest );
}

/*****************************************************
 * average() returns the arithmetic mean average    *
 * of the contents of an array of integers.   It     *
 * requires to have passed to it the address of     *
 * the array and the number of elements involved.   *
 *****************************************************/

float average( int array[], int members );

main()
{
        int values[5],number;
        float mean;

        for ( number = 0; number < 5; number++ )
        {
                values[number] = number + 1;
        }

        mean = average( values, number );

        printf("Average is %f\n",mean);
}

float average( int array[], int members )
{
```

286

```
        float  mean;
        int  i,  total;


        for  (  i  =  0,  total  =  0;  i  <  members;  i++  )
        {
                total  +=  array[i];
        }

        mean  =  total  /  members;
        return  (  mean  );



/*****************************************************
  progression()  returns  the  total  value  of  an      *
  arithmetic  progression.    It  needs  three           *
  values  passed  to  it.    The  start  value,  the      *
  number  of  terms  and  the  common  difference.        *
******************************************************/
#include  <stdio.h>

float  progression(  float  start,  int  number,  float  difference  );

main()

        float  first,  change;
        int  num;

        printf("Enter  first  value  ");
        scanf("%f",&first);
        getchar();
        printf("\nEnter  number  of  elements  ");
        scanf("%d",&num);
        getchar();
        printf("\nEnter  common  difference  ");
        scanf("%f",&change);
        getchar();
        printf("\n\nThe  total  is  %f\n",progression(  first,num,change  ));


float  progression(  float  start,  int  number,  float  difference  )

        float  total;
        int  i;

        for(  i  =  0,  total  =  start;  i  <  number-1;  i++  )
```

```
        {
                start += difference;
                total += start;
        }
        return ( total );
}


/*****************************************************
* std_dev() returns the standard deviation for    *
* the contents of an array.  It is passed two      *
* values, the address of the array and the number*
* of elements.                                     *
*****************************************************/
#include <stdio.h>
#include <math.h>

double std_dev( int array[], int members );

main()
{
        int values[99],number;
        double standard_dev;

        number = 0;
        while ( 1 )
        {
                printf("\nInput number 99 to exit ");
                scanf("%d",&values[number]);
                getchar();
                if ( values[number] == 99 )
                {
                        break;
                }
                number++;
        }
        standard_dev = std_dev( values, number );
        printf("SD = %f\n",standard_dev);
}

double std_dev( int array[], int members )
{
        float total, square_tot, variance, average;
        double dev;
        int count,i;
        count = 0;
        total = square_tot = dev = 0;
```

288

```c
        for ( i = 0; i < members; i++ )
        {
                total += array[i];
                square_tot += ( array[i] * array[i] );
                count++;
        }

        average = total / count;
        variance = ( square_tot / count ) - ( average * average );
        dev = sqrt( variance );

        return (dev);
}
/******************************************************
* reverse() reverses the letter order in a          *
* string which is passed to it.                      *
******************************************************/

void reverse( char *string);

main()
{
        char word[] = "TESTING";

        printf("%s \n",word);
        reverse( word );
        printf("%s \n",word);
}

void reverse( char *string )
{
        int i, j;
        char hlet;

        j = strlen( string ) - 1; /* reduce by one to avoid
                                   * swapping terminating zero.
                                   */

        for( i = 0; i < j ; i++, j-- )
        {
                hlet = string[i];
                string[i] = string[j];
                string[j] = hlet;
        }
}


/******************************************************
* min_max() is basic statistical tool.  It is       *
* passed an array of integers, the number of         *
* elements in the array and pointer to two           *
* integers to return values to.                      *
******************************************************/
```

```c
#include <stdio.h>

void min_max( int array[], int elements, int *min, int *max );

main()
{
        int  values[10],count,highest,lowest;
        highest = lowest = 0;

        for ( count = 0; count < 10; count++ )
        {
                printf("\nEnter a number ");
                scanf("%d",&values[count]);
                getchar();
        }

        min_max( values, 10, &lowest, &highest );
        printf("\n\nLowest is %d and highest is %d ",lowest,highest);
}

void min_max( int array[], int elements, int *min, int *max )
{
        int i, low, high;

        low = high = array[0];

        for( i = 0; i < elements; i++ )
        {
                if ( array[i] > high )
                        high = array[i];
                if ( array[i] < low )
                        low = array[i];
        }

        *min = low;
        *max = high;
}

/***************************************************
* mem_rep() returns the amount of memory on the  *
* system.  This is done with a call to the        *
* Memory Size Service using the ROM BIOS inter-  *
* rupt call 18 ( hex 12 ).                         *
***************************************************/

#include <stdio.h>
#include <dos.h>

main()
```

```c
{
        printf("Memory %d K \n",mem_rep());
}

mem_rep()
{
        int  mem;
        geninterrupt( 18 );
        mem = _AX;
        return ( mem );
}

/****************************************************
* fill_mem() fills the memory starting from the  *
* location passed to it as start for the number  *
* of bytes passed in length with the value        *
* passed in ch.                                    *
* This technique is often used to fill a buffer  *
* with zeros prior to using a raw disk sector    *
* write to fill the disk sector with zeros.  A   *
* process used for security to overwrite data    *
* which is sensitive.                             *
****************************************************/
#include  <stdio.h>
#include  <stdlib.h>

main()
{
        char  *ptr;
        int  i;
        ptr = malloc( 100 );
        fill_mem( ptr, 100, 'A' );

        for ( i = 0; i < 100; i++ )
        {
                printf("%c",*ptr);
                ptr++;
        }
}

fill_mem( char *start, int length, char ch )
{
        int  i;
        for ( i = 0; i < length; i++ )
        {
                *start = ch;
                start++;
        }
}
```

Appendix 4

ANSWERS

```
/****************************************************
* Answer 1                                          *
*                                                    *
* This program takes the input of two single        *
* digit integers.  It divides the first integer     *
* by the second and prints the result of the        *
* division and the remainder.                       *
*                                                    *
* Input stdin                                        *
* Output stdout                                      *
*                                                    *
* N. G. Backhurst May 1987                           *
****************************************************/

#include <stdio.h>

main()
{
      int f_num, s_num, *pfnum, *psnum;
    /* declare two integer variables
     * snd pointers to them.
     */

f_num = s_num = 0;
/* initialize variables to zero/ */

pfnum = &f_num;
psnum = &s_num;

get_nums( pfnum, psnum);
/* call function to get numbers. */

printf("\n%d divided by %d is ", f_num, s_num);
printf("%d with a ", ( f_num / s_num ) );
printf("a remainder of %d.\n", ( f_num % s_num ));

}
```

```
/*****************************************************
* get_nums()                                        *
*                                                   *
* The function get_nums recieves two pointers       *
* to integers as arguments.  It takes the input     *
* of two integers and assigns them to the           *
* address pointed to by the pointers.               *
*****************************************************/

get_nums( int *fp, int *sp )
{
        int a, b;

        printf("\nEnter two single digit numbers.\n");
        printf("\nFirst Number     : ");
        a = getchar() - '0';
        getchar();
        printf("\nSecond Number    : ");
        b = getchar() - '0';
        getchar();

        *fp = a;
        *sp = b;

    /* Assign integers to addresses pointed to by the pointers
     * so making the values known to the calling function.
     */
}
/*****************************************************
* Answer 2                                          *
* Function to convert upper case to lower           *
*   ***********************************************/

char make_lower ( char let )
{
        if ( let < 'A' ) return (let);
        if ( let > 'Z' ) return (let);
        return ( ( let - 'A' ) + 'a' );
}

/*****************************************************
* Answer 3                                          *
* Function to return a string, the number of        *
* characters which can be inputted being            *
* limited to the value passed as num.               *
* Use cgets( char*, int ).                          *
* There is no provision in this version to allow    *
* for use of delete or backspace.                   *
*****************************************************/
```

```
cgets( char *array, int num )
{
        char let;
        int i;
        i = 0;

        while ( 1 ) /* Endless loop */
        {
                let = getch();  /* get character from keyboard */
                if ( let == 13 ) /* carriage return */
                {
                        *array = 0;  /* Terminate string */
                        printf("\n");
                        return;        /* and return. */
                }
                if ( i < num )    /* maximum number not entered */
                {
                        i++;       /* increase count */
                        *array = let;
                        printf("%c",let);
                        array++;  /* increase pointer */
                }
        }
}
```

Appendix 5

SOURCES

The following list of companies provide goods or services referred to in this book.

Aldebaran Laboratories Inc, 3339 Vincent Road, Pleasant Hill, CA 94523, United States of America:
>Source Print, Tree Diagrammer.

Grey Matter, 4 Prigg Meadow, Ashburton, Devon, TQ13 7DF:
>C Compilers, Development Tools and Libraries.

Iansyst Ltd., Omnibus Building, 41 North Road, London, N7 9DP:
>VICAR, Variables in Context Analyst and Reporter.

1512 Independent Users Group, P.O. Box 55, Sevenoaks, Kent, TN13 1AQ:
>Public Domain C Software - Available to Members Only.

Interspike/Intersoft, Holtrichtersveld 709, 7327 DD Apeldoorn, Netherlands:

>C Consultancy and support service and Public Domain Software in Northern Europe. Also have an English Language book supplier service which includes C books.

Seltec Computer Products Ltd., "Farley Hall", Wokingham Road, Bracknell, Berkshire, RG12 5EU:

>Commercial Distributors of Public Domain and Shareware products with a large C range.

Appendix 6

BIBLIOGRAPHY

Books

Advanced Graphics in C Programming & Techniques, by N. Johnson, published by McGraw Hill.

C from A to Z, by B. Costales, pubished by Prentice Hall.

The C Programmer's Handbook, by T Hogan, published by Prentice-Hall.

C Programming Guide, by Purdum, published by Que.

The C Programming Language by B. Kernighan and D. Ritchie, published by Prentice Hall.

The C Toolbox, by W. J. Hunt, published by Addison Wesley.

Computer Handbooks, C Language, by F. Wagner-Dobler, published by Pitman.

Debugging C, by Ward, published by Que.

Dr Dobb's Toolbook of C, by The Editors of Dr. Dobb's Journal, published by Prentice Hall.

The Peter Norton Programmers Guide to the IBM PC, by P. Norton, Published by Microsoft Press.

Solutions in C, by R. Jaeschke, published by Addison Wesley.

System Management Under Unix, by N.G. Backhurst and P.Davies, published by Sigma Press

MSDOS Technical Reference Manual - This is not available to the public being an internal document for Microsoft and their licencees. Many of the computer manufacturers who use MSDOS put out their own version of this document. One of the best is Philips Programmers Reference Manual, so if your manufacturer does not

296

produce a version for his implementation of MSDOS, try getting hold of the Philips copy.

Magazines

There are a number of magazines which contain interesting sections on C. Two magazines though are generally recognized as being the magazines for C programmers, unfortunately they are both American and in England can generally only be obtained by subscription, though in Germany and Holland they can be purchased in a computer shops and some newsagents.

Dr Dobb's Journal of Software Tools - 501 Galveston Dr, Redwood City, CA 94063, United States of America

Micro/Systems Journal - Box 3713, Escondido, CA 92025-9843, United States of America

INDEX